Defiant Sisters

DATE DUE

Studies in Ethnic and Immigration History Series

Gathering Place: Peoples and Neighbourhoods of Toronto, 1834-1945. Edited by Robert F. Harney

DP: Lithuanian Immigration to Canada After the Second World War. By Milda Danys

Studies in Ethnic and Immigration History

Defiant Sisters

A Social History of Finnish Immigrant Women in Canada

Varpu Lindström-Best

1988
Multicultural History Society of Ontario
Toronto

We wish to thank the Multiculturalism Directorate, Office of the Secretary of State for its assistance in the preparation of this volume.

Canadian Cataloguing in Publication Data

Lindstrom-Best, Varpu
  Defiant sisters

(Studies in ethnic and immigration history)
Bibliography: p.
Includes index.
ISBN 0-919045-36-7 (bound) ISBN 0-919045-38-3 (pbk.)

1. Women immigrants — Canada — Social conditions.
2. Finns — Canada — Social conditions. 3. Women —
Finland — Social conditions. I. Multicultural
History Society of Ontario. II. Title. III. Series.

FC106.F5L56 1988   305.4'8894541'00971   C88-093441-7
F1035.F5L56 1988

Cover photo: Washing day in British Columbia,
          n.d. FCHSC 1868/MHSO/AO

I dedicate this book to a very special Finnish
immigrant woman – my hardworking, understanding,
and loving mother

ÄIDILLE

Contents

Tables

Acknowledgments

Over the past fourteen years I have had the special privilege to research the story of the Finnish immigrants in Canada. I treasure the happy memories of the times spent with friends, colleagues and family members who gave their honest criticism, valuable help and encouragement to this project. Despite my deep sense of gratitude to all those who are very much a part of this book, it is impossible to thank here everyone who has contributed. This book, however, is an abridged and popularized version of my 1986 York University PH. D. dissertation which included extensive acknowledgments to all the people whose help I so appreciate. I hope that the bibliography of this book clearly indicates how much I owe to other scholars in this exciting field of immigrant studies.

Working with Finnish immigrants has been a wonderful experience because of their spirit of co-operation and their willingness to share information. All of the Finnish congregations and organizations in Canada allowed me free access to their collections and every individual I approached was willing to give an interview and share often painful memories. Several communities organized special events and helped me finance some of my travels which I did by giving numerous speeches and slide shows. The community leaders directed me to often obscure sources and to interesting, friendly people. This is how, over the years, my list of immigrants interviewed grew to nearly five hundred. Only about half are used directly in this dissertation. All the men and women with whom I have laughed, cried and drank thousands of cups of coffee with *pulla* (sweet bread) have had an important impact not only on my work but also on my life. I have especially grown to respect and honour the unassuming, courageous Finnish immigrant women without whose assistance this book would simply not exist. *Kiitos!*

Financing a long-term research project that spans two continents is not easy, even with the help of a supporting community and family. I have been fortunate to receive over the years several scholarships, stipends and research grants from York University, Secretary of State Multiculturalism Directorate, Social Sciences and Humanities Research Council of Canada, Ministry of Education International Affairs Branch in Finland, Suomi-Seura (Finland Society) Finland, and the Canadian Friends of Finland. I would also wish to extend special thanks to the scholars in Finland, especially in the universities of Helsinki, Turku and Joensuu, to the staff of Migration Institute in Turku, Finland, and to the numerous archivists and librarians in Canada, the United States and Finland for their professional and friendly assistance.

Throughout the research, the Multicultural History Society of Ontario has been most supportive of my work and provided the valuable links to other scholarship in the field. All of the materials, tapes, photographs, diaries, letters and articles which I have amassed in the last fourteen years are now part of the MHSO collection. Anne McCarthy patiently edited the drafts of my dissertation and Diane Mew has helped to turn it into a book. Her judicious cuts of tables, graphs, reference material and lengthy academic discussions have made this a much shorter and more readable book. Mauri Jalava, whose own scholarship is evident on the following pages, agreed to prepare the index in record time. This team effort has made it possible to now present to you the *Defiant Sisters: Social History of Finnish Immigrant Women in Canada, 1890-1930*. On these pages I simply wish to give the Finnish immigrant women a recorded past, a place in Canadian history.

Varpu Lindström-Best
Toronto, November 1987

Introduction

The hallways of the Finnish rest home in Vancouver were sparkling clean. The visitor was greeted with a faint fragrance of lemon-scented polish mixed with the appetizing smell of *pulla* and coffee from the cafeteria. "How can you keep this place so clean?" I asked the nurse who was directing me down the ramp to the common area. "Our residents have spent most of their lives scrubbing, cleaning, polishing, washing and cooking," she laughed, "they are the professionals when it comes to cleaning, and they would accept nothing less now."

A large rectangular room opened up at the bottom of the ramp where about thirty women and two men were vigorously swinging their arms, bending, twisting and kicking to the rhythmic tunes of the piano. Their serious expressions revealed that these senior citizens were defying the physical restrictions imposed by old age and were giving their utmost effort to the exercise class. They were not about to be interrupted by a curious onlooker. The long walls of the recreation room were covered from floor to ceiling with thousands of books – novels, scientific, political and religious volumes – some written in English but most in Finnish. These books, showing the signs of constant use, were the precious possessions of the literate residents who had clung on to them when they moved into the home. The bell rang; it was coffee time. In an instant the large room was empty. "Punctuality," said the nurse, "they do love punctuality, order and routine."[1]

The visit to the rest home raised many questions. Who were these women? What experiences filled their long lives? What hopes and disappointments had carved the deep wrinkles in their faces? What characteristics made these women survivors? Above all, why has their past been such a tightly kept secret?

The quest to understand the Finnish immigrant women's experience in Canada leads directly to two new areas of historical research. In the past two decades important scholarly advances have been achieved in the fields of immigration and women's history, both of which reflect the growing emphasis on social and labour history in North America.

Since the Second World War, the most heated debates in the historiography of the immigrant experience in North America focus on Oscar Handlin's epic, *The Uprooted,* and its theme of alienation. Are the immigrants "uprooted" wanderers? Do they suffer from the "shock of alienation" and degenerating values because the moral restraints normally imposed by families are absent? Or are they "transplanted" people who are happily adjusted to their new environment, complete with old structures and kinship ties reinforced by mutual interest in the ethnic neighbourhoods, as Rudolph Vecoli, Handlin's fiercest critic, argues?

The new immigration history has played a vital role in balancing the often distorted image of various ethnocultures, adding structure, organization and caring to community life. Often it is conducted by descendants of the ethnic groups with specific language skills which allows scholars access to the community's own hidden sources. Oral testimony has been a fundamental pillar in this research.

This book builds on histories which critically examine Canadian immigration policies. Several ethnic groups have boldly exposed the injustices they have experienced at the hands of racist or anti-semitic Canadians and others have complained of their treatment during periods of economic crisis and war.[2] Donald Avery has argued that the government's immigration policy after 1896, despite pronouncements to the contrary, was, above all else, to recruit cheap and mobile industrial workers for Canada. In addition, heightened interest in the cultural aspects of working-class history has prompted some scholars to explain workers' ethnically determined behaviour and its impact on class solidarity.[3]

The current scholarship on Finnish immigrants has followed these trends, concentrating on Finns as workers and radicals. To this literature can be added several local or regional studies, many of which have been sponsored by specific groups or individuals. J. Donald Wilson was the first scholar in Canada to develop seriously a structure and a concentrated research effort in order to integrate the Finns into Canadian history. Following his lead, studies of Finnish radicalism have appeared, and several larger communities with significant Finnish populations have been examined by historians, geographers, anthropologists and community members. Some historians in Finland are also turning their attention to Canada instead of simply bypassing it on their way to the greener pastures of the United States. The availability of translators has allowed a few Canadian historians to incorporate the Finnish immigrant experience into their own work. Thus, a healthy and growing, but definitely male-oriented, history of the Finnish immigrant experience in Canada is now emerging. It does not, however, answer any of the riddles related to Finnish immigrant women.

Like the history of immigration, the study of women has also changed. Much of the early emphasis concentrated on resurrecting and reassessing those women previously lost to the record and finding source materials to bridge missing gaps. By the early 1970s the connecting theme of this "historiography of compensation" was the use of the feminist viewpoint as the conceptual framework. No longer was it necessary to legitimize women's studies; the field had become independent and meaningful in its own right. Yet women as a category of historical study are at once clearly distinct and hopelessly indistinct from men and their activities. Nevertheless, feminist theory can still be useful if its purpose is more encompassing than merely as depictions of oppressed women fighting their oppressors. Judith L. Newton, Mary P. Ryan and Judith R. Walkowitz in *Sex and Class in Women's History,* argue: "After half a decade of research, moreover, we have moved beyond a one dimensional emphasis upon the oppression and victimization of women and have also come to recognize and explore the lines along which women have shaped their own history and that of men" (p. 1).

Women's history has been examined from two distinct viewpoints. In North America the emphasis has been on the role of ideology in shaping women's life experiences. Historians have explored the impact that tradition and religious beliefs have on women's consciousness. They have carefully constructed a "theory of gender" focusing on those aspects shared by all women. Part of this more maternal feminist theory is the belief in universal "women's culture." On the other hand, many scholars in England and some in North America focused on class and linked women to labour history, thus creating the framework for marxist feminist studies. It was argued that women's efforts at liberation can only be understood if all four structures that dominate women's lives are examined: production, reproduction, sexuality and socialization. Joan Kelly was hopeful that both the gender-dominated explanations and those based on class interpretation would come together. She called for the integration of "the doubled vision of feminist theory," the simultaneous operation of class and sex.[4]

This book will attempt to further clarify the feminist vision by adding a third element – ethnicity. The term "ethnicity" has been adopted by immigration historians as a convenient tool to describe various groups of people. It has many inherent problems and is used cautiously in this connection to describe the Finnish culture group (both Swedish- and Finnish-speaking) from within the political boundaries of Finland, Finnish-speaking people from Soviet Karelia, and the people who identify themselves as Finns in northern Norway and Sweden. This work will not view women in a vacuum, nor will it lament their oppressed situation. Instead it will assume that the "true history of women" is the history of their continued functioning in a male-defined world *"on their own terms."*[5] This "triple vision" will examine class, sex, and ethnicity, or more specifically the impact of culture on Finnish immigrant women. This three-layered theoretical framework then will provide the structure for the knowledge vacuum which exists in the field of Finnish immigrant women's history in Canada.

Locating new primary sources is one of many challenges facing researchers into immigrant women's history. One can of course take advantage of women's history in general, since women of all ethnic groups and geographic areas have much in common. For example, women's input into the labour market has been conditioned by family needs as well as their station as a secondary pool of labour. They have suffered further discrimination from employers and government. Recent Canadian writers have penetrated into women's personal lives, charted the importance of life cycles, birth control, and the juggling of women's multiple duties as wives, mothers, workers and members of a community.

As well as the life experiences all women share, it is important to recognize the differences immigrant women face. The recent award-winning collection of essays on immigrant women, *Looking Into My Sister's Eyes,* edited by Jean Burnet, is an indication of the many possibilities to be explored. Most of the articles indicate that immigrant women are clearly set apart from immigrant men. The common problems which emerge from the studies include the imbalanced sex ratios, language difficulties, discrimination, and changing roles within the family. Women's own organizations and their informal networks further attest to women's rapid adaptation of old world customs to the new world setting.

The experiences and problems Finnish immigrants faced were not significantly different from other immigrant women but their responses were. It is this culturally influenced behaviour of the Finnish immigrant women in Canada that is the focus of this book. Why did Finnish women react differently from other immigrant women, or from Finnish men? Why did many of their defence strategies mark them apart from their sisters? To understand the Finnish women's responses to their immigration experience, one must forget the middle-class reformers and their Victorian ideals, which most Finnish women simply did not share. One must explore the background and tradition of the women in Finland in order to discover what kind of culture influenced their world view and behaviour in Canada. It is significant that the age and sex structures of the Finnish communities were distorted. The community was bulging with twenty to thirty-year-old males and noticeably lacking in extended or even nuclear family structures. This unnatural imbalance forced the women to re-evaluate their strategies.

Furthermore, Finnish immigrant women were almost exclusively members of the working class and their economic priorities dictated many of the decisions women made. Since upper- and middle-class Finnish immigrant women were largely absent, no hierarchical structures that existed in the rest of Canada or in Finland were applicable to the immigrant women who built a distinct hierarchy of their own. The elite women in the Finnish immigrant communities could be domestic servants; the eloquent speakers at rallies were often lumber camp cooks; and the defiant suffragists might also be bootleggers.

The difference between women who decide to emigrate and the impact of the immigrant experience on these women are less tangible. It should be pointed out, however, that Finnish immigrant women can under no circumstances be viewed as typical Finnish women. Only a tiny minority of women became emigrants and the "typical" Finnish women stayed in their homeland. Thus, those who left were distinctive.

The primary emphasis in this book is on those adult Finnish women who emigrated to Canada between 1890 and 1930. There is not adequate space to deal with all females: girls under the age of sixteen are discussed only in relationship to their mothers. Second-generation adult immigrant women are also excluded, except when they are indistinguishable in government statistics.

Many important subject areas have also been left out. Regrettably the book does not explore the flourishing women's cultural activities in arts, literature, music, theatre, and sports; women's significant contributions to the cooperative movement; or their participation in the Industrial Workers of the World. Instead, the book will chart the cultural background of Finnish immigrant women and their distinctive settlement patterns. It will focus on the more intimate aspects of women's lives: health, marriage patterns, and family responsibilities. Women are also examined as workers and as active participants in the community. This work, then, is only a beginning which will, I hope, spark future interest in the field.

The strategies and survival techniques created by Finnish women were often coloured by defiance. This defiance could be directed against the old country and its conditions, against their own bodies, against the traditional Lutheran religion, or against Canadian society and ultimately against its legal and political systems. Despite the relative economic success, the spirit of the defiant sisters and their optimistic outlook on life, in many important aspects their immigrant experience was indeed an alienating one which ultimately forced them to adapt and adjust on their own terms, but not without many personal sacrifices. A ninety-eight-year-old woman in the Vancouver rest home remarked stoically from her exercise bike:

> I made the decision to emigrate so why blame anybody else? I never looked back. My life has been an endless string of working days, but over the years I have learned to grin and bear....In sixty-seven years in Canada I never went hungry and I laughed a lot too. It is as the [Finnish] proverb states: everyone is the smith of her own happiness.[6]

CHAPTER 1

Women in Finland, 1890-1930

The Finnish women who emigrated to Canada at the turn of the century spent their formative years in a different social, political, economic, and geographic environment. From earliest childhood they were trained to have respect for the established social order and were educated according to the designs of the state. These early influences extended beyond such tangible and easily identifiable behaviour as cultural practices, language, occupational skills, and religious conformity. All adults brought with them the prejudices, memories, and attitudes they had acquired "back home."

It would be a mistake to assume that all Finnish women experienced identical primary socialization. But although there was much cultural and geographic diversity, there were also strong common elements which had an impact on their lives and future decisions. Some knowledge of Finnish geography, culture, and history helps to understand the development of Finnish-Canadian communities, their geographic distribution, and the women's attitudes to work, family, and organizational life. This chapter will therefore examine the traditional role of women in Finland and the advances of the late nineteenth and early twentieth century which altered their educational, legal, political, economic, and social position, and encouraged some to emigrate.

Geographical and Cultural Divisions within Finland

Finland is, after Iceland, the most northerly country in the world. Its southern point falls well north of Churchill, Manitoba, near the border of the Northwest Territories. One-third of its total length lies north of the Arctic Circle. Habitation is made possible by the Gulf Stream, which has a tempering effect on the Finnish climate. Hence much of the land resembles northern Ontario. The far north, Lapland, reaches beyond the tree-line and even the most tenacious attempts at cultivation have proved unsuccessful: the land is beautiful but, for agricultural purposes, barren. The eastern part of Finland, Savo and Karelia, is littered with lakes, swamps, and thick forests; western Finland, the coastal areas, and the far south offer better prospects for agriculture. The country has over sixty thousand lakes, and thirty thousand islands adorn its coastal regions. Dense forests cover about 65 per cent of its surface area, and even with today's modern agricultural methods, only about 13 per cent of its land is good for agriculture. Such an environment presents a severe challenge to those trying to force a living out of the land.[1] Life in pre-industrial Finland was a constant struggle for survival. Crops were frequently obliterated by early frosts, and starvation and disease checked the population growth. In the late seventeenth century, following a great famine and a long war, Finland's population was a mere quarter of a million people. The last "starvation years" were recorded in 1867-68 when the population of the country was 1.7 million.[2]

As late as the nineteenth century, Finland was not a unified country socially or culturally. After six hundred years of Swedish political domination, Finland was reluctantly ceded to Russia in 1809 and henceforth became its autonomous Grand Duchy. Nevertheless, within the country many different peoples continued to carry on their own traditions—the Finns proper, the Tavastians, Ostrobothnians, Savo people, Karelians and, in the north, the Lapps (Saame people). In addition, those Finns who had adopted the Swedish language, together with those Swedes who had migrated to Finland, formed their own cultural group, the Finn Swedes. The cultural divisions were most sharp between the western and eastern parts of the country. A 1868 British travellers' guide vividly described the contrast:

> There is a most striking difference between the inhabitants of the Finnish provinces to the west and those to the east of Wyborg, more recently severed from Sweden, whose customs and manners, and even language, they had almost universally adopted ... nearly the same dress and the readiness with which they all speak Swedish, make the traveller almost forget that he is in the land that owns the sovereignty of the Tsar. Beyond Wyborg the traveller is suddenly thrown among a strange people: beards become almost universal, from the post-master to the driver – sheepskins are worn, and low-crowned hats with a profusion of buckles; the loose trousers are tucked into the boots. Swedish is scarcely understood, and dollars and shillings are no longer current.[3]

The differences between the two regions encompassed social structure as well. In eastern Finland, extended families were more prevalent. The Karelians, for example, often built large dwellings where several family units lived together and supported each other. Slash and burn agriculture dictated that the population spread out, always looking for new areas to cultivate and thus moving further to the east and northeast. They were isolated from western influences and were able to maintain the ancient customs of the country. It is among these people that the record of the old mythology of the Finns, which had been preserved by oral tradition only, was collected during the first half of the nineteenth century. In the great legend, the *Kalevala*, the constant struggle with nature, the fear of spirits, and trust in the power of magic is reflected.[4] It is clear that the life of the eastern Finns continued to be an endless struggle throughout the nineteenth and early twentieth century. In this struggle women were expected to contribute their hard labour; it was simply a matter of survival.[5]

Women in eastern Finland were less likely to leave their homes, and were bound more by the family unit. Those that did leave usually went to the east, especially to the city of St. Petersburg, which offered opportunities for women in domestic service and in its growing commercial establishments. Immigration to North America was not a popular choice. While there were some communities that sent immigrants to Canada, generally emigration did not take a strong hold in these areas of Finland.

Northern Finns, on the other hand, had no room for expansion, no new forests to burn, and they were the hardest hit by climatic fluctuations. These people from the provinces of Lapland and Oulu were the first to emigrate. They initially moved to Sweden, Norway, and southern Finland and later were among the first to migrate to North America when Finns eventually discovered this alternative destination in the 1860s. This early migration was almost exclusively to the United States, with only a few individuals pioneering the Canadian wilderness, or working on railway and canal construction. The Finns, like other Scandinavians, avoided Canada. In 1882 a disgruntled Canadian immigration agent reported from Scandinavia that "so great is the prejudice against Canada, so systematically has the country been plied with antagonistic matter, that acting upon the advice of the most successful agents I omitted [in a newspaper article] to mention 'Canada' at all."[6]

Thus the major emigration area and the one from which Canada received the vast majority of its Finnish immigrants after 1880 was western Finland: the provinces of Vaasa, Turku, and Pori, and the southern parts of the province of Oulu. The coastal area known as Ostrobothnia (Pohjanmaa) sent as many as two-thirds of all Finnish-

Canadian emigrants, most of them from the southern, most fertile areas of the region.

Ostrobothnian life was coloured by its proximity to Sweden and western culture. It had enjoyed relative wealth because of the fertile farmland, and also because the coastal towns benefited from lucrative trade in pitch and tar with Stockholm's merchants. By the middle of the nineteenth century, however, this trade was in decline and farmland was becoming scarcer. The many independent farmers, instead of migrating elsewhere in Finland, made room for their offspring by dividing up their farms or by looking for opportunities outside the country, mainly in Sweden.

The Lutheran Church was the centre of most rural communities. As well as spiritual leadership, it was responsible for education, health and social services, and also provided the local government. The minister's approval was needed in such civil matters as obtaining a permit for wolf hunting or holding a dance. The high literacy in Ostrobothnia by the middle of the nineteenth century was largely due to the church. Indeed, in order to be confirmed, Finnish Lutherans had to be able to read the catechism; and without confirmation, a Finn was ineligible to marry or to obtain an exit visa from the country. The general understanding among the Finns was that everyone was expected to learn to read and write, if not in the two-week cramming sessions at the church, then independently, under parental supervision at home. It was not until the 1870s that the church and local government in the parishes were separated and public schools became independent of the church. The school curriculum, however, was still based on "Christian principles," and study of religion was compulsory. Old customs lingered on till the turn of the century, and Lutheran pastors continued to wield power in civil affairs. Total separation of church and state and consequent freedom of religion did not occur until 1923. Even then, the Lutheran Church was given special recognition and status as the national church, and church taxes were automatically deducted from everyone's income.

Throughout the major emigration years, the Lutheran Church continued to be a powerful force in the daily lives of its parishioners. Even today, over 90 per cent of those Finns who belong to a church are Lutheran. But the church was not without its critics, and strong revivalist movements took root, especially in Ostrobothnia, beginning in the 1830s and 1840s.

At first the Lutheran Church responded by banning these movements and imprisoning some of their leaders, but by the 1850s the church had come to the conclusion that reform was necessary. It adopted many of the more solemn practices, and the emphasis was on individual salvation. The truce was only temporary, however. By the 1880s a new revivalist movement spread to Ostrobothnia from northern Finland and Sweden. The Laestadians fought against what they considered a corrupt world and growing materialism. It is no coincidence that this movement appeared when industrialization and socialism were taking root in Finland. The strength of the Laestadians, coupled with a growing evangelical movement in the south, forced the church once again to re-evaluate its position. The effect of these revivalist movements was apparent in Ostrobothnian society, which became staunchly conservative, in favour of temperance, and intolerant of secular entertainment.

The majority of Ostrobothnians were Finnish speaking, but within the region, especially in the coastal cities, strong pockets of Swedish-speaking communities could be found. Because this area of Finland was densely populated, it was influenced more by village culture than strong family ties. The young people banded together to form village cliques, to identify with and be influenced by their friends. It was common to have the youths of the entire village join together in one group. Within the group or organization the young men and women were equal partners although they might be assigned separate tasks. The strongest manifestation of this identity with the village came in the form of youth gangs and their attacks on neighbouring "outside" villages. These outbursts appeared most frequently in Ostrobothnia where village solidarity was vigorous.

Thus the young women of Ostrobothnia grew up in an area that was losing its preferential economic position, which was running out of land, and becoming more socially intolerant. They also grew up literate and with a strong sense of village culture. When they chose to leave, they usually did so in groups with other villagers. They were more likely to seek an escape route that took them across the sea to the west than to the southern cities. About two-thirds of the women who emigrated from Finland between 1880 and 1930 came from this region.

Demographic Factors and Occupational Changes

Following the demographic trends of northern Europe, Finland's population had also increased rapidly since the eighteenth century. Despite the many wars and periods of starvation between 1750 and 1865, Finland's population quadrupled. In 1865 only 7.4 per cent of the population lived in urban areas, and as late as 1920 Finland was still overwhelmingly a rural nation with only 16 per cent living in cities. At first, the people were able to expand their farms by clearing new fields out of the virgin forests; but by the end of the nineteenth century there was no further room for expansion in western Finland. Population growth, however, continued unabated until the First World War when 3.1 million people lived in Finland.[7]

The farmers of Ostrobothnia were growing reluctant to divide their land amongst their children, and with no possibility for agricultural expansion, overcrowding became a serious problem. The number of landless peasants, cottagers, and surplus sons and daughters of farmers increased at an alarming rate, forcing many to abandon their familiar surroundings and villages to look for wage work in the towns and cities. In 1901 the number of landless people reached 48 per cent of the rural population, and by 1910 this had risen to 59 per cent. Although Finnish women had won the legal right to inherit land in 1878, in reality women were seldom landowners. As late as 1920, for example, only 13 per cent of landowners were women. Thus, the pressure for women to move to the urban areas was even greater than for men.

Historically Finnish women were expected to work hard. They were to be seen alongside their brothers in haying fields and during harvesting. They were mainly responsible for the care of the domestic animals, hauling the water, splitting and carrying the firewood, as well as the more traditional domestic chores: child rearing, cooking, spinning. According to Finnish mythology, women's work was clearly defined in the *Kalevala,* "Instructing the Bride." Among her tasks were also included the warming of the sauna and the making of beer:

> When the evening bath is wanted,
> Fetch the water and the bath-whisks,
> Have the bath-whisks warm and ready,
> Fill thou full with steam the bathroom.

> Thou must brew the ale of barley,
> From the malt the sweet drink fashion,
> From a single grain of barley,
> And by burning half a tree-trunk.[8]

While hunting was usually man's work, it was not uncommon to find a Finnish woman with a gun on her shoulder. She also participated in fishing, minding the nets, hauling and cleaning the fish. Life for all women was constant work, and the independent nature of Finnish women and their relatively respected position within the family can be partially explained by their self-sufficiency. Men were often absent from homes for long hunting and fishing trips or working in the forests. Under Swedish rule, they were drafted for years to fight in frequent wars.[9] Out of necessity, therefore, women became self-sufficient; strength, hard work and tenacity were glorified as the ideal attributes of a good wife. Single women, too, were expected to show strength of character. Ample evidence of the image of Finnish women is found in the literature. Tuulikki Hosia describes the main attributes of Finnish women in the following manner:

> A familiar picture in the Finnish scenery: wife is rowing and the husband sitting in the rear, takes us to the origins of our female idols. We have always demanded from Finnish women almost unnatural physical strength. There, where the physical strength has waned or where illness has taxed the woman we find that much more *sisu* and tenacity. Our cold country is incapable of admiring a woman who is lacking in both physical and spiritual strengths, be she however sophisticated.[10]

If women were not needed at home, they were expected to earn their living elsewhere. They were traditionally hired by nearby farmers as baby-sitters, maids, or to work in the barns. But in the latter part of the nineteenth century they began to migrate to the coastal and southern cities. There, too, they primarily worked as live-in domestics. As Finland began to industrialize during the 1860s, new opportunities in the service industries, cotton mills, needle trades, textiles, manufacturing, commerce and teaching opened up for them. A new female migrant worker, a single woman living independently far from home, became part of the economic structure.[11]

In Helsinki, the capital of Finland, 39 per cent of working-age women were employed as early as 1870, and this increased to 55 per cent by the turn of the century. By 1920 the proportion of women in the "economically active population" in Finland was 41 per cent. This is exceptionally high in comparison to other western countries. The proportion of working women continued to grow, and today Finland has the highest percentage of women of any western nation working outside the home. In 1870 over 76 per cent of female workers were domestic servants, but with increasing industrialization, this figure declined dramatically to 40 per cent by the turn of the century.

Finnish working women in urban areas were overwhelmingly single. In Helsinki around the turn of the century, for example, 61 per cent of the twenty-five to twenty-nine year-old women were single. One explanation for this is that the internal urban migration was higher among women who had fewer opportunities in agricultural areas. In many of the larger cities the proportion of women was higher than men. However, the number of single men also increased at the same time, and one can only conclude that for some reason there was great reluctance or obstacles in the way of marriage. The trend to remain single was most pronounced among upper-class women. Therefore, economic hardship was not the only reason for postponed marriages. Difficulties in finding a suitable husband, coupled with economic independence, helped to create the large number of single upper-class women so prevalent in western Europe.[12]

Single, working women who had migrated to the cities made ideal candidates for overseas emigration. They were not obstructed by husbands, were more independent of restrictive family ties, and they had already made the break with their familiar village environment. Many women had managed to save enough of their wages to purchase a steamship ticket despite the fact that they were paid, on average, 50 per cent less than men.[13] Others received prepaid tickets from prospective employers, friends, and relatives already in North America.

Not surprisingly, married women were less disposed to work outside of the home or to emigrate. Their economic contribution was high in agricultural communities, and their participation in home industries added to the family income. While only about 10 per cent of married women between 1900 and 1920 worked outside the home, recent studies indicate that the majority of all home industries were performed by women with families, especially among the working class. Other opportunities were limited. Before 1919 married Finnish women required their husbands' permission if they wished to operate a business of their own.[14]

Until 1910, when Finland's birth rate began to drop dramatically, those women who did marry had sizable families. In comparison to other European countries, family limitation came to Finland relatively late. Upper- and middle-class women were the first to practise birth control, but they were a very small percentage of the population. In 1890 the Finnish aristocracy made up only 0.1 per cent of the population, the clergy 0.3 per cent and the bourgeoisie 3.1 per cent. But, after 1910 Finnish women were practising birth control on a large scale, in a decade reducing the number of children born per thousand Finns by one-third. Surplus women from the rural areas were migrating to the cities, breaking many of the familiar traditions and bonds and creating a new, mobile female work force.

Educational Reform and the Suffrage Movement in Finland

Women's activism outside the home and their political participation started in Finland during the 1880s and then spread like wildfire. The last half of the nineteenth century, especially its final two decades, were exciting years in Finland. The Finnish national identity, its folklore, music, and language flowered, and its political institutions enjoyed exceptional autonomy under tsars Alexander II and III. The people were ripe for new ideas and implemented reforms in industry, politics, and society. As the national consciousness rose, so too did the desire to establish an independent nation state, to gain freedom from Russia. This desire was fueled by the Pan-Slavic movement, which was spreading simultaneously in Russia. The next tsar, Nicholas II, introduced repressive measures in Finland, enforced censorship, compulsory conscription and failed to respect the wishes of the Finnish Parliament. Everywhere Finns were discussing freedom from oppression. This atmosphere and willingness to fight for freedom were advantageous to women who could argue that they were also asking for more freedom – freedom of their own identity and actions, freedom of opportunity in social participation.

By the turn of the century, the people were in open resistance against the restrictive legislation which curbed Finnish freedom. In 1904 the tsar's hated governor general, Nikolai Bobrikov, was murdered. When the Russo-Japanese War broke out in 1905 and drained the resources and manpower of Russia, Finland staged a successful general strike, demanding constitutional reforms. Women were actively insisting that they be included as full participants in the reformed Parliament. The timing was right. The tsar relented in 1906, and Finland was granted the right to reform its government. In one bold move, Finns created a unicameral Parliament elected by universal suffrage. Finnish women became the first in Europe to receive full franchise and the first in the world to have the right to hold public office. This seemingly swift and effortless victory was in reality preceded by a whole generation of women's activism.

The first grass-roots activism which involved women was the rural revivalist movement. Many women were among the religious critics of the Lutheran Church. In the urban areas, on the other hand, free churches were gaining a foothold. Some of the intelligentsia began to view religion as something that belonged to the past superstitious era. One critic summed up the thinking of the time: "We do not fight against Christianity we simply forget it." To guard against the internal and external threats, the Finnish Lutheran Church established home missionary work in 1905 and its own newspaper, *Kotimaa* (Homeland).[15] The church also tried to modernize its appeal by actively increasing its work among the youth and the needy. Women, as volunteers and as deaconesses, were gaining some respectability within the very patriarchal Lutheran Church of Finland, which until very recently had firmly rejected women as ministers.

After 1865, when the Finnish government established public schools which were independent of the church, the educational level of Finnish women improved considerably. The last quarter of the nineteenth century witnessed a rapid increase in rural public schools, which were aimed at nine to thirteen-year-old children who had already acquired basic reading skills on their own. For example, during the school year of 1875 there were 285 rural public schools with ten thousand students. Thirty years later, in 1905, there were 2,400 rural public schools with one hundred thousand students. Primary education was extended to both sexes, but girls were in an inferior position in the country's secondary schools and universities. The first Swedish-language high schools for women were opened in 1844, and women were admitted to teachers' college when it opened in 1863. The first Finnish-language high school for girls opened in Helsinki in 1869. Higher education was only possible by special permission, first granted in 1870. Finnish women gained legal equality in university studies in 1901, by which time 14 per cent of the students were women.

Literacy increased the flow of information and made it possible for new ideas to spread rapidly. Along with the public schools came public libraries. By 1880, 481 libraries had opened their doors in all regions of Finland. Finns were also avid newspaper readers. In 1876 there were 46 newspapers, and thirty years later there were 256 newspapers, many of which were specifically oriented towards women.[16] Among them were three papers supporting women's emancipation: *Koti ja yhteiskunta* (Home and Society) (1889), *Nutid* (New Times) (1895), and *Naisten ääni* (Women's Voice) (1905).

The political awareness and activism of Finnish women rose hand-in-hand with their higher education and their increased participation in the work force. Unmarried women had been declared free from guardianship in 1864, and during the same year wealthy women were given the right to vote in municipal elections. In 1884 the first feminist organization, *Suomen Naisyhdistys* (Finland's Organization for Women), was founded. Its members were mainly upper- and middle-class women, most typically wives of prominent Finnish men who also supported new reform movements such as temperance, youth organizations, and parliamentary reform.[17]

The promotion of temperance appeared in Finland as early as 1840. During the seventeenth century Finns had made drastic changes in their drinking habits, moving from beer and wine to spirits. Although Finnish nobles owned stills obtained in Sweden during the sixteenth century, the custom of manufacturing spirits in larger quantities from grain was brought to Finland by returning soldiers from Russia. The problem was acute, not only because of drunken behaviour and lost work days, but also because the use of rye for the manufacture of spirits was making a significant dent in the food supply. At first the promoters of temperance advocated drinking within reasonable limits, but by 1884 the total abstainers had taken over the temperance movement. The executive of the first nation-wide temperance organization – *Raittiuden Ystävät* (Friends of Temperance) – contained fifteen women. In 1905 the temperance organization counted thirty-four thousand members, and was lobbying for prohibition.

At the same time as the temperance movement was involving women in social action, a youth movement to promote self-education in the arts, literature, and theatre and to encourage sports activities attracted many female members. This movement, founded in 1881 in Kauhava, spread rapidly. In 1905 it had forty thousand members, most of whom came from southern Ostrobothnia. Within this movement could be found members of all social classes who tried to emphasize the importance of national unity. In this way the youth of Finland were drawn into organized activity and were taught social and cultural responsibility.[18]

The women's rights movement was also acquiring younger members and soon found its greatest strength in single women. In 1892, a new women's rights group, *Unioni Naisasialiitto* (Union League of Women's Affairs), was established. This more youthful group was also quite closely allied with Swedish-speaking Finns. The third women's rights group to be formed was *Suomalainen Naisliitto* (Finnish Woman's League), founded in 1907. The first groups initially rallied around the question of equality of education for women, and female teachers were among the most active and numerous members. From the education issue they moved to demand equality in legal matters, better opportunities for women in the labour force, and increased political participation.

Despite the fact that, in general, the women's rights movement in Finland was an upper-class movement, in its initial stages it allied itself closely with working-class women, and many of its members embraced socialist ideals. One-quarter of the women in 1884 were members of both a worker's organization and a women's rights group. It is always difficult, of course, to estimate the impact of these relatively small activist organizations and their energetic leaders. However, from the ranks of the women's movement rose spirited and influential writers who were able to reach a much larger audience through their novels and plays. Prominent Finnish women, such as Minna Canth, whose activism started in the early temperance movement, spoke out boldly against the system. In her sensational drama, *Työmiehen vaimo* (Worker's Wife), first performed on the Finnish stage in 1885, she exposed the evils of the marital system, alcohol, and the plight of the poor. Despite her superior skills, thrift, and temperance, the heroine was at the mercy of her drunken husband. Society, especially its legal system, had failed to protect her.[19]

Like Minna Canth, turn-of-the-century feminists were focusing on women's powerlessness within marriage, lamenting the loss of individuality, and counselling women to remain single if they wanted any measure of independence. Among outspoken feminists a single woman was seen as something to emulate. Miina Sillanpää, well known for her tremendous efforts in promoting the rights and better working conditions of maids and for her thirty-seven years as a member of Parliament (following her first election in 1907 to represent the Social Democratic Party), declared bluntly: "Nothing beats the life of a spinster. I can go wherever I want and I never need to think about my spouse. To get married! I, a clever woman! No, you know, I must accomplish my work alone! It is my only chance to participate fully!"[20]

Most women's rights supporters, however, did not go that far, and the Finnish women's movement held on to the importance of the family. They were generally in agreement with John Stuart Mills's *Subjection of Women*, a book which was often quoted and read at their meetings. Their main aim was to increase women's opportunities outside the home in order to make them better participants in society at large. Equality of opportunity in all spheres of life was necessary, but so too was women's role in the family. These women's rights groups chose the more liberal and evolutionary, rather than revolutionary, path to achieve their goals. Like Mary Wollstonecraft, they emphasized the need for women to educate themselves in order to be equal partners with men. They stressed the importance of self-study, self-improvement, night schools, and educational reform.

In 1899 activist women in Finland, led by Lucina Hagman, started a women's mass organization. Its aim was to improve the lives of rural women and to bring "civilization" to the most remote homes. The organization, which was first called *Sivistystä Kodeille* (Civilization to Homes), later took the name *Marttaliitto* (Martha League) after the biblical figure. Through all kinds of self-help programs, sewing circles, courses in health, child rearing, cooking, chicken farming, and so on, the organization promoted women's awareness in their ability to participate in and improve their family's condition. These rural women were also drafted to the suffrage cause and made aware of their civic responsibilities. The message was first spread by friendly visits from the "civilized women" and later by the organization's own newspaper, *Emäntälehti* (Magazine for rural housewives) first published in 1902. This organization had a significant impact on raising women's awareness in remote areas. By 1911 there were 143 Martta locals with a total membership of 11,156. The organization's head, Lucina Hagman, was one of nineteen women elected to Parliament in 1907.

After 1907 when women in Finland had achieved two of their important goals—equality in education and the right to vote—the women's rights groups lost much of their initial enthusiasm and failed to attract many new members. Instead, active women were integrating into the existing political parties, trade unions and reform movements. The focus of activity now shifted to the working-class women and to the rapid growth of socialism in Finland.

Women and Socialism

Nineteenth-century Finland was open to political and social change; but of the new ideas and reforms, socialism had the greatest impact. It grew rapidly and enlisted tremendous enthusiasm. The increasing number of landless peasants and the new industrial proletariat, including women, were its staunchest supporters.

The first workers' organizations were founded in Finland in 1883. These followed the Bernstein style of reform socialism and advocated "liberal humanitarianism." In 1893 these organizations held their first nation-wide meetings to present their reform platform, and the working-class press was started a year later. The workers' movement was soon split as newer, more radical, revolutionary ideas gained strength. At a meeting in 1903 the *Suomen Sosialidemokraattinen Puolue* (Social Democratic Party of Finland) adopted an explicitly marxist platform and became strongly anti-religious and materialistic. It was soon clear that the greatest danger to the authority of the Lutheran Church came from the socialists. Both sides entrenched their positions, and cooperation between the two became almost impossible.

Within a decade of its founding in 1899, the Social Democratic Party had become the largest political party in Finland. Socialist halls appeared in even the most remote communities, equipped with libraries, readings rooms, stages, and sports fields. From the beginning, women had been involved in the party, and by 1906 about a quarter of the card-carrying members were women.

The *Suomen Sosialidemokraattinen Naisliitto* (Finland's Social Democratic League for Women) had been founded in 1900, although some women in the movement were against the splintering of the women's efforts. Nevertheless, in the first elections held under the reformed universal suffrage law, in 1907, the Social Democratic Party won eighty of the country's two hundred seats and became, in relative terms, the largest socialist party in the world. Among the new members of Parliament were nineteen women -- of whom nine were Social Democrats. In subsequent elections the socialists increased their strength until they held a majority in 1916 with 103 seats.

As the country became more polarized along political lines, women, too, were divided. Working women could not relate to the middle-class women's "right to work" movement. To them work was not a pleasure but an absolute necessity for survival. Socialist women were also taught to forget about their individual goals and to work for the collective good, a new society where men and women would be equal. Their position was thus somewhat problematic. On the one hand, they felt the need to improve themselves, their knowledge of the class struggle, economic conditions, and the social position of women, to organize separate women's groups and to start their own newspapers. On the other hand, they wanted to integrate into the socialist movement. Ultimately, socialist women flocked to their own organizations. After a few false starts, the maids' organization, which had been founded to promote the welfare and skills of the domestic servants, published the first socialist women's newspaper in Finland in 1905, *Palvelijatar* (Maid). Its editor was the chairman of the organization, Miina Sillanpää, who was elected to Parliament in 1907 as a Social Democrat. In the same year a more encompassing and far-reaching newpaper, *Työläisnainen* (Woman Worker), was established and supported directly by the Social Democratic Party.

Simultaneously, non-socialist women became increasingly more conservative. By the time the socialists formed the majority in Parliament in 1916, the split was total and affected all organized activity. Workers founded their own temperance, youth, sport, and women's groups.[21] The divisions and discords within the organizations reflected the overall heightened tension within Finland and the breakdown of communication and trust among Finns.

On December 6, 1917, when Russia was in the midst of the turmoil of revolution, Finland decided to declare its independence. The excitement of achieving political freedom was soon marred by a bitter civil war between the Finns who were socialists (reds) and the conservatives (whites). Both sides were supported by women's organizations which helped distribute food, nurse the wounded, and deliver information. In some red army units, women were also issued weapons and engaged in fierce battles. The *Lotta Svärd* organization, which rose to support Marshal Mannerheim and his white army, was led by many early suffragettes.

The atrocities and murders that are such an inevitable part of any fratricidal struggle left deep wounds in the young nation. An estimated four to five thousand women were among the red prisoners of war who suffered starvation, disease, and terror, while many *Lotta Svärd* women died or were wounded in action. Those affected remained forever either red or white. The heroines of one side were harlots to the other.

After three months and eighty thousand dead, the whites emerged victorious and many of the defeated reds decided to flee to Russia. The vast majority were repatriated, but a small group of "blacklisted" red refugees (forty-three men, eight women, one child) who were army leaders, nurses, and soldiers, including Finland's first socialist prime minister, Oskari Tokoi, came to Canada and worked in the New Liskeard, Ontario, lumber camp. They were led by a Finnish woman who had served as a nurse for the red brigade. Aini Wetton remembered the episode:

My father had been murdered by the whites and I was told that they were now after me. I had heard that two of my brothers had managed to escape to the "Murmansk Legion" in northern Russia. I left Rovaniemi on foot and walked across Finland, alone, I was only seventeen at the time, cold, hungry and terrified. I only walked at night and hid during the day, there were many times I was nearly caught . . . I found my brothers and hundreds of other Finns who had joined the British forces and were serving a Canadian Lieutenant. He fell in love with me and insisted I marry him and move to Canada. I absolutely refused unless he agreed to bring with him my brothers, and all other red Finns who could not return to Finland because they would be executed.

Aini Kauppinen was as good as her word and married Lieutenant T. C. Wetton only after the red Finns were safely in England and had been promised passage to Canada. Oskari Tokoi was best man. Numerous other disappointed socialists and disillusioned workers left for North America. Many travelled alone and in secret. Some arrived with false passports, some escaped Finland through Sweden.[22]

During the twenties and early thirties right-wing organizations flourished in Finland: nationalism and patriotism was equated with conservatism while the socialists were viewed as traitors. The pendulum, which had earlier so strongly swung to the left, was now swinging with equal strength to the right. The farmers of Ostrobothnia were among the most reactionary wing of this conservatism. The Communist Party was banned in its infancy and Social Democrats were harassed. In 1932 the country narrowly avoided becoming a fascist state when an attempted coup of Mäntsälä failed. Many women, especially those graduating from high school and university, gave their hearts to the nationalist cause. This patriotic fervour, the nation's political swing to the right and the harassment of the left, coloured Finnish social and cultural life during the years of greatest emigration to Canada (1920-30).

CHAPTER 2

Geographic Distribution of Finnish Women in Canada

Finns appear as a separate group in the Canadian census for the first time in 1901, when they numbered 2,502.[1] Finnish communities, however, date back to the mid-1880s when various recruitment programs were launched by the Canadian Pacific Railway and the Canadian government to encourage Finnish workers and farmers to migrate to Canada. It is generally assumed that very few women were part of this early work force, and hence their experiences have not been investigated. Yet it is possible to piece together an early migration pattern for Finnish women, who arrived in Canada from the more established Finnish communities in the United States as soon as the men found permanent work.

These women established a pattern of rooming-house keeping, which made them central figures in the early communities as providers of vital services to promote the growth of the settlements. Women also proved a tremendous asset in the pioneering stages of homesteading, and few men dared to dream of transforming the prairie sod or the dense forests of northern Ontario into a farm without a strong, healthy woman to help them. Indeed, the first white women in many a desolate frontier community were Finns.

While much of the early information must be gleaned from scattered and lean sources such as letters, oral history, and records of church congregations and temperance societies, the 1911, 1921, and 1931 census data provide the means for a more accurate analysis of the settlement patterns. A primary concern here is to discover how important gender was as a factor in settlement patterns.

Recruitment of Workers

Recruitment of immigrants, enticing them to leave their homeland, was strictly forbidden by Finnish authorities and little information remains on the clandestine operations conducted by Canadians in Finland during the 1870s and 1880s. It is known, however, that by 1874 a book about Canada appeared in Finnish. Written by Colonel H. Mattson, the book "praised Canada to the skies," and excerpts were published in Finnish newspapers. Most vigorous of the early advertisers was the *siipiiaari* (CPR), which had lured Finns from the United States to the Thunder Bay area, as early as 1876. During the most intensive period of transcontinental mainline construction, from 1881 to 1885, the railway recruited Finnish workers from the northern parts of the United States.

Typically, the records of this early Finnish recruitment seldom mentioned women. The railroads, canals, mines, and lumber camps did not hire women, and the settlements that were built around construction sites consisted of men only. The immigrants were either single or had left their wives in Finland or the United States. Their lives and dreams revolved around work and money.

The first women who broke this pattern usually followed their men as wives or sisters. The only work opportunities for women in these frontier conditions involved catering to the male population as rooming-house keepers, cooks, laundresses, bootleggers, and prostitutes. Women's fortunes were linked to their male supporters, so as long as the men avoided ill health, injury, or death and managed to find work, the women survived. Such sparse information as we have indicates that most of the early Finnish immigrant women in Canada moved here with their husbands from the United States.

When the first Finnish Lutheran congregation was founded in 1893 in Nanaimo, British Columbia, it recorded twenty-one wives, one single mother with children, and seven single women.[2] Photographs of the first Finnish organizations in Canada, the two temperance societies – Lännen Rusko (Western Glow) founded in 1890 and Aallotar (Maiden of the Waves) founded in 1891 on Vancouver Island – show at least a dozen women with one or two young children tugging at their skirts.

The married women who travelled from the United States were often part of the early family migration from Finland. In 1882, for example, 20 per cent of all emigrants were couples.[3] In addition, some had come as single women and found husbands in the Finnish communities in the United States, while a few came to Canada alone and married in British Columbia. One of these was Susanna Ahonpää, who came to North Wellington to stay with her brother. There, sometime in 1896, she married Kusti (August) Tiensuu, and together they had at least six children. Tiensuu was a coal miner, who later opened a grocery store which was run by his wife. The store burnt down in 1907, and sometime later Kusti went back to work in a lumber camp where he died in an accident two weeks before his youngest son was born. According to the written source, "Mrs. Tiensuu did not have an easy life after that."

Life was difficult, but the Finns found comfort in each other's company. Two Finnish spinsters, tired of being alone, made the following appeal in a British Columbia handwritten Finnish newspaper, *Säde* (Ray), in 1901:

> Hei, Hei You Finnish Boys!
>
> Here are two happy maidens who would like eternal guides to their life here on the Canadian shores. Because we are lonely as a bird on a wind-swept branch, we would like to leave this loneliness and begin a friendship with single men. We are not too tall and not too short, eleven feet all total and eighty-seven years...so that we are not too young and not too old, but in the best sale condition to tie those love knots. Letters from all are welcome.
>
> Searching in Extension
> Longing in Canada

Women were also arriving to join their husbands who had worked on the CPR's Rocky Mountain track, and were now settling in the Solsqua and Salmon Arm districts as farmers. In 1901, according to the census, 780 Finns lived in British Columbia.

The situation was similar in Ontario, home to 1,225 Finns. As the men found steady employment they tried to bring out or find a wife.[4] Among the first Finns who arrived in Port Arthur from the United States in 1876 was Andrew Johnson and his wife Katherine from Minnesota. Katherine, who spoke English and Swedish fluently, immediately opened a rooming-house/restaurant that same year on Pearl Street. By 1882 at least eleven married Finnish women lived in the area, among them Mrs. Erkkilä who had come from New York. The Erkkiläs founded the Windsor Hotel, also on Pearl Street, and for many years it was a traditional Finnish gathering place. Turn-of-the-century photographs of the hotel show several women working in the kitchen and as hotel cleaners. By the 1890s the population was augmented with newly arrived immigrants from Finland. Seven weddings are recorded for 1901, all of the brides being born in Finland. These single women may have come independently to Canada, or they may have been the grown-up daughters of the first immigrant families.[5]

The desire to own land, to become more self-sufficient, prompted many Finns to claim homesteads, whenever possible, within commut-

ing distance from Fort William and Port Arthur. As the vast majority
of Finnish immigrants were of rural background, the stones and
rocks of northern Ontario were all too familiar to them from the old
country. An immigration agent reported in 1901 that, "indeed, in one
day Finlanders, aggregating one hundred persons, men, women and
children, applied to me for land in Lybster."[6] The women who had
moved to the rural areas with eager anticipation soon discovered that
they were left alone to tend to the stumps: "In the forested, rocky
land of Northern Ontario, it was usually possible for a farmer to do
no more than grow vegetables and grain for his own use and enough
feed to support a few cows, pigs and chickens...extra cash had to be
made from bush work and road construction."[7]

Life for the women was one of endless toil, selling their meagre
crops for a few pennies while denying the family all but the most basic
necessities. While the men were away, women battled the elements,
wild animals, and loneliness through hard and constant work. Still,
optimism, memories of a rural life in Finland, and the feeling of security, of living on one's own land, spurred the turn-of-the-century
Finnish families in Thunder Bay to work farms. These communities
often displayed pioneer enthusiasm in their Finnish names: Intola
(Place of Eagerness), Tarmola (Place of Vigour), Toimela (Place of
Work).

As was the case on Vancouver Island and in Thunder Bay, Finnish
women were quick to follow their men to Copper Cliff. The minute
books of the temperance society, *Oikeuden Ohje* (Direction to Justice
[Golden Rule]), list nine women among its first members in 1898, and
an additional twenty-six by 1901. With two exceptions they all came
from Ostrobothnia. Reverend Pikkusaari, a Lutheran pastor, reports
that the first white child born in Copper Cliff was a Finn. The baby's
mother had arrived in 1888 to join her husband and to work in Johnson's rooming-house.

In the Sudbury area, the families also seemed to seek a rural setting,
trying to transform the forests and bush of Beaver Lake, Waters
Township, Long Lake, and Wanup into small farms while maintaining
their commuting distance to the mines. The first three Finnish homesteads were claimed in 1888, and in all cases the men had brought
their wives to Copper Cliff. Here, too, a farm was insurance against
economic disaster, providing plenty of food but not much money.
"The Finnish immigrant is warned by those who have come before
him, and who write back, to keep away from the city because unemployment always exists there."[8]

Some Finns did not heed the warning, but settled in Toronto. This
community was unique in its occupational structure, as all of the ten
men who had settled in Toronto before the end of 1901 were tailors.

Otherwise, the early history of this community follows the familiar pattern. With only one exception, the men had immigrated first to the United States. Seven of them were married and brought their wives with them to Toronto. There were also two single women; both worked as live-in maids and one had a brother in the city. As new immigrants arrived, they boarded with the earlier immigrants. In Toronto, too, one of the women, Johanna Heinonen, started a restaurant and a rooming-house around 1892.

The early recruitment of immigrants to Toronto was done entirely by the Finns themselves, especially by Jaakko Lindala, the first Finn to settle in Toronto in 1887. Lindala, a tailor from Vähäkyrö, Ostrobothnia, enticed his childhood friends and new acquaintances in the United States to come and join him. Lindala ended his bachelor days during a visit to New York in 1893, where he found his seventeen-year-old bride, Charlotte, through a newspaper advertisement. In Toronto Charlotte opened a grocery store and helped manage the community sauna while Lindala was busy organizing a cooperatively run tailoring shop. All of the Finns clustered together in the south-central area of the city.

Recruitment of Farmers

Officially Canadian immigration authorities in Ottawa were not looking for coal miners, loggers, railroad workers or skilled craftsmen, but for farmers and agricultural workers in order to hasten the settlement of the sparsely populated prairies. The promise of free land, however, was not open to women unless they were the single heads of a household. Therefore, women were mainly brought there by their husbands or persuaded through advertisements to come and look after some man "with serious intentions."[9]

In 1893 the office of the Canadian high commissioner in London authorized the printing of thirty thousand emigration folders for distribution in Finland, and the following year an additional sixty thousand. During the next decade, forty-five hundred Canadian atlases were distributed to Finns in the United States, and the following recruitment booklets were translated into Finnish: *Work, Wages and Land, Canada the Land of Opportunity*, and *North Upper Land*. All this effort was expended, despite the fact that the distribution of the pamphlets in Finland was still illegal.

Nevertheless, in 1899 James Mavor was sent to Finland to investigate the possibilities for large-scale immigration. His favourable reports on the efficient operation of Finnish steamship lines and their agent, Lars Krogius, his sense of the tense political climate in Finland, and the fine character reference he was willing to give its "highly intelligent," "literate", and "freedom loving" people promoted the idea that mass emigration from Finland was possible.

The Canadian authorities were most impressed with the peasant backgrounds of the prospective settlers who were accustomed to cold climates and had centuries of experience in clearing wilderness. In 1899 Krogius received a letter offering to give all prospective settlers 160 acres of free land if they were male and over eighteen, or if they were female heads of families. This is the first time women are mentioned in the recruitment letters or literature.[10]

Disconcertingly, Canadian government officials noted that despite their best efforts and extensive advertising in Finland, the Finns stubbornly continued to emigrate to the United States. Something more substantial had to be done to change this pattern. In 1899 a Finnish delegation was invited on an all-expenses-paid tour of Canada in search of a suitable area to establish an extensive Finnish agricultural colony. After examining several locations, the four delegates chose the district of Red Deer, Alberta, and optimistically promised to provide four thousand settlers annually. In fact, only a few hundred came to settle the area, and among them were several families from the United States.

Arthur Aho recalled that his father was working in a mine in Ishpeming, Michigan, when the mine closed. Together with his twenty-five-year-old wife, Maria, and two young children, the father decided to leave the hazardous mining business and resettle on the Canadian prairies. A fellow Finn, Jeremiah Kautonen, was encouraging others to come to a settlement he had founded in southwest Saskatchewan in 1888 and nostalgically named "New Finland." The story of Maria Aho as retold by her son is quite typical of the pioneering prairie women:

> My mother was so homesick, she never allowed us to dismantle her trunk insisting that she would not stay in this bush with no roads, nothing, just a small two-room hut with branches as a roof. The roof leaked. But every second year she had a new baby until there were twelve of us. She worked all the time, I never saw her sleep and still she kept insisting we act civilized. I was not allowed out to the nearest town till I could read and write. She taught us all that and she told us about Finland, her hometown Lapua. We dug a well by hand, but it kept drying up. Still we had a sauna every week and we were all scrubbed. Then we read the Bible and sang from the hymn book....Mother never saw Finland again, she died at seventy-six, and I have never seen that country, but still if people ask me I tell them that I am a Finn.

Between 1888 and 1901, at least forty-six families and twenty single people moved to New Finland. These homesteaders clearly found a large family to be an asset. With one exception all of the married women had children, if not their own, then adopted. By 1901 there were already 125 children in New Finland, many of these old enough to start their own households. As in Toronto, here too, the sex ratio was quite balanced.

As women arrived, it became clear that their work patterns were totally different from those of men. By 1901 there is already a hint that women preferred the more densely populated areas. The necessity to find wage work led many to the resource towns. If gender was a factor, so too was ethnicity. Finnish women sought the proximity of other Finns, and preferably access to both rural and urban living. Furthermore, the climate and geography of Finland had conditioned them to survive in the north.

Geographical Distribution of Finnish Women by 1911

According to the census figures based on racial origin, 15.497 Finns lived in Canada in 1911. The majority of Finns were now sailing for Canada directly from Finland:

Table 1: Immigration from Finland to Canada, 1901-1911

Year	Number
1900–1901	683
1901–1902	1,292
1902–1903	1,734
1903–1904	845
1904–1905	1,323
1905–1906	1,103
1906–1907	1,049
1907-1908	1,212
1908-1909	669
1909-1910	1,457
1910-1911	2,132
Total	13,498

SOURCE: *Census of Canada, 1911, Special Report on the Foreign-born Population* (Ottawa, 1915), table 13, pp. 30-31.

In addition, Finns continued to cross the border from the United States; the 1911 census lists 807 American-born Finns. Of these 42 per cent are women. No age breakdown is given for females, but the statistics show that 80 per cent of the males were under twenty-one. This indicates a strong family migration of Finnish-born parents who are bringing with them their American-born children.

Unlike the women who arrived from the United States, many of the new Finnish arrivals were single. Estimates on the percentage of single people among all emigrants from Finland vary from 60 to 83 per cent. In 1905 – the only year that specific information on emigrants destined for Canada during this decade is available – the percentage of single people was even higher, ranging from 83.6 per cent to 89.9 per cent. Between 1900 and 1909, 35.2 per cent of the emigrants were women and at least 60 per cent of them were single.

Single women did not have a husband to follow to a predetermined location. Yet, despite this independence, the women were drawn to the established Finnish settlements. Ontario continued to be the most popular province for both men and women, followed by British Columbia. In all provinces, women were in a minority.

Table 2: Percentage and Number of Females of Finnish Racial Origin in Canada and Provinces, 1911

	Per cent	Number
Quebec	9	20
Ontario	32	2,796
Manitoba	48	521
Saskatchewan	44	442
Alberta	43	675
British Columbia	32	904
Canada	35	5,393

SOURCE: *Fifth Census of Canada 1911*, II (Ottawa, 1913), table 10, "Origins of the People," pp. 342-66.

Only twenty-eight Finnish-Canadian women lived in the three maritime provinces, seven in the Yukon and four in Quebec. In Ontario Finnish communities continued to grow in the northern part of the province, in the Algoma, Nipissing, and Thunder Bay districts. Except for Toronto, where the sex ratio was almost normal, women were outnumbered by men nearly three to one, the most serious imbalance being in the Algoma East and West districts which attracted large numbers of men to the lumber camps and mines. In the prairie provinces, the near normal sex ratio remained constant. The husband-and-wife farming teams and natural increase helped to balance the population.

New farming communities in more arid sections of the prairies were established toward the end of the decade. The Coteau area, by the Saskatchewan River near Moose Jaw, attracted a few Finnish settlers who claimed homesteads on both sides of the Saskatchewan River by Outlook and Elbow. By 1909 more families migrated from the United States, and the Finnish communities spread westward to Dunblane and Dinsmore – some of the harshest and most barren of the last prairie lands to be settled. Women were among the pioneers who braved these conditions, beginning their new lives in dug-outs and sod huts.

> My mother and father regretted that they had ever come, eventually father escaped back to Finland leaving mother with five children. Then mother just walked the prairie bush and cried....When they came [1899] to New Finland father immediately took a most miserable quarter of land, full of stones and old bush, stone on top of stone. We spent many weeks every spring just clearing the stone....We left New Finland and moved to Dinsmore, there we were in at least three different homesteads, but always we had to give them up because it didn't rain and there were no crops. [FANNY MUSTAMA, New Finland, Saskatchewan]

Finns were not experienced prairie farmers, and the farm sites they chose or were placed on were often of poor quality. They looked for treed areas, and they were not wary of the presence of rock and stone on their lots, already being used to the same in Finland. Many of the hardships they endured and the failure in later years to attract more immigrants to the prairies were aggravated by their poor choice of land.

The decade between 1901 and 1911 was one of significant growth for the prairie communities. The prairies benefited from the Finnish family migration from the United States. Some Finns were also moving directly from Finland to the prairies or from other Canadian communities. Still, less than four thousand Finns lived in Manitoba, Saskatchewan, and Alberta.

British Columbia's geographic distribution of Finnish women closely resembles that of Ontario. Great variations within the province existed. The extreme imbalance occurred in the sprawling district of Comox-Atlin where women were outnumbered four to one. In Vancouver and in the older, more established Finnish communities near Nanaimo, however, they made up 40 per cent of the population.

One noteworthy new Finnish settlement in British Columbia was established on Malcolm Island off the coast of Vancouver Island, across from Knight's Inlet. Named Sointula (Place of Harmony) by its founder Matti Kurikka, who wished to establish a utopian socialist community, it was given to the Finns in 1901 by the province of British Columbia, which was eagerly promoting settlement. The first woman, Anna Wilander, moved to Sointula in 1902. She came from New York where she had just been married: "We asked comrade [Anna] Wilander to stay away from our boat and to come later with a larger boat, but this sprightly, young woman who was not afraid of danger refused to stay and came with us. The trip was most hazardous."[11]

Upon arrival in Sointula, Anna became the cook for the dozen men who were constructing buildings for the expected influx of settlers.

Dozens of married women came from the United States and Finland, drawn by the dream of a harmonious settlement where everything was shared equally. Within a year the community had over a hundred people, among them several single women. But some women found communal living a difficult adjustment and left: "The winter of 1902 was a time of misery and of great trials. The wretched housing conditions made people, especially the women, dissatisfied, and members began slowly to move out of the island."[12]

While the attempt to develop a utopian community had failed by 1905, several families remained on the island. They divided the land into homesteads and turned to fishing for a living. The dissatisfied members of the Sointula settlement tried once more to establish a cooperative commune, this time near Vancouver in Webster's Corners. The cooperation only lasted a couple of years, but here too a permanent settlement of farmers remained. Between 1903 and 1917, another seventeen families moved from Malcolm Island, to Gibson's Landing and became "the single largest identifiable ethnic group in the area." They promptly erected a socialist hall.

One more agricultural settlement at White Lake, British Columbia, was started by five Finnish squatters on "lumber company lands" near Carlin station. By the spring of 1911, twenty-two Finnish families were squatting in this area.

By the end of the first decade of the twentieth century, however, Finnish women were showing increasing reluctance to move to remote areas or to become farmers' wives, preferring a locality closer to the urban centres. The period was characterized by a distinctly uneven ratio of men to women. Of the Finnish-born immigrants there were 252 males to every 100 females in Canada. The shortage of women was most acute in British Columbia and Ontario. In these provinces there were 304 and 253 males respectively for every 100 females, a fact that made the Finnish immigrant woman's experience significantly different from that of women in Finland.

Geographical Distribution of Finnish Women by 1921

The second decade of the twentieth century was ushered in with brisk immigration from Finland, but during the war years the number of immigrants was reduced to a trickle. Between 1911 and 1921, 9,827 Finns sailed directly to Canada.

Table 3: Immigration from Finland
to Canada, 1911-1921

Year	Number
1911–12	1,646
1912–13	2,391
1913–14	3,183
1914–15	459
1915–16	139
1916–17	249
1917–18	113
1918–19	2
1919–20	44
1920–21	1,401
1911–20	9,827

SOURCE: Mauri A. Jalava, "Radicalism or a 'New Deal'?" table 2, p. 13.

In 1921, 21,494 Finns were reported living in Canada. The number of females had increased significantly, now making up 44 per cent of all Finnish immigrants in Canada. Not surprisingly, emigration statistics confirm that single women were now leaving Finland in much greater numbers. Between 1910 and 1914, 40 per cent of Finnish emigrants were female, between 1915 and 1919 this had increased to 48 per cent. These females were mainly mature women, only 12 per cent being under the age of sixteen. Proportionately more female emigrants were likely to leave from the urban areas.

In Canada, in 1921, women were distributed as follows:

Table 4: Percentage and Number of Females of Finnish
Racial Origin in Canada and Provinces, 1921

	Per cent	Number
Quebec	45	33
Ontario	44	5,703
Manitoba	43	218
Saskatchewan	44	851
Alberta	48	1,384
British Columbia	40	1,239
Canada	44	9,461

SOURCE: *Sixth Census of Canada, 1921*, I, Part 2 (Ottawa, 1924), table 26, "Population, male and female, classified according to racial origin," pp. 360-81.

In all provinces, the percentage of women had increased dramatically. This was due both to the balancing effect of natural increase as well as to the growing number of women emigrating to Canada. Ontario was the primary destination for Finnish women, with 60 per cent; Alberta and British Columbia attracted 15 and 14 per cent respectively. Finnish women continued to ignore Quebec and the maritimes, and their number in Manitoba at this time was actually cut in half, while Saskatchewan showed slow growth.

Within the provinces the variation in male-female distribution was becoming evident. The 1921 census indicates that 40 per cent of Finnish females, compared to 30 per cent of Finnish males, lived in urban centres in 1921.

Ontario had become the focal point for all Finnish immigration. In addition to the great increase in numbers, the former imbalance in the sex ratio was narrowing. In Port Arthur and Fort William the number of women was beginning to equal that of men, and in Toronto women were now in a majority. In Temiskaming, however, they still lagged far behind. Some of the new Finnish settlements in Ontario were created near Timmins–South Porcupine just prior to the great fire. Women were there as part of the pioneering community. Despite the northern location and the dense forests and swamps, here, too, Finnish couples established mixed farms. Miina Knutila was one of the first women in Timmins where she worked as a cook in a rooming-house and later watched all her savings and possessions go up in smoke when the building burnt to the ground. She describes her move to a homestead:

> We took a "homesteetti" in 1914. It cost 50 cents an acre and it had to be cleared. We just marched there, Jallu and I and one cow that kept tripping, into the dark, dense forest. There was nothing there but bears and wolves which kept howling right near us. Then with our bare hands we proceeded to make a hut from the spruce trees, everything by ourselves except the window frames and the tar paper for the roof....But it was a beautiful place right on the shores of Lake McIntosh [near Timmins], and it was our own – we didn't have to give a tenth to the landlord, didn't have to work three weeks for rent.... Voi, voi that feeling when I saw the first crop sprouting, never again would I have to beg.

Finnish immigrants were attracted to Ontario because here they could combine wage work with a setting similiar to Finland. The women described the clear lakes, the beautiful birch trees, and the moss on the smooth granite rocks. "It was just like home!" But beauty was not enough, and economic considerations superseded aesthetic ones. If, however, the Finns could combine both, as they did in many localities in northern Ontario, it was a happy occurrence. One Saskatchewan woman remembers:

> I couldn't stand it. Flat, flat, flat. No waterfalls, no trees. I had to see a tree, I could almost taste the smell of a pine tree. I longed for enough fresh water to have a good bath. Eventually it became an obsession, and I left my job [in Regina] with a good family

and pretty good wages too and moved to Sault Ste. Marie [HELMI VANHATALO].

For single women like Helmi Vanhatalo, the decision to move was simpler than if it had involved uprooting an entire family and coaxing the often reluctant husband to leave the farm. No matter how poor the quality of the soil, the farm still represented thousands of hours of toil and sweat. However, Manitoba's two major Finnish areas were shrinking in size, and women seemed more eager to leave than men.

The same phenomenon was evident in Saskatchewan. The increase in the New Finland area was mainly due to the large number of children being born, some of whom continued to farm the land. The Coteau Finns were still receiving new immigrants at the beginning of the decade, making their claims for free land grants. The number of Finns in Alberta remained stable with the exception of Edmonton which was now attracting more women. British Columbia continued to be the province with the greatest settlement differentiation for men and women. By 1921 women equalled men in Nanaimo and were in the majority in New Westminster, but Vancouver was still male-dominated, as were all other Finnish communities in British Columbia.

Distribution of Finnish Women in 1931

Long awaited by the pioneer community, a wave of Finnish mass migration became a reality between 1921 and 1930 when 37,448 Finns emigrated to Canada. The most important reason for this sudden desire to come to Canada was the restrictions placed on immigration to the United States.[13] By 1924 the American alternative had almost disappeared, and prospective emigrants turned their gaze to a more northerly destination. The impact of chain migration, letters home, prepaid tickets, and photographs sent from established Canadian communities also served as inducement for Canadian immigration. Besides, many Finns were devastated by their civil war and sought a safer country with more economic promise and political freedom. The First World War had created a temporary bottle-neck for prospective emigration; but once the seas were safe again for sailing, there was an initial rush of immigrants.

Table 5: Immigration from Finland
to Canada, 1921-1931

1921	274
1922	1,171
1923	7,640
1924	4,261
1925	1,864
1926	4,811
1927	5,167
1928	3,758
1929	4,712
1930	2,811
Total	37,448

SOURCE: As table 3.

During the twenties the proportion of women among all Finnish emigrants dropped slightly from 43 per cent between 1920 and 1924 to 40 per cent between 1925 and 1930. According to Finnish sources, the emigrants of this decade were somewhat older, especially those from urban areas. In 1923, 62 per cent of all female emigrants from Finland were between the ages of sixteen and thirty, while 12 per cent were girls under sixteen.[14]

By the time of the 1931 census the Finnish-Canadian population had doubled to 43,885, of which 42 per cent were females. Ontario was once again the most popular destination: 62 per cent of Finns had settled there by 1931 and 16 per cent had chosen British Columbia. The combined population of the three prairie provinces made up only 15 per cent of all Finns in Canada. During this decade, Quebec attracted Finnish immigrants in large numbers, 7 per cent having chosen to settle there.

Table 6: Percentage and Number of Females of Finnish
Racial Origin in Canada and the Provinces, 1931

	Per cent	Number
Quebec	46	1,352
Ontario	43	11,709
Manitoba	43	441
Saskatchewan	44	1,020
Alberta	45	1,491
British Columbia	37	2,547
Canada	42	18,628

SOURCE: *Seventh Census of Canada, 1931. Population by Areas,* II (Ottawa, 1933), table 31, "Population classified according to sex and racial origin," pp. 294-97.

In ten years, the number of Finnish females in Canada had doubled, Ontario benefiting most as its Finnish female population rose by more than six thousand. Both British Columbia and Quebec increased their female population by about thirteen hundred. British Columbia's older Finnish communities were a natural magnet, but proportionately fewer women than men were settling there. The percentage of women in British Columbia dropped by 3 per cent during this decade. The prairies continued to be shunned by the newcomers, Alberta barely holding on to its Finnish population and losing 3 per cent of its females. Manitoba and Saskatchewan increased their female population by a few hundred, but proportionately Manitoba experienced the greatest loss of women – 5 per cent. Their interest in Quebec was a totally new phenomenon, and the fact that so many women settled there on arrival needs to be explained further.

The new Finnish communities which were established in Quebec during this decade were mainly in Montreal. On Montreal Island women were clearly in the majority in the Finnish community. The other Finnish enclaves in Quebec were more or less temporary. They grew up around large construction projects, particularly the hydroelectric projects developing along the rivers. Finns were also working in the lumber camps. In addition to Beauharnois, Timiskaming, and Papineau, men could be found in Abitibi, Chicoutimi, and Quebec. Only a few Finnish women were reported in these resource centres. Montreal, then, was the desired destination for women who arrived in the twenties. Urban life and good working opportunities induced them to stay in this major port of entry.

In Ontario most of the Finnish women could be found in the Thunder Bay area, where they continued to live in Port Arthur–Fort William and in nearby farming regions. Toronto had become the second largest community of women. Still, it should be noted that even as far north as Cochrane, there were 842 Finnish women. Finnish communities had grown around Timmins–South Porcupine, Kirkland Lake, Cobalt, and North Bay, and hundreds of Finnish women made their living in these communities. In the male-dominated mining towns, the arrival of women was most welcome.

By 1931 the urbanization of Finnish women was clearly established. Comparing cities with a population of thirty thousand and over, it was apparent that Toronto, Montreal, and Vancouver held the greatest attraction for the immigrants. In Winnipeg (53 per cent), Toronto (60 per cent) and Montreal Island (54 per cent) Finnish women were in the majority. Of the large cities only in Vancouver (42 per cent) was there a noticeable imbalance with women in a minority. In Montreal nearly all of the females were born in Finland and were the most recent immigrants. The fact that only half of the Finnish females in Winnipeg were born in Finland supports the argument that the city was the recipient of farmers' daughters born on the prairies. In Toronto and Vancouver there was also a small proportion of North American-born Finns, but overall it was clear that the females in the large cities were overwhelmingly immigrants who were born in Finland.

In many other urban centres of ten thousand or more inhabitants, Finnish women also outnumbered the men. Cities provided opportunities for women to work as live-in maids or in the service industries such as restaurants, hotels, and hospitals. Here women were not necessarily dependent on the Finnish community for employment, but rather worked for Canadian employers. Finnish men, however, found it more difficult to get work in the cities and preferred the resource industries and locales.

Table 7: Population of Finns in Selected Urban Centres of 10,000 and More, 1931

Place	Males	Females
Calgary	50	60 (55%)
Fort William	492	503 (51%)
Hamilton	99	111 (53%)
New Westminster	71	77 (52%)
Outremont	1	25 (96%)
St. Catharines	25	48 (66%)
Victoria	18	26 (59%)
Westmount	9	147 (94%)
Windsor	107	148 (58%)

SOURCE: As table 6, see table 32, pp. 298-319.

The larger urban areas where women were in a minority were for the most part the mining and lumber centres of northern Ontario:

Table 8: Population of Finns in Selected Urban Areas, 1931

Place	Males	Females
North Bay	99	24 (20%)
Sault Ste Marie	608	502 (45%)
Sudbury	777	597 (36%)
Timmins	321	248 (44%)

SOURCE: As table 7.

Overall, 52 per cent of Finnish females were classified as urban compared to 45 per cent of the men. If we remove all children and older people from these calculations and consider only those Finns between the ages of twenty and twenty-nine, the difference is more striking: 68 per cent of Finnish women in this age group lived in urban areas compared to 44 per cent of men in the same age group.

Should we be surprised by the geographical distribution of Finnish women? After all, increasing urbanization was a common phenomenon in Canada, and Ontario was its most populous province. In these terms the behaviour of the Finnish women is not markedly different from the rest of the population. They were immigrant women, however, and when compared to other immigrant groups, great variations appear. Ethnicity seems to have determined the location of the Finnish communities. According to the declared destinations of immigrants who arrived to Canada in 1929 (the last year before immigration was virtually stopped through restrictive legislation), the Finns acted in total opposition to the norm.

Table 9: Intended Destination of Immigrants to Canada, 1929

Place	All immigrants	Finnish immigrants
	%	%
Ontario	26	60
Quebec	11	28
British Columbia	4	8
Prairies	57	4
Atlantic Provinces	2	0

SOURCE: Dominion of Canada, *Report of the Department of Immigration and Colonization* (Ottawa, 1930), table 30, pp. 38-39.

While other immigrants were still destined for the prairies, the Finns moved to Ontario despite the professed immigration policy of the Canadian government to accept only farmers or agricultural workers. Their social and cultural background had prepared the Finns to accept the living conditions in northern Ontario, and their economic goals pushed them to the resource towns. Women were allowed into Canada as farmers' wives and daughters, or as domestics. The latter category opened the doors wide for single Finnish women who wished to settle in Canada. In 1929, 39 per cent of all Finnish immigrants to Canada reported that they were female domestic servants. If it is an accurate assumption that about 40 per cent of Finnish immigrants were women, then virtually all Finnish women, single or married, came under this category. This explains why such a large percentage (66 per cent) of the twenty to twenty-two-year-olds lived in urban centres, where the majority of positions in domestic service were located. Their settlement pattern was thus determined not only by their gender and ethnicity, but also by their position as unskilled wage workers.

In subsequent chapters, as the impact of immigration on Finnish women is discussed, it is important to remember that there were three distinct categories of Finnish immigrant women, the largest group being urban women, often single, and mainly domestic servants. A second group encompassed those who lived in or near the resource towns and catered to the needs of the male labourers. These women had to show great flexibility in the job market. Often they created their own work, or braved the distant lumber camps. In this group I would also include the "stump farmers," those rural women who lived within commuting distance of cities such as Sudbury and Thunder Bay. The third group, and the smallest, were the women on the prairies.

CHAPTER 3

Quality of Life:
The Health and Welfare of Finnish
Immigrant Women and
Their Children

Traditionally women have been responsible for maintaining the health of the family. They have administered herbal cures, acted as midwives, and stood vigil at the bedside of a sick child with a raging fever. Only in dire cases and if money was available would a professional male doctor be called. Women were also responsible for the cleanliness of the household and the preparation of nutritious food. When the women fell ill, the family's support network, especially that between the other female family members, was crucial. Relatives could step in temporarily to tend to the children, household tasks, and the patient.

In Canada, Finnish immigrant women seldom benefited from family support systems. The women who arrived, especially the young single women, were gambling that they could survive alone by staying healthy. Novels created around immigrant themes often highlighted the plight of women: many heroines were defeated by life's harshness.[1] In 1928 the Consul of Finland, Akseli Rauanheimo, wrote a critical and pessimistic letter to Canadian immigration agents:

> The old homeland from which the emigrant left healthy and strong receives him back a wreck who is insane or otherwise disabled for life. Many dozens who were healthy and able to work when they came here are yearly returned as wrecks. The nerves could not resist the loneliness, the fight for existence in a strange country without anyone to care, proved too much.[2]

In ascertaining whether Finnish women suffered from these maladies as much as men, we must evaluate the causes of death and consider whether health is also determined by ethnicity and sex. At the same time, we must consider the working conditions and the community organizations that battled the apparent physical and psychological disintegration.

Was the number of unnatural deaths from accident, murder and suicide greater than might be expected? Were women less vulnerable to violent deaths than men? Which diseases were frequently found among the Finnish population? What was the average life expectancy of Finnish women and how did it compare to men? Was rural living healthier for women than men? Was the child mortality rate exceptionally high? Were women better able to survive the problems of alienation than men?

The Welfare of Children

Bertha Heikkinen, a Finnish maid working in Rosedale, Toronto, sat down one day to record the number of deaths among Finnish children in the city. She published her findings in the local handwritten newspaper, *Toiwo* (Hope):

> This year [1903] seven Finnish children were born in Toronto, but, at the same time, six Finnish children died, the oldest of whom was about seven. This is ample testimony to the harshness of life that we Finns here in Toronto must endure.

According to the thorough census of the Toronto community enumerated by the Finns themselves in 1903, there were forty-eight Finnish children in the city who were six years of age or under. Thus, the number of dead represents 12.5 per cent of the total number of children in this age group. This is a staggering annual loss, but quite within, or even below, "normal" expectations. While no accurate Canadian statistics are available for the turn of the century, it is estimated that one out of every five to seven babies died in the first two years of life and continued to be very vulnerable to diseases at least till the age of six.

Twenty years later, when infant mortality and child welfare had become a serious concern of the social reformers, children were still most vulnerable during the first six years of their life. According to the 1921 census's special study, which compares infant mortality among people of different racial origins, the Finns were among the lowest in this category. That year 496 Finnish children were born and 33 infants (6.6 per cent) under the age of one died. This is considerably less than the national average (8.0 per cent) or the mortality rates for Italian (8.2 per cent), Ukrainian (9.8 per cent) or Hungarian (18.2 per cent) infants and about the same as that of Irish (6.7 per cent) and Swedish (6.5 per cent) infants. In order to determine why the Finnish infants had a better chance of survival, we must examine their mothers' family health regimen.

The records of the Jackson and Barnard Funeral Home at Copper Cliff offer statistics on the deaths of Finnish immigrant children between 1913 and 1930. Excluding stillborn babies (fifteen), 146 children under the age of sixteen died. The youngest were most vulnerable, seventy-two being infants under one year old. In the Sudbury area, also, about half of the children who perished before the age of sixteen died during their first year.

In New Finland, Saskatchewan, where the sex ratio was most balanced and where the rural economy promoted larger families, the records of the Lutheran Church show that the proportion of children among dead Finns is a staggering 52 per cent. Once again the first year was most precarious, accounting for eighteen deaths (or 58 per cent) in the period from 1897 to 1913. Life on the prairies was no kinder towards infants; in fact, proportionately more children died in their first year in New Finland. Two sad, admittedly extreme, examples are the families of John and Maria Lauttamus and Matti and Maria Mustama. The Mustamas arrived in New Finland in 1891 with a three-year-old son, Ernest. In August 1891 their second son, Emil, was born. In the family history Emil wrote later he relates the death of his four-year-old brother, in January 1893, from "brain fever." "This was a great sorrow for my parents, especially my mother, for Ernest had been her constant companion." The situation was made worse by the knowledge that earlier in Finland, two of her children had died in infancy. In August 1893 a sister, Sophia, was born, followed by seven more children in the thirteen years between 1893 and 1906, but only three survived to adulthood: William, Lempi, and Tyyne. Lempi died, however, at the age of twenty.

The story of the Lauttamus family is not much better:

> After Lempi died [John's first wife who left him with 6 children], John married Maria Laitinen, born 1876. She had children from her first marriage: John Arthur Laitinen, born 1899, and Reino Laitinen, born 1901. John and Maria's children were Kusti Toivo, born 1910, died 1926. His twin Vieno Lydia died an infant. Aili Katariina, born 1911, died an infant. Eino Akseli (Alex) was born 1913. Jenni Katariina, born 1912, died one year old. Bertha Johanna, born 1915. Jaakko Benhar, born 1916, died an infant. Maria [the mother] died in 1916 too.[3]

Thus, of the last seven children, two survived to adulthood, one died at sixteen and four during their first year of life. Prairie life could be devastating to children; primitive living conditions and isolation added to the hardship. Even so, some women had a dozen healthy children who lived to adulthood. The census takers noted that in the prairies, the Finns had a lower than expected mortality rate among infants and partially attributed this to their literacy and access to information.

The Thunder Bay area Finnish children had a slightly better chance of survival. The church records indicate that of 596 age identifiable deaths in the period from 1909 to 1930, 243 (40.8 per cent) were children; of these 124 died during their first year.

Despite the regional differences and the urban-rural mix, no glaring inconsistencies emerge. In proportion to the Finnish adult population, the number of child deaths is much higher than that of adults; in New Finland, children make up 52 per cent of the dead. According to the 1931 census, 32.3 per cent of Finns in Saskatchewan were under the age of fifteen. In Ontario, where Finnish women had smaller families, the percentage of children in the overall population was even less, 22.3 per cent in rural areas and 17.8 per cent in urban areas. Bearing in mind that these statistics are estimates and that many Finns fall outside official census figures and the above sample areas, it is difficult to make an accurate summation. It does appear, however, that Finnish immigrant children in northern Ontario and Saskatchewan were twice as likely to die as the adults.

The death notices in the *Vapaus* newspaper are not a reliable source of information on child mortality. If the infants died during their first month, the parents seldom spent the money for a printed announcement. Only 19.3 per cent of the children found in the newspaper's obituary columns were under the age of sixteen, and 77 per cent of these were children between the ages of ten and fifteen. For the parents, the death of a new-born infant was not as newsworthy as that of an older child. In fact, it is impossible to determine the actual number of infant deaths, as many were buried quietly at home "in the garden under the green grass without any ceremonies."[4]

Infant deaths were expected and often announced in a matter-of-fact way. When an infant died, the ministers, undertakers, or parents who reported it seldom bothered to explain the cause of death. This is in direct contrast to the death of older children and adults whose illnesses are described in great detail. Still, evidence indicates that the death of a child was felt by most as a tremendous loss. The agony of parents who described the "most horrible pain suffered by our beloved and only child," the comforting words wishing the infant "beautiful, restful sleep," the laments over "losing our most precious darling who fell in the water barrel" and the terms of endearment that accompanied the obituaries all speak to the emotional commitment of Finnish immigrant parents toward their children.[5]

Infanticide was not common among the Finnish population. If it existed at all, it was without regard for the sex of the child, as the male-female ratio among children fourteen and under is about normal.

After the age of fifteen, the number of girls was higher than the number of boys as many immigrated from Finland at this tender age to work as baby-sitters, housekeepers, and maids. Overall in 1931, 55 per cent of the fifteen to nineteen-year-old Finns in Canada were female.[6]

Children died of many natural causes. Those children who survived the first two weeks of life and then died commonly succumbed to stomach ailments, pneumonia, or tuberculosis (contracted from their mother). After the first year, pneumonia continued to be a major killer. Added to this were various fevers (Spanish fever, scarlet fever, measles), influenza epidemics and "tooth aches." Children were also accident-prone. Among older boys gunshot wounds were the most common cause of death, followed by drowning (including drowning in a well) and burning. Girls who accompanied their mothers on washing days were sometimes poisoned or severely injured by eating the lye balls used as whitener in the laundry. Teenage girls also died of tuberculosis.[7]

The living conditions of rural immigrant women, who were burdened with frequent pregnancies and large families, and of women wage-earners in the cities, who were simultaneously trying to nurse their infants and work, increased the risk of accidents. Children were frequently left without adult supervision and at times boarded out to other families while the mothers were scratching a living in remote lumber camps. The lack of a readily available family support network for baby-sitting often forced women to leave their children in less than satisfactory care.

One social reform movement in Canada at that time which touched the lives of the Finnish immigrants was public health. Nurses toured remote communities, visited schools and homes, and promoted family hygiene, cleanliness, and a nutritional diet. When the public health nurses in Ontario braved the remote districts of Rainy River and Thunder Bay, they encountered many Finnish families. There they spoke, usually through children who acted as translators, to the "suspicious but friendly" Finnish women whom they found at home alone. The men were labouring in the fields, forests, or on construction sites. The nurses diligently recorded their observations during these field trips. Following are some of their observations. In 1926 the report from Marks Township stated: "The Finnish people live very simply and plainly as to diet; their homes are clean and airy and even the poorest of them have a bath house which is used almost daily...." Another report from Pearson Township stated: "The majority of the Finnish children seen are healthy and well nourished." This specifically mentioned that, "even in the most remote corners one finds the Finn with cows and a garden." One nurse visited a school in Nipigon where the vast majority of pupils were Finnish. She was impressed with what she discovered:

> The outstanding feature of this large school of New Canadians was the personal cleanliness of the pupils. Not one unclean head was found in those 120, and even the fingernails were kept short and clean.

"On the whole," concluded a nurse from her tour of Lybster Township, "the Finns live more naturally than the Canadians." She described their traditional habits of eating coarse, brown bread, little meat and candies, and drinking plenty of fresh milk. This report echoed the sentiments of the other nurses commenting on the healthy respect Finns had "for the cleansing properties of soap and water, most families, however poor, possessing a steambath."[8]

No doubt cleanliness and a wholesome diet contributed to the relatively low infant mortality among the Finns in Canada. The Finnish culture promoted cleanliness, and the tradition of a weekly sauna was deep-rooted. The sauna was also useful during childbirth. If at all possible mothers would retreat to the sauna, usually a separate building away from the main dwelling, when their labour started. This age-old practice had several advantages. First, it isolated the mother from the rest of the family and gave her the needed peace and quiet to concentrate on the birth. Secondly, the sauna could be heated to a comfortable temperature for the mother and new-born infant, and there was always plenty of warm water available for washing. The afterbirth was easily disposed of in the sauna oven. Furthermore, the carbon present in the old-fashioned smoke sauna prevented bacterial growth. Thus, the midwives and the women giving birth had ideal sanitary conditions and privacy.

In Finland, midwives were held in high esteem, and Finnish women in Canada continued to prefer their services even if doctors and hospitals were available. Many of the Finnish midwives in Canada were trained in Finland, but others learned their skills by observation. Oral accounts offer great praise for the local midwives. Anna Petäys from New Finland is credited with assisting in over three hundred deliveries, and Elizabeth Luoma with another two hundred. Their duties were described as follows:

> When the baby was about to be born, a midwife was sent for, and a hired girl would also come in, as neighbourhood girls were always available. After the midwife left, the hired girl would stay and help look after the new mother and baby as well as run the household. In the event that the baby was sickly, the midwife would perform a lay baptism.[9]

The midwives are praised for their dedication, walking, skiing, bicycling to their destination regardless of weather and spending endless nights at the side of a woman in labour. Midwives also operated in the cities, where, however, the warmth and isolation of the sauna was not usually available. Fathers or hired help were expected to tend to the family and run all errands which the midwife deemed necessary. In the absence of a midwife, the husband, a neighbour or a friend would be called in to help.

But the news was not all good. Because Finns trusted to their own methods and avoided institutional medical care, their children did not always get the best available treatment. In fact, very rarely did the obituaries for Finnish children indicate that they had died in hospital. Doctors were expensive and used only in extreme cases. When finally summoned, it was often too late. Furthermore, the remote location of many Finnish settlements made the journey to the doctor hazardous and often impossible. The stark reality faced by many poor immigrant families is illustrated in this nurse's account:

> In one of the homes visible in Forbes lives a little girl of eight years of age with a tubercular knee. She walks to school on a little crutch (which is too short for her) when the weather is not too cold. The parents say they cannot afford treatment. Also they do not want the child to suffer. They live about 30 miles from the city and even to get an opinion of a Doctor on the case, under the circumstances, would mean time taken to convince parents of its necessity, and to arrange transport in and out. The further difficulties are by no means the least, involving writing, interviewing, begging and perhaps sending the child away to some other place. Therefore without time and favourable weather etc. nothing is done except speaking to the Doctor who diagnosed the condition four years ago, who said "to bring the child in."[10]

The nurses also commented on two obvious social issues: the plight of single-parent families and the employment of young, working-age daughters. The high number of widowed (or abandoned) women who had to cope with large numbers of children in utter destitution, but who were ineligible for charity because they were not naturalized Canadians, was listed as one of the major obstacles to good health for Finnish children in the area. Here two immigrant problems converge: their official "foreign" status, which denied immigrant women equal access to benefits, and the social conditions within the Finnish immigrant communities, discussed in more detail in the next chapter.

The concern of the Anglo-Saxon nurses arose from the apparently immoral practice of hiring young Finnish girls to "keep house" for the many lonely bachelors in the area. This practice explains one reason for the high number of teenage brides found among the daughters of Finnish immigrants; the other reason was the shortage of women, common to many immigrant communities at the time. Furthermore, daughters from rural areas were sent off at an early age to earn their living in the cities, usually as domestics, while sons remained at home longer as their labour was more useful on the farm. By 1931 only 52.5 per cent of the Finnish females in the fifteen-to-nineteen age group were listed as "rural," as compared to 65.2 per cent of males in the same age group.

The predominant concerns of many Canadian social reformers and public health nurses – ignorant mothers inadvertently killing their infants, ragged, filthy, and impudent immigrant children, abused and overworked, who introduce contagious diseases into the schools – do not seem to apply to Finnish immigrants. Despite problems created by socio-economic conditions in the immigrant communities, Finnish mothers seem to have clung to the traditional values of cleanliness and health care and invested considerable effort in the welfare of their children. Pioneering conditions, poverty, and isolation did not hamper the women from carrying out their duties in an orderly fashion, boiling their laundry in the sauna tub, scrubbing the seemingly unscrubbable pine floors, and feeding the children "proper food." The children benefited and, as a consequence, enjoyed better health.

Health of the Adult Population

After reviewing newspaper accounts of deaths among the Finnish immigrants, a depressing scenario of mangled bodies, murder victims, suicides, and accidents begins to emerge. There are many women among them whose dreams are extinguished by a sudden, unnatural death at an early age. Headlines can be misleading, and, therefore, to force some objectivity into the picture of horror presented in the media, a statistical analysis of the recorded deaths of Finnish women is helpful. To determine whether sex was a factor in the cause of death, comparable statistics on men are also included here. From them we are able to calculate the average age at the time of death for Finnish immigrants sixteen years and over:

Table 10: Finnish Adults' Age at Death

	Number	Average age	% of adults
Jackson and Barnard Funeral Home			
Women	73	37.6	27.4
Men	193	34.9	72.6
Thunder Bay Church			
Women	129	39.9	36.5
Men	224	39.0	63.5
New Finland Church			
Women	16	53.2	55.2
Men	13	44.0	44.8

NOTE: Only those whose age is given are included in these calculations. The age is calculated by rounding the years to the last birthday, for example: 28 years 8 months and 8 days is calculated as 28, and then to the final average of all people 6 months is added. This method is necessary because often the available information is already rounded to the last birthday.

These statistics indicate that life expectancy for Finnish women was longer than that for men. Life in the Sudbury–Copper Cliff industrial region seemed to be especially dangerous for Finnish men, and women in New Finland who survived beyond the age of sixteen could expect to outlive both urban women and their own farming husbands. Although this sample is small, the nine-year discrepancy in male and female life expectancies is significant. Even at the end of this survey period (1930), the Finnish population density was highest in the twenty-five to thirty-five age group, while the number of older people was minute. Thus, the very low average age at the time of death for adult Finns is partially due to this disproportionate age structure. On the other hand, only the adults are included here, those who are living the safest years of their lives, and, therefore, some further explanation must be offered for the high mortality rate at a young age.

While women managed to live longer, their proportion of deaths was about equal to that of men. As we have noted in Chapter 2, the sexual imbalance was the greatest among adult Finns in northern Ontario. Women in this category often comprised only about one-third of the population: hence the lower number of deaths. However, if the number of men and women who died was proportionately equal, their cause of death was strikingly different. Three sources have been selected for a comparative study of the causes of death based on the criterion that each source must contain information for at least 80 per cent of the cases. From these fragments of information the following picture emerges:

Table 11: Causes of Death for Finnish Adults

	Women		Men	
Jackson and Barnard Funeral Home, 1913-1930				
Unnatural causes	3	(4.7%)	81	(45.0%)
T.B.	11	(17.2%)	23	(12.8%)
Childbirth	3	(4.7%)	—	
Other	47	(73.4%)	71	(39.4%)
Thunder Bay Church, 1914-1919				
Unnatural causes	4	(14.3%)	12	(27.3%)
T.B.	3	(10.7%)	9	(20.5%)
Childbirth	5	(17.9%)	—	
Others	16	(67.0%)	23	(52.3%)
Vapaus *Newspaper, 1921-1925*				
Unnatural causes	10	(17.9%)	69	(51.9%)
T.B.	8	(14.3%)	19	(14.3%)
Childbirth	1	(1.8%)	—	
Others	37	(66.1%)	45	(33.8%)

NOTE: These calculations include only the persons whose cause of death is known. There is no unknown or other category. Therefore, the samples used here were selected on the basis that they give accurate information in at least 80 per cent of the cases. This limits the Thunder Bay Church records to a period of six years, from 1914-19.

These statistics indicate that women were much less likely to suffer an unnatural ending to their life and confirm the suspicion that many men's lives were cut short by accidents and violence. To explain this difference we must take the analysis one step further and study these causes.

The highest percentage of unnatural deaths for women was reported in *Vapaus,* which would be more prone to publish the dramatic stories of suicide and murder than common disease. Still, less than one-fifth of the women died as a result of suicide, abortion, murder, or accident. The newspaper reported that over half of the Finnish men met an unnatural early death. In the Copper Cliff–Sudbury region, where they were involved in dangerous mine work, the percentage was 45 per cent, while the Thunder Bay Church recorded only 27.3 per cent. The low percentage of unnatural deaths in the church statistics also reflects the fact that murderers and suicides were less likely to receive the minister's blessing and, with few exceptions, are missing from these records. Similarly, many of the lumbermen who were susceptible to work-site accidents shunned the church because of their political beliefs. Yet even the most conservative estimates would indicate that, while the percentage of unnatural deaths among women was about 10 to 15 per cent, the same percentage among men ranged from one-third to one-half of the total known causes of death:

Table 12: Unnatural Causes of Death for Finnish Adults

	Suicides		Murders		Accidents	
	women	men	women	men	women	men
Funeral Home	2	8	—	3	1	70
Church	—	2	—	—	4	10
Newspaper	6	20	1	8	3	41
Total	8	30	1	11	8	121

Unnatural causes of death for women in these samples were just about equally divided between suicide and accident. Only one woman was a murder victim: she was killed by her husband. Life then seemed relatively safe for women. The accidents that were likely to kill them usually happened at home. Only one died at her place of employment, the others either fell down stairs, accidentally shot themselves (while hunting), were poisoned, or died as a result of an abortion. Interestingly, not a single adult woman in this sample was listed as a drowning victim.

Since suicide is viewed as one of the clearest symptoms of disintegration in a society, the high number of Finnish women in this category indicates serious distress. This small sample, which in all probability lists only a few of the suicides, reveals that Finns had an exceptionally strong tendency to commit suicide. For example, during the year 1923 newspapers alone reported that thirteen Finns committed suicide in Canada that year. This sample, we must remember, does not include any suspicious deaths by drowning, being run over by a train, poisoning, or accidental shooting. Yet already the suicide rate was about seven times the national average in Canada for the same year and at least three times the expected number of suicides in Finland.

Is this a sign of social disintegration in Finnish-Canadian communities? Is the shock of the immigrant experience so devastating and the living conditions so wretched that death is preferable? Does Finnish culture, coupled with an abnormal socio-economic balance and a feeling of alienation, cause the high incidence of suicide? To answer these puzzling questions we must try to probe the actual causes. Once again, invaluable detail is provided by the Finnish press. The primary motive for female suicide appeared to be illness. Women who had suffered and lost any hope of regaining their health decided to end their misery rather than be a burden to their family and prolong everyone's suffering. One woman dragged herself from the bed to the front porch where she hanged herself on her children's swing; four others were reportedly suffering from chronic illnesses before they hanged themselves. One destitute woman with three children hanged herself in the stairwell of her home, and two others shot themselves. The youngest female suicide was sixteen and the oldest thirty-nine. With the exception of the sixteen-year-old, the women seemed to be living with a permanent partner, or they were single mothers.

Poverty and illness then were the obvious reason for suicide among Finnish women. Perhaps these can be linked to the trauma of immigration. It might well be that if the support systems of the extended family were present to look after the sick women and if they had received medical attention, fewer would have committed suicide. But there is also the cultural transference of a tradition of suicide. Lutheran Church records bear this out, and the people themselves have not felt pressured to hide their suicidal intentions. Since 1910 all suicide victims have received a normal burial in a consecrated graveyard. The act of taking one's own life in Finland is seen by many as a private decision, an ultimate act of independence. Preventive legislation has proved totally ineffective. The tradition is long-standing: the heroines and heroes of Finnish folklore often killed themselves. Finland's best-known composer, Jean Sibelius, wrote his first symphony around the theme of suicide. When this tradition is combined with the personal trials of immigrant life, the loneliness, isolation and inability to seek help, then the suicide rate is bound to increase. While Finnish immigrant women frequently made this calculated decision to end their wretched existence, Finnish men were four times as likely to make the same choice.

Not only were Finnish men more likely to kill themselves, but their motives were also different. At least six of the thirty suicides listed in table 12 were related to alcohol. Three others were murder/suicides. Another man killed himself in the "almshouse," and four other victims were reported to have had lengthy illnesses. The others were simply found hanging from trees or shot in the forest. Men were also known to throw themselves in front of trains, blow themselves up with dynamite, or drown themselves. Unlike the women who committed suicide, at least one-third of the men were bachelors. Many had no known family, sometimes even an accurate name was missing, the dead being known only by some nickname. The men seemed to be even more disrupted by the abnormality of immigrant life; poverty, illness, alcoholism, and loneliness, in the end, drove them to suicide:

> Outside of Port Arthur there was a famous tree called "the last stop" because that's where the Finns hanged themselves. It seemed that almost every week someone was dangling there from his neck. They were considerate, you know, if somebody was missing you knew where to look first. It was much more difficult to go to the forest and find the pieces of those who shot themselves – wild animals often got to them first. But when you know one is hanging from a tree branch, this isn't such a problem.... Life was so rough, unemployment, hunger churning in the stomach, lonely men, not even money to go back to Finland. You can see why they would

choose to kill themselves... when you are a foreigner your life isn't worth a damn, and soon you start to believe it too.

This summation was made by William Eklund, who edited *Vapaus* for thirty-five years and who collected the history of the Finnish Organization of Canada. He, perhaps better than any other Finnish immigrant, was familiar with the reality of immigrant life.

We have already noted that accidents were rare among Finnish women, but for men the case was different. While women seldom drowned, 23.1 per cent of the men in our sample of unnatural deaths did. Alcoholic poisoning claimed another 8.3 per cent and 5.8 per cent died in train-related accidents. However, the biggest killer of Finnish men were industrial accidents. Of all the unnatural deaths, 43 per cent happened at the work site. The work Finnish men were engaged in was extremely hazardous. Women were almost totally spared this kind of death, but they did suffer the consequences, losing sons and husbands in their most productive years. The life of a young immigrant widow with children was fraught with economic and emotional difficulties.[11]

The only category of accidental death where women seem to equal men was accidental shooting. Finnish women frequently went hunting, and many never left the house without a gun on their shoulder in case they saw a rabbit or a grouse. Miina Knutila from Timmins, Ontario, remembers:

I have been hunting and catching grouse [*pyitä*]. I always carried a gun. Of course, it was often illegal, but sometimes you have to do things you are not supposed to in order to have food. If we got moose we put it in a barrel in the forest, salted it and put the ice on the bottom. The whole village could get food from one moose....

With guns so readily available, accidents were bound to happen. Not only were adults killed by misfired guns, but children, especially teenagers, fell victim as well. When access to firearms was mixed with excessive use of alcohol, the number of accidents increased even further.

Women, then, were spared most of the violent and accidental deaths common to Finnish men. Except for those instances of suicide, female adjustment to their new environment was smoother. Alcoholism affected their lives when they fell victim to abuse, battering and, at times, murder by their drunken partners. The women's work place was also more accident free. Nevertheless, they died, in proportion to their numbers, as frequently as men. What then was the cause?

General Health of Finnish Immigrant Women

On arrival in Canada, immigrants were expected to be healthy. Ever since the introduction of cholera with the Irish immigrants of the 1830s, all foreigners have undergone at least a cursory health inspection. Canada's first Immigration Act in 1869 contained legislation against the entry of lunatics and idiots. By 1902 on-the-spot medical examinations were instituted at several ports of entry, and the medical officers were asked to screen out persons with a specific physical disability, and those suffering from mental disorders and disease. By 1910, when the new Immigration Act expanded the prohibited classes, the list included idiots, imbeciles, feeble-minded, epileptics and the insane; those afflicted with any loathsome disease or with a disease which is contagious or infectious, or which might become dangerous to the public health; the dumb, blind, or otherwise physically defective. The examination, however, was not thorough.

It is unlikely that people would venture on the long and arduous journey to North America in anticipation of a life of hard work if they did not feel physically capable of the task. Women, accompanying their husbands, were an exception to this rule. Some wives were several months pregnant and probably in a weak state by the time they reached land, but women were expected to be pregnant and tired.

Deportations of Finnish women on arrival were rare, but just because they slipped through did not necessarily mean that they were healthy. In addition, when a man was deported it often reflected on the lives of other family members. A commissioner of immigration wrote the following plea on August 4, 1903:

> A Finlander ...with her three children landed at Halifax ex S.S. Tunisian on the 4th of January 1903. Her husband was returned to Finland on account of being a victim to trachoma, and as they had tickets to Whitemouth the mother and the three children came forward during the winter, but one child died since coming to Whitemouth. The mother has no means of support, and they are totally dependent upon charity. The father is too poor to send money for their return to Finland. I think this is a case where the woman and her two children – one boy of six years and the other a girl of four – should be sent back to Finland as soon as possible.[12]

During the height of Finnish immigration to Canada (1923-24), only ten Finns were deported, all men. When the nation's economy took a downturn and immigrants were seen as a financial and political burden to the community, Finnish deportations multiplied. In 1931, 221 Finns were deported, but only 29 of these were women.

The majority of Finnish women deported suffered from ill health or extreme poverty. The assumption that women were more susceptible to insanity in the unfamiliar new environment is not borne out by the deportation statistics. Eighteen insane men, as compared to only two insane women, were deported. Women were also less likely to be public charges as they could manage to find shelter and work as live-in domestics. Most vulnerable, once again, were single mothers who were forced to rely on public charity. If they were not yet Canadian citizens, they could face deportation. Even during the exceptionally active year of deportation in 1931, only thirteen women as opposed to forty-four men were forced to leave for health reasons. Deportations of criminal Finnish women were also rare, but one-third of the deported men were criminals. While some people were happy enough to be leaving (some might even have engineered their own deportation), to many others it was a sudden end to a life built on hope, a signal of failure, a disgrace felt by the entire family.

The foremost natural scourge on the health of Finnish women in Canada was tuberculosis. Canadian social reformers were particularly keen on eradicating this disease, which was seen as "the most exact measure we have of the social status of an individual, family, community or state."[13] By 1882 it was known that tuberculosis was contagious and most prevalent in overcrowded, dirty, industrial, urban areas. It seemed to strike first the people in poor health, although no one was immune to the disease. If it was contagious and if environmental factors increased the chance of contracting the disease, then, the social reformers reasoned, it was curable. Finns seemed to be especially prone to this "social disease with a medical aspect." If we examine only those cases in the above samples that were definitely identified as TB, the percentage of all deaths for women from this disease ranged from 10.7 per cent to 17.2 per cent. This range was about the same for men, 12.8 per cent to 20.5 per cent. These figures leave out all other illnesses that could have been linked to tuberculosis, such as respiratory problems or, as described by the grieving families, a "cough," "blood in the lungs" and a "tight chest." It could be assumed that since men worked in the mines, they would be more likely to develop TB. In fact, the Finns nicknamed the disease "the miner's illness" *(mainarin tauti)*. But why did so many women die of tuberculosis? Was it crowded quarters, or perhaps poor overall health? If so, why did farm women contract this disease? A notation in a prairie family's biographical history reads: "Vilhelmiina Myllymäki died in 1896 about the same time as her year old son, Einar and Kaarlo died at the age of 15 of TB, which plagued the family for the next two generations."[14]

Wherever Finns had settled, tuberculosis was killing them off steadily and surely. The city solicitor of Sudbury sent an urgent plea to the Deputy Minister of Immigration in 1931:

Sanna and J.K. Lauttamus, the first couple to settle in New Finland, Saskatchewan, in 1890. (New Finland Historical and Heritage Society Collection)

Many Finnish women worked as cooks and dishwashers in the remote and isolated lumber camps. North of Thunder Bay, Ontario, 1927. (Sakari Pälsi Collection, National Museum of Finland 158:43)

Infants were most vulnerable to disease and death and the child mortality was staggering. Sudbury, Ontario, *c.* 1914. (Fin 7391-13/Oiva Svensk/MHSO/OA)

Finnish women were well recognized for their hunting skills. Northern Ontario, *c.* 1900. (FCHSC 2049/MHSO/OA)

Women were able to supplement the family income by raising poultry. British Columbia, n.d. (FCHS 1428/MHSO/OA)

Washerwoman, 1927. (Fin 10971-Elsa Sillanpää Collection/ MHSO/OA)

Large Quebec construction projects attracted women who worked in the roominghouses, restaurants and stores, *c.* 1928. (Pertti Kaski, private collection)

Lumber camp cook taking a rare moment of rest, North of Thunder Bay, Ontario, 1927. (Sakari Pälsi Collection/National Museum of Finland 158:44)

FSOC Women gymnasts marching in the July Parade in Port Arthur, Ontario, 1912. (FCHSC/OA)

Despite the austere surroundings, young immigrant women were full of optimism and enthusiasm. Northern Quebec, *c.* 1928. (Pertti Kaski, private collection)

Lower left: At the photographers. Northern Quebec, *c.* 1930. (Pertti Kaski, private collection)

Lower right: Two Finnish hospital workers posing on the roof of the Toronto General Hospital, 1927. (Olga Fagerlund Collection/Migration Institute, Turku, Finland)

Newly arrived maids on the steps of the Finnish Immigrant Home in Montreal, Quebec, *c.* 1929. (PA 127086/Victor Kangas Collection/PAC)

After the wedding of Lieutenant Wetton and his wife Aini in London, England, in 1919. Former socialist Prime Minister of Finland is the best man and the members of the Murmansk Legion, who are on their way to a Canadian lumber camp, form the honour guard. (Varpu Lindström-Best, private collection)

The first modest home, Whitefish, Ontario, 1920.
(Fin 12680/Martta Huhtala/MHSO)

Co-operative Finnish Restaurant, Rouyn, Quebec, 1926.
(Fin 7387-Niilo Nissilä/MHSO/OA)

Toronto's Finnish maids after their English lessons in front of the Church of All Nations of the United Church of Canada, 1928. (MHSO)

I wish that you could send up a representative to Sudbury to go into this matter [tuberculosis] as we have quite a number of Finlanders in the Sanatorium. They seem to be a race susceptible to this complaint and they are becoming a burden to this municipality, and we would like to find out just what could be done in a matter of this kind.[15]

The Finns, too, tried to ascertain what could be done. They stacked the libraries with available information on TB, scrubbed the floors once more, moved those who were ill into sunshine, and slept with their windows open. Women tried to convince the men that spitting, especially in the sauna, should be avoided, and once again fresh milk was seen as a cure. Rather than obtaining their information from Canadian women's organizations and public health nurses, the Finns trusted their own medical pamphlets. Their methods did not, however, differ from those recommended by Canadians. According to Katherine McCuaig, the women of IODE and WCTU waged an unceasing war against "indiscriminate spitting, the common drinking cup, dry sweeping, flies, [and] impure milk." But they also addressed more deep-rooted social problems, such as "poor housing, long working hours, low wages, over-crowding, poor nutrition, and alcoholism." By the end of 1930, the incidence of TB was declining, even though it continued to be a serious threat to the health of Finnish immigrants. The slow agonizing illness, the long wait for the almost inevitable death, caused much suffering not only to the patients, but also to those close to them. No wonder some women chose suicide to free themselves and their family from the economic burden of health care and the psychological agony of seeing a loved one suffer.

Finns preferred to treat their own ailments if possible. The knowledge of home remedies was passed on from one generation to the next by women, who were the healers. An old Finnish proverb states: "If sauna, tar and spirits are not a sufficient cure then death is imminent." One lonely Finnish trapper in Canada remembered his mother's advice when he was suffering from chest pains, possibly pneumonia. He wrote:

Now I am staying at home, I heat up the sauna and bathe and I inhale the vapours from heated tar into my lungs so that I can kill all the bacteria from my lungs. ...I can cure all bad coughs, it is the only way to kill the needling pain in my chest, I breath also vapours from turpentine and again tar... you remember mother the way I used to do it at home. [LAURI NURMINEN, Kirkland Lake].

Though they lived in a relatively accident-free environment, Finnish immigrant women did fall prey to a host of physical ailments, usually only described as a pain in the stomach, weakness of blood, or internal infections. Heart failure and cancer claimed some. The rest died of influenza, fever, and pneumonia. Childbirth claimed up to 17 per cent of the women in Thunder Bay, but the funeral home records indicate that less than 5 per cent died while giving birth. Accurate statistics here are difficult to obtain; many of the "bleeding to death" cases or "high fevers" could be caused by childbirth or abortions. Church records reveal several instances when the mother's death was followed a few days later by the death of her infant. Since no accurate cause of death is given, these women remain outside the calculations. After suicide and tuberculosis, childbirth was the third most common cause of death. Very few women reached old age. Occasionally the cause of death was documented as "senility," the old woman having reached sixty years. After sixty death was considered as natural as that of newborn infants and causal explanations were omitted.

Mutual Aid

In Finland men and women in the prime of their life were hardly concerned with planning their own funeral arrangements. Families, friends and, in destitute cases, the state, were there to rely on in that event. Once in Canada, however, many people became preoccupied with the prospect of dying. Having seen unmarked shallow graves where "some foreigner" was hastily buried – no name, no place of birth to identify the victim – they feared meeting the same fate. Who would send a message to Finland to my old parents? Who would see to it that my remains were disposed of with dignity? The Jackson and Barnard Funeral Home, for example, sold the bodies of single men with no known families to the medical departments of Queen's University and the University of Toronto. Between 1926 and 1931, twenty Finns were shipped off, identified simply as "a blond, blue eyed, Finnish male, about forty, found on the railroad track near Sudbury." The funeral home received $150 per cadaver and saved themselves the search for relatives or the bureaucratic process of obtaining funds for pauper funerals. It is most interesting to note that not a single Finnish woman buried by the Jackson and Barnard Funeral Home met this fate – all of them had an identifiable family or friend. Finnish women were known and recognized as individuals and maintained their own support networks. Some men, on the other hand, led a transitory existence, often on the move, using a variety of names and living as loners.

To obtain some security in case of injury or ill health, the Finnish immigrants quickly organized sick benefit societies. The mining communities, naturally enough, were the first to pool together and develop their own form of mutual aid. The first concern was the danger of sudden death and inadequate burial rites, and the second was the possibility that an industrial accident or debilitating illness would have a devastating impact on the remaining family.

The oldest surviving regulations of a Finnish mutual aid organization come from North Wellington, British Columbia, a Vancouver Island coal-mining community. The rules of the "Organization to Aid in Case of Injury or Illness" were dated October 11, 1891, the same day as the Aallotar temperance society held its founding meeting. From the beginning the two groups were united in their action. All those who had turned sixteen and did not suffer from a chronic or venereal disease were eligible to join. The membership fee was one dollar for men and fifty cents for women. In addition the monthly dues were fifty cents for men and twenty-five cents for women. All members had to give the names of their immediate relatives and in the case of a member's death, all others had to pay seventy-five cents to cover the funeral costs. Women's cheaper fees reflected their lower salary levels and their safer working conditions. In the event women fell ill, they were expected to survive on half the money of the men, who would receive one dollar per day for the first sixty days and fifty cents per day for the next sixty days. The people were not paid for the first week of illness, nor were they paid for illnesses lasting less than two weeks. In case of death, the organization arranged a funeral for $60, or gave the money to the closest relatives or friends to take care of the funeral. Subsequent minutes of the association show that the task of caring for the ill more often than not fell on the women and their work was on a voluntary, rotating basis. The organization not only paid the sick benefits but also tried to arrange for house-keeping, food, and nursing for those immigrants who were single.[16]

In addition to the many structured mutual benefit organizations, communities banded together more informally to help individuals in distress. For example, the Finnish Organization of Canada paid for the funerals of the many victims of industrial accidents and organized fund-raising events to send women suffering from TB or other long-term illnesses back to Finland. The Finnish Consul in Toronto, Adiel Saarimäki, raised funds in the local Finnish community, and especially through the Toronto Finnish United Church, to obtain legal aid and hospital costs for two maids badly injured when their place of employment blew up in Toronto on October 1, 1927, killing several of the occupants. The explosion was caused by fifteen gallons of gasoline which were brought to the house for "fall cleaning." The two Finnish maids, Lyydia Hietikko and Esteri Kallio, did not receive the sympathy of Canadian authorities; instead they were threatened with deportation since they had become a burden on the city, unable to cover their hospitalization expenses. The women, who had not only lost their health and appearance (they were badly burnt and cut by glass), had also lost all their private possessions, including their savings. The cruelty of this threat, published in the *Globe,* once again exposed the vulnerability of single immigrants and mobilized the Finnish community. This particular story had some positive aspects as the women, thanks to community efforts, received $3,000 and $600, respectively, for their injuries from the estate of their employer. Without this support network these immigrant women faced almost certain deportation.

Finally, private individuals also helped each other during times of difficulties. A sentimental poem written by a Finnish lumberjack who watched as his friend was crushed by a log, records the dying wishes of his workmate. A few translated verses of this poem, written in a forest near Montreal, illustrate the concerns of the dying man, his need to be remembered by his mother and girl-friend:

> "You were my best comrade"
> Uttered Kalle Koski.
> "Our roads will separate.
> I remain here, this is my last wish:
>
> Search for my photograph, you remember it,
> It's somewhere in my wallet,
> Take it with my greetings,
> To my fiancee in Toronto.
>
> My golden watch is yours.
> Tear my shirt open,
> I hid my dollars inside,
> Send them to my old mother in Perho.
>
> Write her a little, and tell her:
> I remember her and my childhood."
> Then his head sunk,
> He went through the gates of death.
>
> So ended his wandering,
> One Kalle Koski,
> Born in Perho, died now,
> In the forest, under Canadian skies.[17]

Not all girl-friends or mothers received a poem, but many did receive at least a letter written by someone who knew the address of the next of kin. Usually the men did not have much property to dispose of; the gold watch, their symbol of respectability and success, was carefully wrapped and sent to the grieving mother in Finland. Some photographs, worn-out letters, and a few tools usually made up the entire fortune of the itinerant worker. The practice of sending the remains of the deceased to the homeland, common to some immigrant groups, was not a Finnish custom.

Despite the various levels of mutual aid, pre-planned sick benefit organizations, spontaneous community involvement, or the helping hand of a friend, some Finns simply "disappeared," meeting the anonymous death they so feared. Occasionally the Finnish consulate would publish lists of names whose mailing address was unknown and who had mail left for them at the consulate. About 95 per cent of the missing people were men. In the list of 271 missing Finns, just prior to Christmas 1924, there were only fourteen women. Women, in general, benefited greatly from community assistance. But there were still some women, especially single mothers with children, who did not receive support in time.

Most Finns in Canada received simple funerals where the body was laid to rest in the local graveyard or farm while friends, neighbours, and family looked on. But because some Finns were devout socialists, they refused the final blessings of the church:

> Good-bye mother darling,
> My beloved spouse,
> Your life was one of endless battle,
> For your family, for your loved ones.
> You didn't ask much for yourself,
> But for your class, for your comrades,
> You sacrificed everything.
> Sleep in peace comrade, mother dear, beloved wife.[18]

Because of such radicalism among the Finns, the Jackson and Barnard Funeral Home found it necessary to mark in their records the former political beliefs of the deceased. In the corner of the form would be scribbled a warning, "a socialist, no minister!" The tradition of politicizing funerals also marked the Finnish women apart from most other Canadian women.

The religious Finns and those who were non-political were buried by the local Finnish minister, if he was available. Many socialists also opted for the traditional funeral, and ministers reluctantly performed the last rites on people who spent their entire lifetime denying the church. Others had second thoughts when sick and dying and reportedly "found Jesus" in time to merit a church service.[19]

In direct contrast to these quiet, peaceful burials were the showcase funerals for the "victims of class war." These were strategically planned to maximize political gain for the workers' movement. Some of the largest political demonstrations and parades in northern Ontario were staged around Finnish victims of industrial accidents. Politically aware women participated in the funerals, marched, and gave speeches. The martyrs, however, were men. Finnish women in domestic service, who died in a fire or explosion, were not deemed worthy of such ceremonies, no matter how supportive of the workers' movement they had been.

All of the above evidence indicates that the health and welfare of Finnish women in Canada was influenced by their ethnicity, class and gender. The mutual benefit societies which they organized in Canada were not part of cultural transference for the Finns but rather were radically modified institutions created to respond to the immigrant's special needs. Community assistance was invaluable, but it was not enough. Social problems common in the old country were further exaggerated in Canada.

CHAPTER 4

"Canada Is Hell for Men, Heaven for Women": An Examination of Marriage and Birth

Throughout history women's lives have been greatly influenced by their marital status and their reproductive capacity. The norm for traditional Finnish women was to find a partner and build a strong family unit. The immigrant experience and the changed economic, social, and working conditions, however, forced women to rethink and re-evaluate some traditions which directly affected them. The majority of Finnish women in Canada were between the ages of twenty and thirty-nine. In their natural life cycle, all faced the inevitable decisions about courtship, marriage, children, and separation. The old traditions in their homeland were also changing. After the turn of the century and before the Great Depression, Finland had a high percentage of single women and relatively late marriages and a sharply declining birth rate. Did the women who came to Canada continue to follow the cultural patterns of marriage and birth established in Finland, or did the immigrant experience influence their decision in these matters? How strong were environmental, economic, and social factors in formulating their options?

The available data on women from other cultures are lean, but do allow for some comparison. The study of the Finnish immigrant woman must take into consideration regional variations, sex imbalance, and the structures and values of the Finnish immigrant community. It must also encourage the immigrant women to discuss their most intimate and difficult decisions to determine if ethnicity was a factor in their decision-making.

Courtship

Marital opportunities in Canada were definitely in the women's favour; this was the complete opposite of the situation in Finland where years of emigration and war had produced "surplus women." It has been suggested that some of the single women who moved to America between the world wars came in pursuit of the eligible bachelors who had left the homeland earlier. While this is difficult to substantiate, there were some examples of "mail-order brides." Usually these were women who had responded to advertisements placed by lonely Finnish men in their village newspaper in Finland. Aili Grönlund Schneider provides an enlightening depiction of this custom in the 1920s:

> Mail-order bride! That had an unhealthy sound. There had been many embarrassing situations concerning these amongst the Finns. Starry-eyed girls came from Finland to meet men they had written to, exchanged pictures with, but never seen. Often one or the other party found reality too hard to take. A couple of years ago, seven brides came over all from the same village in Finland. The whole Finnish population of Timmins turned out to meet the train, to watch this mass meeting of grooms and brides who had never laid eyes on each other before....They all married, though there was some gossip about some trading back and forth, but actually, nobody knew who had come for whom in the first place.[1]

The Finnish mail-order brides came on their own accord. There is no indication of any parental involvement, except some attempts to discourage them from making such a reckless decision. To be a mail-order bride required courage, a spirit of adventure, and a dose of optimism. At times, the brides brought a child with them. Canada, they had heard, was good for women, and there is no question that once in Canada the shortage of women was a great social advantage. One woman describes her initial response to the wealth of men in Timmins:

> 'Kanaatas' [In Canada] it was easier to be a woman. I left to seek adventure in Timmins and I went to work in Härmä boarding-house – you know – the people from Härmä have founded it. It took me four hours to find a man, there was no need to look for them, just to pick and choose. I arrived on the four o'clock train and at eight o'clock I left to dance at the organization's hall [TYYNE PIHLAJAMÄKI].

A quick partnership culminating in a fast marriage or common-law relationship was one response; the other was to take advantage of the situation, prolong the days of being single and enjoy the attention. One shy woman wrote from Copper Cliff: "Yes, there are all kinds of boys here too, even I the quiet type could get as many as I would like without trying at all, even now I have one such boy to whom I must write a Dear John letter tomorrow night."[2]

During the courtship, women seemed to have the upper hand and were quick to note the difference in mood between Finland and Canada:

> Oh Toini, it is much different in here from Finland in all ways I have not been homesick at all yet because I have had so much fun right away during the first night when I arrived to *nipikkaan* [Nipigon] we went to the hall and then almost every second night we were at the hall while I lived there and I could get car rides as much as I wanted to and here you don't have to walk to the dance place they just take you in fine style with a car and then there is one thing here a person is appreciated be she good or bad you don't see anybody's face in a cynical smirk as some young boys do there in Finland everyone here is so polite as could possibly be *voi* Toini it would be so much fun if you too were able to come here uncle here asked me right away if Niko has sent you a ticket yet....[3]

Toini, however, was getting conflicting advice. While her girl-friend was bubbling with enthusiasm and happiness, her boy-friend sent more pessimistic reports. Life for men seemed more difficult:

> ...are you not going to leave soon to come and see me don't you want at all to come I guess we could somehow manage here but it is much more fun there in the land of birth in my opinion and in the opinion of many others yes this place is praised too much but it is not proper to complain either since I have immigrated...I would be so happy if you were here speaking to me....[4]

There were several factors which contributed to the favourable social conditions for women. The most important, a high percentage of surplus males, was common to most immigrant groups. The Italian community was hard hit; the almost total lack of women had a demoralizing effect on single men. Ukrainians and Hungarians, on the other hand, came mainly as family migrants, and while they too had a shortage of women, their communities were not as severely affected. The Irish, who had immigrated to Canada in large numbers since the end of the Napoleonic Wars, had reached a near normal population gender balance by the 1920s. But in their initial immigration, they, too, experienced a great social sexual imbalance. The Swedes, even more than the Finns, had mixed communities. They were not characterized by temporary migrant life, nor were they happily balanced communities which encouraged normal marital patterns.

The shortage of women in the new Finnish communities in Canada was most acute in the over twenty-one age category. In 1921 the proportion of surplus males who had been born in Finland reached 68 per cent. An age-specific calculation based on the 1931 census shows that until the age of twenty-five, Finnish women were often in the majority; but among those over twenty-five, the shortage of women became apparent.

Finnish men magnified their own problems by insisting on acquiring a Finnish wife. Of those who were married and had a child in 1921, 91 per cent had a Finnish spouse. Finnish women also showed a preference for Finnish men. They did marry non-Finns as well, however, in greater numbers. Only 83 per cent of Finnish women were endogamous. This trend added another 8 per cent to the male surplus. The Scandinavians and the Irish showed much greater willingness toward integrated marriages, while nearly 100 per cent of the Italian women married Italian men. In fact, Italian women were often married on arrival, or were brought over for this explicit purpose. Ukrainians also married each other while the Hungarians had a similar pattern to that of the Finns.

Why did 17 per cent of Finnish women choose to marry non-Finns despite the great demand for them within the Finnish community? One explanation lies in the diverse geographical distribution of Finnish men and women. Many women lived in cities where they worked with non-Finns, were often able to learn at least the rudiments of the English language, and were more often exposed to men of other nationalities. In any case, Finnish men were not the only ones looking for partners. Across Canada there were 6 per cent more males than females in 1921. In addition, in many of the larger urban centres there was actually a shortage of Finnish men – a situation which encouraged the women to look elsewhere.

Finnish men were not at all happy to see Finnish women courting "foreigners," and some men tried to stop it:

> ...The Finnish men set up guards by the dance hall in order to keep out the "German engineers." Sometimes there was serious trouble and fights, especially when the Finns were drunk. They just couldn't stomach seeing a Finnish girl under the arm of some *kielinen* (one who speaks the language) [MARTTA KUJANPÄÄ, TYYNE LATVA, Toronto].

A recording of a popular song has survived which humorously describes the attempts of the Finnish men to keep their women. It also pokes fun at the frivolity of the women who were courting non-Finns – lips thick with red paint, sitting on park benches arm-in-arm with strangers, trying to hold discussions in English. The song reflects many of the strongly held prejudices within the Finnish communities against the *pusut* (literally "kisses," Polish or Slavic men), *petturit* (literally "traitors," French Canadians) and *saksalaiset insinöörit* (German engineers). Estonians and Scandinavians were more easily tolerated, and when Finnish men and women chose partners outside their community, they were usually from the preferred ethnic groups. About one-third of them also married "British stock."

Marriage

Despite this often obvious, and perhaps exaggerated, courting of Finnish women by non-Finnish men, it is still significant that ultimately 83 per cent of the women married their own countrymen, preferring an endogamous relationship. It was easier to converse in the mother tongue, to share the same culture without explanation, and to have a partner who could also converse with other family members and friends. Ethnic ties bound the husband and wife together. One woman described her initial difficulties with her Slavic boy-friend:

> On Saturday night, I took him to a sauna – well – he thought that he was in hell, and when I jumped into the icehole, he ran screaming to the house convinced that I was possessed by the devil. That ended that, you couldn't make him into a Finn and no way was I going to give up my Saturday night sauna – no, not for any man [MAIJA PETERSON].

Organized life within the Finnish-Canadian communities – the halls, youth groups, dances, picnics, sports events, and theatrical performances – provided the necessary backdrops for social encounters within a Finnish milieu.

Enough Finnish-Canadian church records have survived to examine marriage patterns, especially the age of Finnish brides. The most complete records come from the largest Finnish community in Canada, Thunder Bay, which list 1,367 marriages between 1901 and 1930. These records will be supplemented and compared with information from congregations in New Finland, Saskatchewan; Copper Cliff, Sault Ste. Marie, and Toronto, Ontario; and Montreal, Quebec.

When Port Arthur women are compared to women in Finland, we note that during the first phase of settlement they married at an earlier age in Canada, but by the twenties, a pattern of exceptionally late first marriages was also evident among the Canadian Finnish women.

Very little information exists on the women from other ethnocultures which would allow for easy comparison. One exception is a 1935 study of Montreal's Italian and Ukrainian women. The average age

Table 13: Average Age of Finnish-Born Brides in Port Arthur and Finland, 1901-1930

Time Period	Average Age		Number in Canada
	Finland	Canada	
1901–1910	24.9	23.4	241
1911–1920	25.2	23.6	403
1921–1930	25.3	25.1	475

SOURCE: Finnish statistics are from Haavio-Mannila and Kari, "Changes in the Life Patterns of Families in the Nordic Countries," table 6, p. 25; National Evangelical Lutheran Church of Port Arthur Marriage registers, 1901-1930.

NOTE: The average age of a Finnish-born husband compared to males in Finland marrying for the first time also indicates a tendency to marry younger during the early years of Finnish immigration and gradually shifting to delayed marriages.

of a Finnish bride at the only Finnish church in Montreal at that time was 31.1, remarkably late. Three-quarters of the forty-seven Finnish women chose to wait till they were over twenty-five before they married, while the opposite was true of Italian and Ukrainian women, over three-quarters of whom married between the ages of sixteen and twenty-five. While generalizations about other ethnocultures cannot be based solely on this study, it does appear that the immigrant experience and the imbalance in the sex ratio were not the only explanations for late marriages. Had this been the case, the Italian women should have married even later than the Finnish.

The pattern of late marriages among the Finns was not uniform nation-wide. The Port Arthur and Montreal statistics should also be compared with the rural community of New Finland, Saskatchewan, northern Ontario resource towns like Sault Ste Marie and Copper Cliff, and Toronto.

Table 14: Age of Finnish Women at First Marriage in New Finland, Sault Ste. Marie, Copper Cliff, and Toronto

Place	Time period	Average age	Number
New Finland	1896–1910	20.7	17
Sault Ste. Marie	1896–1914	26.3	8
Copper Cliff	1909–1920	23.0	51
Copper Cliff	1921–1928	26.1	9
Toronto	1929–1930	25.7	15

SOURCE: New Finland Lutheran Church Membership Register; St. Mary's Lutheran Church Membership Register; St. Timothy's Lutheran Church Marriage Register; Toronto Finnish Bethlehem Evangelical Lutheran Church.

Seven of the Finnish brides in New Finland were teenagers: (two were only fourteen) and only one woman was over twenty-five at the time of her first marriage. In rural communities women had few options other than marriage. The situation was vastly different in Montreal, however, where women worked outside the home, usually as live-in maids, and marriage could mean the loss of economic independence.

In the male-dominated northern Ontario communities of Copper Cliff and Sault Ste Marie, Finnish women continued to marry late. The availability of a willing suitor did not seem to matter. In Copper Cliff, as in Thunder Bay, at the turn of the century women married at a younger age; then, after the large numbers of single women from Finland arrived, at a later age. The very small Toronto sample is also slightly higher than the national average in Finland.

These records indicate that, except in farming communities, Finnish women were marrying even later in Canada than in Finland despite the great number of willing suitors. Their desire, or the necessity to work and the nature of their occupation as maids, can provide part of the explanation for the postponed marriages. Other factors include delays in the emigration process itself. Independent, single immigrant women often first worked in Finland until they had the means, maturity, and courage to emigrate alone. The Finnish immigrant home records in Montreal for the year 1928 indicate that the average age of the 634 women who visited the hostel on their arrival in Canada was twenty-seven. Unless the women were travelling as daughters or close relatives of established settlers, they seldom ventured to a new country until they had obtained a degree of work experience and confidence.

Finally, the cultural heritage of Finnish women, specifically the desire to be independent, must also be considered. There was no great social stigma attached to being single in the Finnish community, and many immigrant women were making calculated decisions to prolong their period of independence. One woman wrote from Shreiber, Ontario, in 1926: "I have had so many chances to get married, but I just thought that there is plenty of time for that in the future because first I want to make some money." Many decisions to stay single were based purely on economics. A woman confided to her friend in Finland from a lumber camp near the Algoma Central Railroad Mile 198 in 1929:

> Do you like being married, I ask you only because you are such a good friend....I feel differently, I am going to keep the designation of old maid in the church books....It is not because I have no chances, there are plenty of opportunities, imagine just now I look after nine men in a lumber camp as a cook and soon more men are coming....I can't help it I just want to make money, I keep thinking how I would like to shake off that old country poverty as you know I was an orphan and so poor over there [HILJA LAHTI].

Women who decided to stay single encouraged others, through writing in the Finnish newspapers, to follow suit. They scorned the question "how to get married" and instead provided answers on "how to stay single." While anti-male and anti-marriage articles were more pronounced in the socialist newspapers, the right-wing paper *Canadan Uutiset* also published articles promoting spinsterhood. In one example in 1920, an article entitled, "Old-Maid's Confession," the author concluded that it was much better to stay single as happy marriages were very rare. Another woman prophesied in *Toveritar* that if women only knew how miserable it was to be married, they would never get into the predicament in the first place. Several incidents of wife-beating by drunken Finnish husbands were actually brought to court, and these stories were used to underline the point that, "a married woman was nothing but a slave."[5] Women were told that only the most independent, the most courageous and defiant of them could ever hope to have a measure of equality within the confines of marriage.

If the decision to marry late was largely a cultural phenomenon, then it should follow that the Canadian-born women whose mothers came from Finland might also prefer late marriages. The church records totally destroy this assumption. In fact, in all of the Finnish congregations studied, the Canadian- or American-born daughters married at an extremely young age. In most congregations the samples are too small to be representative, but from Copper Cliff and Port Arthur a clear image of the young bride emerges: in Copper Cliff in the years 1912 to 1928 the average age was 19.5, in Port Arthur for a similar period, 17.8. Six non-Finnish women were also married in Port Arthur to Finnish husbands between 1923 and 1928, and their average age, 19.2, was comparable to the North American-born Finnish brides.[6]

We have already noted the Finnish habit of sending their daughters to keep house for lonely men at an extremely young age. Economic necessity drove the surplus farm daughters either into service industries in the cities or into the hands of local bachelors. The second generation did not suffer from language difficulties which broadened their choice of men. Some mothers strongly disapproved of the early marriages and dating:

> "This place swarms with males, like ants, they are all over. Girls who are still much too young, are constantly asked out to picture shows, dances and parties when they should be attending to schoolwork and learning something about housekeeping." Mother complained constantly about our busy social life to everybody in general and to father in particular. There were at least thirty men to each woman in Timmins. Competition for a date with a girl was keen indeed.[7]

Late marriage, then, was a phenomenon unique to Finnish immigrant women, a result of cultural transference among first-generation women and time delays inherent in the emigration process. It was more prevalent in communities where alternatives to marriage were available to Finnish women. It was a product of the first generation, not transmitted to the North American-born children.

Widowhood

Many of the women married in the Finnish congregations were widows. At the beginning of this century, the average life expectancy was short, and because of the hazardous nature of their work and their tendency to drink to excess, Finnish men were especially susceptible to accidents. In 1931, 56 per cent of Finns who had lost their spouses and remarried were women. Happily for the widows, there seemed to be no problem in finding new husbands. Of the eighty-five widowed women married in Port Arthur, 56.5 per cent were older or the same age as their husbands. It was possible to find a forty-year-old bride who married a twenty-five-year-old man. In fact, men seized this opportunity to entice women to come to the less popular Canadian settlement areas. Advertisements in *Vapaus* for women often included children:

> Attention Women!
> I would like to get a middle aged woman to come to my farm to do the general housekeeping, which would be: cook for two men, keep clean three rooms and if possible milk one cow. I think that a woman who has 1-2 children can well manage these chores. If out there is such a brave woman who dares to come to a prairie farm to the home of a single man, please write immediately.

This prairie farmer from Abbey, Saskatchewan, in 1921 had plenty of competition. Advertisements for Finnish women could be found in most issues of the newspapers. Some tried a humorous approach to catch the attention of women. For example, that same year a lonely man in Nickelton, Ontario, advertised:

> So now that Nickelton's family sauna is ready – and all the families have their own women to wash their backs, except I the undersigned. That is why I decided to turn for help to the women. With the intention etc. etc. etc. The old maids and the widows of living or dead men get the first chance (I am the latter myself too).

The widows of "living men" were women whose husbands had left them or who themselves had walked out on their husbands. Many men were not as tolerant as the above writer and definitely did not want replies from such women. Even the preferred political outlook was specified, some stating that, "those who dream under the influence of the church" need not bother replying, others advising the "immoral people who deny the existence of God" to save their stamps. The business of matchmaking was subsidized by these ads. Enterprising Finns in the United States started special magazines for this purpose. One such paper, *Lemmen Sanomat* (Messages of Love), which claimed to be the best Finnish paper for marriage advertisements, was selling annual subscriptions in Canada for fifty cents. The messages of love, however, seldom included any terms of endearment or romantic illusions; instead men sought a good, strong, no-nonsense worker whose duties were carefully outlined beforehand. If the ad was well written and sent to a newspaper in an area where there were many single women (New York, Toronto, Montreal, or Finland), men could expect a large response.

A man from Alberta recalled how he received more than ninety replies to his advertisement and continued this extensive correspondence through the winter months. In the spring he travelled to New York to "interview" the candidates and chose a woman who met his specifications. His detailed descriptions of the selection process are in themselves informative. Many women rejected outright the notion of going to a small farm in Alberta, others did not please the bachelor because they were "spoiled," "weak," or too sophisticated. When the "lucky" woman was finally found she typified the image of a Finnish farm woman. She was from a poor background, "used to working hard and didn't expect much from life"; she was also described as healthy, brave, and a person who trusted in her own strength and judgment. This prairie farmer's dream woman was also "well proportioned, busty and happy."[8]

The advertisements in *Vapaus* from men outnumbered those from women by a ratio of four to one. But women too, especially widows, used the press to find a partner or employment. A woman from Fort Frances, Ontario, placed the following notice in 1921: "A middle-aged woman would like to be a housekeeper for a lonely bachelor or to go and cook in some camp where a five-year-old daughter can come along." Normally the advertisements specified one or two children, but when a woman was left, through death or desertion, as the sole support of a large family, her plight was pitiable. In New Finland where large families were common, widowed men and women remarried within a year. In many instances women got together, took up collections, held dances, even performed plays to assist those women who were single family supporters and, for one reason or another, had been unable to marry. The insurmountable difficulties, the cruelty of life, and the pain that was the lot of many such single mothers is reflected in some of the distressing stories in the press:

Helmi Mattinen's family is a picture of true misery – four small children in rags – the husband left her and for three years not a word has been heard from him. Helmi took two more children to baby-sit, but these children's father also abandoned his children without paying a penny...what can the county do? The mother is not a Canadian citizen.

Common-law Relationships

Until now we have only considered legal marriages registered in Finnish congregations. But there was a large group of women who entered into common-law relationships. Some of these arrangements were dictated by necessity, others were a deliberate political statement by Finnish socialists who refused to sanction the authority of the church. It is possible that this custom also had an impact on the late marriage age of Finnish women.

Many Finnish immigrant men had come to Canada intent on earning money and returning to their families in Finland, or they brought their wives out to join them in the new land at a later date. This worked if all went well, but if illness or unemployment intervened, their stay in Canada might be protracted for years. The longer the time here, the more distant the wife in Finland became. Immigrants who returned to Finland did so usually within the first five years. According to Keijo Virtanen, 25 to 30 per cent of all Finnish male immigrants returned permanently, while only 10 to 15 per cent of the women went back. This difference can be explained: the men were fulfilling their family obligations, while the women found it easier to adapt to the new country where they had good employment opportunities. Canadian records further support Virtanen's estimates that women were more permanent settlers. Four times as many men returned to Finland, via the Finnish immigrant home, as women.[9]

Many men, however, despite their best intentions, never returned. In Canada men in their prime met other women who were near at hand, who were warmer than distant memories, faded photographs, and increasingly formal letters. New relationships ensued, at first temporary, but then developing into permanent unions. Legal marriage under these circumstances was not possible. Often the families in Finland and Canada didn't know of each other's existence. Betty Järnefelt, the wife of the first consul sent from Finland, wrote a book of short stories based on her Canadian experiences during the twenties. In her stories she highlighted the dangers of unnatural separation, the development of dual marriages and the tremendous guilt experienced by the men. "I am so ashamed," wrote Juho Knaappi to his three orphaned children in Finland ten years after his departure, "that I can't send you any money." In the American Letter Collection of the University of Turku, there are many samples of men who promise, year after year, to bring the family over and never do, and of children who come to find their fathers and end up finding their other families as well. My own grandmother was "an American widow," and her Canadian counterpart had no knowledge of her or my father's existence.

The term "American widow" has been applied only to women, but there are also examples of Finnish women who left husbands and children in Finland and came to Canada alone. Usually, though, they left for good, never intending to return. They wished to escape from bad marriages, or they were single mothers who hoped to make more money in Canada to send to their children. These women left their children with relatives in Finland, diligently sent money home and, if possible, brought their children over later. In many cases married women literally had to "escape" since they required their husband's signature on their travelling documents. One woman, who ran away from an insane husband sighed, "How unfair are the laws that prefer the signature of an insane man to that of a healthy, mature woman." Others left drunken husbands, and some departed purely "to escape a stale marriage" and to seek adventure.[10] But in general these women were only a small minority; family obligations and consequent guilt weighed more heavily on the men.

It is impossible to estimate how many common-law relationships existed because of a legal spouse on the other side of the Atlantic. It was not to the advantage of those involved to advertise such unions, and they usually came to light only when the husband or wife died and notice had to be sent to the next-of-kin. The disaster at the Hollinger mine in Timmins in 1928 was but one example. All eight Finns who died in this fire had families; five had common-law wives, and three also had legal wives in Finland. Another practical reason for common-law relationships was the fact that most Finnish communities did not have a Finnish pastor or a congregation. Getting married was simply inconvenient, a process which could be postponed, sometimes indefinitely.

Ideologically motivated common-law relationships were especially popular during the 1920s. The Finnish brand of socialism, both in Finland and Canada, was extremely anti-religious, and many radicals refused to have any contact with a church. Since the left-wing Finns dominated organized activity in Canada until the 1930s, the social pressures to make a political statement by refusing to marry in the church were considerable. Instead, these Finns would simply hold a party at home or in the local socialist hall and then cement the union by an announcement in the newspaper.

These "free unions" between a man and a woman date as far back as 1902 in Canada, and examples are found in all Finnish communities. During the twenties, however, Finns became more vocal and proud of their defiance of the system. In *Vapaus* between 1921 and 1925, fifty-one large announcements appeared declaring new couples. The language followed a set form in which the couple declared that they had joined together to be comrades to each other according to the laws of nature. It was especially pointed out that, "no black cloth" was visible, or no "sky pilot" present to pronounce his "superstitious spells." At the end of the advertisement as many as fifty people would sign their names, witnessing the event and wishing the new comrades happiness in "the most difficult life ahead."

Most communities were affected by this style of marriage. It was especially common in northern Ontario; one-third of the announcements came from Beaver Lake and Creighton Mine near Sudbury, Timmins–South Porcupine, and Cobalt.[11] These were all communities where radicalism flourished and anti-religious sentiments ran high. An article published in *Vapaus* described the visit of a pastor to Creighton Mine in 1924 in no uncertain terms:

> Pastor Matti Hirvonen stopped around here looking for possible pastures. It's been a long time since our village has seen an agent for the road to heaven, at least not a Finnish-speaking pedlar of souls.... We are a little regretful that the pastor's visit here was an utter failure.... The working class has so many other more important things to do than to run after some story-book figure Jesus, a product of sick imaginations, who supposedly forgives sins. Praying is not going to help us. We demand real action.

When emotions ran this high, it was not easy to kneel at the altar. Still, some radical Finns did secretly marry within the church, in another community, just to protect the legality of the union.

Only a handful of the "newly-weds" could afford to purchase a bold newspaper advertisement. The local news sections of *Vapaus* reported 112 other common-law unions for the period 1921 to 1930. These had no pomp and circumstance, no loud political protest, just a statement: "throwing the rags together," or "jumping under the same blanket." One local historian from White Lake, British Columbia, described such a ceremony:

> The first wedding here was celebrated in 1922 at the school house. At that time we had no pastors around. The young couple just declared in front of the audience that they would become comrades to each other and we danced afterwards and that's it. This marriage has proved to be equally watertight as those blessed by the pastors.[12]

It was not the institution of marriage that was repugnant to these socialists, but rather sanctioning it in the church. Sofia Pontio from Sudbury explained: "I was never legally married. I felt that I would have been deceiving myself if I got married in the church when I didn't believe in it....Anyway free marriages then were so very common in Sudbury." The Finns were eagerly demanding civil weddings, an opportunity to "stop the hypocrisy," and they complained that Canada was the last civilized country in the world to insist on the blessings of the church. In Finland civil marriages were legalized in 1917.

While it surely made no difference to the happiness of the couple whether they were blessed or not, it made a tremendous difference to the women if their husbands died. The issue was brought to the front pages of the press after the Hollinger mine disaster when the wives of Finnish victims were not compensated because they were not legally married. At the Northern Ontario District Women Workers' meeting in 1928, Finnish women from Timmins made the motion to demand that the Workers' Compensation Act be altered so that all mothers and children would be covered. The Canadian Federation of Women's Labour League joined their "Finnish sisters and comrades" in the protest:

> ...we note already a question has been raised concerning ... the right of our Finnish women comrades to this Compensation because their marriage form is not recognized by Canadian law. We ask your League to take this matter up immediately with the Union representatives in Timmins and ask them to see to it that our Finnish women comrades are not put on one side because of this. They have a right for full Compensation and must dispute any decision that is made by the authorities which would rob them of that right.[13]

The mine owners were not the only threat to this form of Finnish defiance. Other employers, who avidly sought an excuse to fire "reds," now attempted to do it on moral grounds: the Finns were "living in sin." In many instances, this information was supplied to them by Finnish pastors who abhorred the practice of free marriage. Needless to say, the "squealing of the black coats" did not bring the Finnish people any closer to the church. The debate received a great deal of publicity in the *Sudbury Star* in 1929, which proclaimed that, "Finnish children are like colts who know nothing of their fathers." The paper, however, made the fatal error of quoting one of the marriage declarations published in *Vapaus*. Unknown to the *Sudbury Star* and to the Finnish pastor who acted as its informer, this couple had also legalized their union. They brought suit against the paper.

These common-law relationships, in the absence of civil ceremonies, were very much a product of immigrant life, but they did have some counterparts in Finland, especially among the working class. During the thirties a newspaper in Finland complained of the "anarchist phenomenon" of the illegal union of couples, "which has been allowed to flourish freely amongst us for decades." Finnish working-class papers also carried advertisements of these free unions. The example, then, was set in Finland, and prevailing conditions in Canada – lack of family influence, weak Finnish congregations, a strong organized socialist movement and, at times, legal wives in Finland – all added to the popularity of common-law marriages.

Free Love

Those joined in common-law unions were not usually criticizing the institution of marriage per se, but rather the necessity of formally sanctioning it. There did exist, however, a small minority of women who advocated "free love" and the abolition of marriage and all unions which were not based on love. Marriage without love was seen as a form of prostitution for women. In Finland this free love movement did not gain any strength. In the United States, among radical feminists, the movement was discussed in the 1850s and found some advocates among the socialist feminists of Greenwich Village around 1910. The basic difference between the free love movement and the advocates of common-law relationships was that parenthood, in the former, was to be removed from the union; child care would become institutionalized, thus freeing the woman for other pursuits.

One of the most colourful advocates of free love among Finnish Canadians was Matti Kurikka, a Finnish journalist, theosophist, and the romantic founder of the utopian socialist community of Sointula, British Columbia, in 1901. While his personal attempts at embracing the free love concept have come under much speculation and criticism within the "Godless colony," and while only fragments of information are available on the single women who practised free love in Sointula, Kurikka's philosophy was carefully articulated in the first Finnish-Canadian newspaper, *Aika* (Time), which flourished from 1901 to 1905.[14] The paper had a wide circulation in both the United States and Canada, and Kurikka's provocative ideas were hotly debated at Finnish gatherings.

In a series of articles in *Aika,* Kurikka lamented how pitiful it was, "that the demands of nature and society's rules were so contradictory." He explained at length the biological necessity to fulfil the sexual needs of men and women in order to keep a balanced nervous system. Women, according to Kurikka, had the most to gain from free love as "presently women exist only to satisfy the male lusts." Responsibility for the destruction of women's sexual pleasure fell upon the church, "which despises women" and makes the wife the subject of her husband. Kurikka begged the people of his commune to forget about unnatural marriage, "the ghostly remnants of an interfering church," and to respect only "unions of love." He also proposed that a woman should never live with her lover – only see him occasionally – but live instead with a friend. Kurikka was not only influenced by nineteenth-century Russian nihilists and American radicals, but also by the Oneida commune whose founder, John Humphrey Noyes, had proposed "communal marriages."[15] Kurikka was especially concerned that women understand the behaviour of their bodies and gave lengthy advice on all aspects of sexuality and childbirth. His information came mainly from Dr. E.B. Foote's *Home Medical Advisor,* first published in English in 1858 and translated into Finnish sometime before 1901.

It is impossible to measure the impact of Kurikka's teachings. Certainly all who read his paper were familiar with his free love arguments. In addition, Kurikka made lecture tours to promote his colony, and he received a great deal of publicity from Finnish pastors who were outraged and denounced his audacity. Kurikka was a handsome man with deep burning eyes, a great orator with a gift for writing and music. He certainly had an impact on all who listened to him. After leaving Sointula Kurikka continued to write, as editor of *New Yorkin Uutiset* (New York's News), and encouraged Finnish women to air their troubles in the pages of the paper under the heading "Nuorten Pakinoita" (Youth Chat), from January 1912 to November 1915. What emerged was a frank, twice-weekly discussion by Finnish women in the United States and Canada. The women, especially domestics, often vented their anger and showed definite anti-male, anti-marriage attitudes. It is impossible to assess how far the resolve "not to be a plaything for men" was carried into their personal lives, but the public voice of many women was militant.

Later, when Alexandra Kollontay, a Soviet diplomat and promoter of communist-style feminism outside the Soviet Union, began to question marriage on ideological grounds, as part of the new communist woman, left-wing Finnish women were quick to listen. After all, these ideas were not totally new to them. Kollontay's *New Morality and the Working-Class,* first published in 1918, was translated into Finnish, and sections of it were published and debated in the women's paper, *Toveritar* in 1922. It became recommended reading among all Finnish-Canadian communist women's reading circles, where the book was analysed chapter by chapter. Kurikka's and Kollontay's influence and the mood of the women who believed that they were entering an era of new morality are clearly reflected in the immigrant writings of Mariana Koivu, who wrote in *Vapaus* in 1921:

Today, a wife is but a machine which makes babies...but slowly and surely women are shaking off the moldy traditions, they are trampling them to the ground and laughing at them.... What is the marriage based on in a communist society? We answer: Free love!... Society will take care of the education and care of the children and youth.

Some attempts were made at communal living in Toronto, Sudbury, Timmins, and Port Arthur during the twenties, but the question of free love seems to have been more a conversation piece than a practical reality. Progressive women needed to be aware of Kollontay and the principles of equality in love and in all other male-female relationships in order to be "modern" and to partake in discussions. But on a practical level, a common-law relationship was the Finnish immigrant women's compromise to free love.

Separation and Abandonment

Divorce was virtually unknown among Finnish women. Of eighteen hundred legal marriages examined, only five women reported that they were divorced. In the 1931 census, fifteen Finnish women were listed as divorced. On the other hand, abandonment (walking away from a legal or common-law marriage) was much more common. Cases where men left large families and sick wives received most attention and the community rallied in defence of the women deriding "the drunken pig"; but women were also known to leave their husbands.

Once again, the Finnish practice of discussing private affairs in the press has provided the historian with valuable information. Between 1921 and 1925 eighteen notices of separation were printed. Eight of these were signed by both husband and wife, who would be as "free as a wave" once the notice had been published. The matter-of-fact explanations of the impending separations included such statements as: "For fifteen years we have tried to live together unsuccessfully – now we are finally free," or "the magic spells of the blackcloth didn't work." Of the remaining ten notices, seven were placed by men whose wives had left them. Perhaps publication of the fact was intended as an off-handed plea for the woman to return, perhaps it was an attempt to settle old scores, to embarrass the wife, or simply to put an end to speculation:

Because my legal wife, Lempi Laaksomaa, has not behaved according to our agreement regarding our joint property, and because she has unsuccessfully tried to court with another man, I shall not have anything further to do with her.

If the union was based on trust, the couple could simply declare it over. At the same time, the woman usually informed the readers of her intention to use her maiden name again. The availability of work for women, even if they had one or two children, and the willingness of Finnish men to court separated women gave some the freedom to leave an intolerable situation.

Surely the decision to leave was not easy and demanded great courage, but the published examples of others must have made it somewhat easier. Those women who embraced socialism found strength from numerous encouraging stories which supported the principle of divorce. There was no question of the validity of divorce for one contributor to *Vapaus* who asked if divorces were necessary. "The question," she writes, "is as strange as asking if it is necessary to remove a rotten boil?" The Finnish churches, while not promoting divorce, did not refuse divorced people access to church membership or to the rituals. The right-wing Finnish newspaper, *Canadan Uutiset*, came out strongly in support of civil marriages and easier divorce laws in 1918. The tolerant mood of the community, coupled with the availability of work opportunities for Finnish women, increased the number of "widows of living men."

Family Size

In Finland the birth rate dropped dramatically after 1910. In Canada, too, despite the strict ban on birth control information, women were limiting the size of their families. Statistical comparisons between Canadian women and immigrants are futile as the immigrant age structure and sex ratio imbalance distort the overall findings. Information on Canadian abortions and birth control is also sketchy, shrouded by illegality. Recent research, however, leaves no doubt that some women had at least a rudimentary understanding of their bodies' behaviour, and that about ten times as many women performed abortions on themselves as were performed by doctors.[16]

Family size was also governed by immigrant social conditions. The newly arrived Finns did not have extended families to rely on for assistance in child care. Because Finnish women showed great determination to work, even after marriage, a small family was more manageable and desirable. In addition, they often married late, so their child-bearing years were limited. But, perhaps most importantly, Finnish women had access to birth control information, contraceptives, and abortion clinics. For every Finnish woman in Canada between the ages of twenty and forty-four, there were 1.2 children. In urban areas this declined to 0.8, while in rural areas it was 2.0. Ukrainian women in the same age group had three times as many children (3.6), while the average for all women in Canada was twice as many (2.4).

However, by examining a 1926 special study on female fertility in the prairie provinces, it is clear that Finnish women there are closer to the average. For every hundred women between the ages of fifteen to forty-nine, Finns had 10.5 births as compared to 9.3 for the Swedes, 11.3 for the Italian, 12.2 for the Hungarian and 15.0 for the Ukrainian women. While the prairie birth rate is still culturally determined, economic factors also play a significant role. Children were an economic asset on the prairie farms and hence desirable in larger numbers.

Unfortunately Finnish congregation records do not provide detailed information on births, age of mother, or number of children they had, except in Montréal, and even there only at the end of the depression, when the average age of a Finnish mother having her first child was an astonishing thirty-four years. The baptismal records of Port Arthur show that as the number of marriages per year was increasing, the number of baptisms was decreasing. Although there were 457 marriages and 1,417 baptisms in the period 1911-1920, in the following decade the comparable figures were 645 and 912. This seems to indicate that the number of children in Port Arthur and outlying areas was declining dramatically. The statistics, however, are blurred by the fact that many Finns, especially during the 1920s, avoided participating in any church rituals. Also, not all of the baptized are newly born, which further complicates the calculations.

Across Canada in 1921 there were three times as many births as marriages recorded, but among Finns less than twice as many. Since Finnish sources are based on church records, they omit all common-law marriages and children born from these unions. We can thus safely conclude that, among the religious Finns at least, small families were the norm. As for socialist Finns and their family size, emphasis on small families was even greater. In a sample of one hundred Finnish immigrant women who belonged to a socialist organization, immigrated to Canada before 1930, and were living with a permanent partner, the average number of children per woman during their entire lifetime was 1.2.[17] Clearly then, Finnish immigrant women made definite attempts to limit their family size.

Birth Control and Abortions

Delayed marriages, abstinence, and breast feeding were the normal methods of birth control in the early twentieth century. In addition, Finnish women had easy access to birth control information and devices. Both national Finnish-Canadian newspapers, *Canadan Uutiset* and *Vapaus,* carried advertisements for Finnish drug stores which promoted birth control apparatus. The cost for male condoms was $3.00 a dozen and for female pessaries $3.50 a dozen. For an additional ten cents these could be mailed in plain wrapping "anywhere in Canada." Such an expense was more than 10 per cent of a maid's monthly salary in 1921.[18]

Since Finnish women were literate, they were also able to read the dozens of Finnish-language medical books sold through the newspapers and available in community libraries. Somehow the medical manuals written in Finnish escaped the careful scrutiny of the censors. One advertisement alone promoted seven different books about venereal disease, women's sexual behaviour, women and marriage, and general medical advice for women. In addition, Finnish-Canadian newspapers frequently published medical questions dealing with sexuality. Through conversations and letters, women advised each other on birth control methods and justified their decision not to have children: "I have decided not to have any children since I have had to look after so many other people's brats and also if I couldn't give my kids a better upbringing than I had I figure it's useless to have kids and let them suffer when it is possible to prevent pregnancy."[19]

Economic struggles were usually cited as the major reason for limiting family size: "What, more than one child, when there wasn't even enough food for the adults? No, you don't understand how difficult life was, all Finnish women had to work, they couldn't come home and feed babies, no and the homes too were so crowded." Because of the chronic shortage of maids and cleaning staff in Canada, Finnish women found that they could often find work when the men could not. In such cases there was no time for maternity leave or any possibility of staying home with the baby:

> Since the man is the head of the household – "so now we go!" said my husband, and there I was six months pregnant. Blindly we came to Montreal just about at Christmas time of '29 and I was seasick the whole journey, didn't eat a thing. Then we went to an employment office in Toronto, I could have found work for fifteen days a week. As soon as I got out of the hospital I went to work in a Finnish restaurant...my husband stayed home and I rushed home to feed the baby but he died at three months of pneumonia, it was a boy, Eino.... Soon my husband died too [TYYNE PIHLAJAMÄKI].

Although farming communities were characterized by larger families, here too the women were aware of birth control methods. An article in *Toveritar* in 1916 entitled, "Thoughts from a Farmer's Hag," vigorously defended the farm woman's right to birth control. In the writer's opinion, limiting the number of children was not dangerous to the health of a woman, nor was it a crime. She mentioned the availability of books with good illustrations and explained methods of birth control by using nature metaphors. "Heavy downpours wash away the seeds," she taught and, "canvas stops their growth." Another prairie farmer from Sprucefield, Alberta, pleaded with the class-conscious workers not to "heap any more stones for her to drag" by criticizing her large family. "Why is it," she asked, "that in this instance too, the blame is put on the woman?"[20]

If birth control failed, the only alternative was abortion – "emptying." In the larger cities of Toronto and Montreal, special abortion clinics were organized where "real" doctors performed the actual operation and Finnish women provided rooms for convalescing. In Toronto "Mamma [Lyyli] Anderson's" clinic, hostel, and job exchange for Finnish maids all shared the same premises. The services of the clinic were not limited to single women and live-in maids but were also available to married women who did not wish to have any more children. According to Tyyne Latva: "You didn't get a bad reputation if you visited Lyyli, the issue of abortion was quite openly discussed. No one that I knew of was ever hurt, except some who had it done in Cleveland."

Other women were not as fortunate and, in the absence of a doctor, relied on each other to induce miscarriages. "It was very common," sighed a Thunder Bay resident, "we just helped each other out." For this purpose, the women were able to purchase special long-handled implements, resembling knitting needles but with "proper covering" on them. "They were not advertised as emptying devices – but everyone knew what they were for! You just picked them up from the shelf." The biggest medical problem experienced by women was post-abortion bleeding. This particular informant listed eight women who had bled to death. "I nearly died myself once," she said, "but what to do, I probably would have died in childbirth as I was so exhausted with five children."

When women were arrested and sentenced for performing abortions, the reaction of the Finnish press was mixed. The arrests usually followed the death of a patient. When a twenty-six-year-old married Finnish woman died of an abortion, it was called "an act of an angel" by the socialist press and "premature birth" by the conservatives. Neither criticized the abortionist or moralized on the issue. The abortionist, a woman, was sentenced to six months in prison. "That always happened," exclaimed Lydia Punni, whose friend died of an abortion in Vancouver in 1924. "The women die or go to prison and the men walk off as if nothing happened. Is that fair, I ask you?"

The risks were high, and every community had its sad story of a desperate woman who died as a result of an abortion. These were supplemented by articles about women who had gone insane or committed suicide when unable to stop the pregnancy. A Finnish man, touched by the suicide of a fourteen-year-old Finnish girl, was incensed at the "stupidity of the religious parents who did not take her to the doctor and stop the pregnancy" and expressed his anger in a private letter.[21]

Perhaps the most revealing article on abortion was written by two Finnish women in an insane asylum near Battle River, Alberta. Inside the thick brick walls, surrounded by "beautiful green hills," the women had time to think about life, to observe the inhabitants and to draw their own conclusions. Together they wrote:

> In ignorance, many wretched mothers do whatever they can so that they won't increase their troubles and workload. They fear creating new life, suffering many long months of pregnancy and then having to do all the work afterwards. So many poor women, ruin their health because of their ignorance, their nerves suffer and their general spiritual life becomes dull. The woman slowly deteriorates until her place too is here. . . . Please come and visit us.

The medical books and literature which contained details on birth control also offered some information on self-induced miscarriages. This usually appeared disguised as "remedies for late periods." Such medical advice was also published in *Toveritar*. Usually it consisted of hot saunas alternated with submersion in cold water (a dip in the ice hole). Swallowing castor oil was another traditional method, so too in "stubborn cases" was fasting. Enterprising "Madam Peton" advertised her "Feminese pills," which were guaranteed to bring back periods. In interviews farm women explained that heavy work, especially lifting sacks of grain or bales of hay, would usually abort the pregnancy. It was only if all other methods failed that the Finnish women sought "abortion with utensils."

Thus, in Canada Finnish women had many advantages and options when making decisions about marriage and reproduction. The common statement among Finnish immigrants that "Canada was hell for men and heaven for women" had some truth to it. Many stories and whimsical reminiscences describe the period of courtship in their lives as one when they could "pick and choose."

Postponed marriages also caused delayed births and smaller families. Finnish women, even in the most remote corners of Canada, took pride in their ability to have some control over their own bodies and practised what they preached by having very few children. The more radical and defiant even passed resolutions in their organizational meetings. In 1925 the Women's Labour League of Finland, Ontario, recorded in their minutes the following discussion: "Roosa Lampi read to us about communism, but we were not really able to discuss any other aspect of it except the question of children. We were of the opinion that if whatever method helps we will not have any children." The control over reproduction had a significant impact on women's lives as fewer or no children left the women with time to work and participate in social and political activities.

Comparisons which can be made with other ethnic groups clearly indicate that in this respect Finnish women were unique. Once again, inherited cultural patterns, universal literacy, and the availability of information, as well as the tendency of Finnish women to seek work outside the home, had an impact on their behaviour distinguishing them from women in many other cultures. It is important to note that despite all the information warning of the dangers of marriage and the cultural glorification of the single, independent woman, the fact remains that ultimately most Finnish women in Canada did find themselves in some kind of permanent union with a Finnish man. They did so at a slightly later age, often in a less formal manner and in the midst of much anti-marriage rhetoric; but in the end they found it the most convenient alternative to spinsterhood or mixed marriages.

CHAPTER 5

Finnish Women at Work

The main attraction Canada held for Finnish women was the lure of economic opportunity. Women who responded to a University of Turku survey stated that they came to Canada in search of a better life, to pile up dollars, to look for gold, to carve gold with wooden knives, or simply, to work. Finnish women anticipated that their salaries would be far in excess of those they received in Finland. In turn, Canadian immigration agents promoted the immigration, bringing women to Canada to do the work other Canadians did not wish to do. At the top of the list was domestic service. It was also hoped though that women would come and settle in the west or in the northern resource towns and that their presence would have a stabilizing effect on the immigrant communities.

By the turn of the century, and certainly by the 1920s, several employment opportunities had opened up for women in Finland, ranging from professional work to industrial labour. Canada, however, mainly received the rural, migrant, working-class women. Furthermore, the women who arrived rarely spoke English. Lack of skills and language difficulties seriously limited their choice of employment. They were shut out from professional work such as teaching, and from other traditional female occupations – clerical work, telephone operators, bank clerks or saleswomen – which required a knowledge of English.

Despite the many negative aspects of domestic service, it was the most common occupation for Finnish immigrant women in Canada. But women who could not work as live-in domestics did have other alternatives. The socio-economic imbalance which existed in the immigrant communities, especially in the resource towns, made women valuable not only as girl-friends and wives, but as camp cooks, laundresses, rooming-house keepers, bootleggers, and prostitutes. Unlike many southern European and Jewish women, Finns shunned working in the factories or doing piece-work at home.

This chapter will first examine the attraction and economic incentives of those jobs popular among Finnish women. This will enable us to determine whether Finnish women's choice of employment was dictated not only by their working-class status, but also by their ethnicity. Three occupations will be examined in detail: domestic service, bootlegging and prostitution. The first, because it was the greatest employer of Finnish women, and the others because they acquired special significance in the Finnish immigrant communities.

Salaries

Single women could not view their occupations as providing supplementary income; they were self-supporting and could seldom rely on family to provide free room and board. Married women also worked, and often their salary was the only steady income the family received. By comparison women's salaries in Finland were very low; for example, the average maid's salary in the United States ranged from five to ten times as much as that in Finland. In 1930 a maid in Finland could receive as little as $2 to $3 per month and "$9 was an excellent salary." This, according to a newspaper report, "was scarcely enough to keep the clothes on one's back."[1]

In Canada, immigrant women had several work alternatives. The minimum wage for women in factories, stores, and laundries during the twenties ranged between $12 to $14 a week. This salary was for an adult woman with one year's experience. The inexperienced workers started at $10 a week, and young girls received even less. For this salary women worked forty-four to fifty hours a week. In Toronto, they had to pay an average of $2 to $3 a week for rent. In 1921, a University of Toronto study concluded that the minimum weekly income women needed to survive was $16.38 ($8 for room and board, $5.12 for clothing, and $3.26 for miscellaneous). This calculation did not include any money for medical expenses. To put the salaries in perspective, at the same time Finnish women were paying $2 for a cook book and $2.50 for a dozen pessaries. The salaries did not increase greatly during the twenties. In 1928 seemstresses were still earning as little as $12 a week for a fifty to fifty-five hour work week. Pieceworkers were earning even less.

A single self-supporting immigrant woman with no immediate family could hardly survive on such wages, let alone save money. Because Finnish women were independent, they had more flexibility and looked for other, more lucrative prospects. All they had to do was to pick up a Finnish newspaper and read the advertisements for dishwashers, maids, cooks, bakers, managers of restaurants, and boarding-house keepers. One of the highest paid occupations for a Finnish woman in Canada was to be a lumber-camp cook. During the early twenties they were already earning $45 to $60 a month, which often included room and board. A government survey in 1928 reported that the cooks were the highest paid at lumber camps, earning $60 to $80 a month. Their working week, however, was seventy hours including Sundays. A lumber-camp cook had no time for relaxation; men had to eat every day, rain or shine. But if the woman's main objective was to save money, then work in a lumber camp was ideal. Women were isolated, there was little opportunity to spend the money, few expenses, and the men held the cook in high esteem. In 1925, a Finnish camp baker, Aino Norkooli, wrote "from the dense forest":

> There are twenty men here and I am here to cook for them...I have one boy as my helper...I get $60 a month wages which is a good salary but I sure have to work hard for it...in the morning I must get up about five o'clock and then I run non-stop till nine o'clock all the time I have to work and try to bake as much as I can manage...I am trying to learn to become a cook because there is always work for them and a good salary I know even now around here on the camps women get sometimes over hundred dollars a month when they cook for fifty men and that is an excellent salary and one day I will get it too and then I will come to Finland because I have decided that when I get $300 then I will come to Finland maybe I will have it by the spring.

Married women also worked as camp cooks and sometimes took their children with them or tried to board them in the city. Aino Norkooli noticed a considerable drop in her income after she got married and had a child. She complained to her mother that she had to pay $20 a month for child care. The wife of the Finnish consul general was especially concerned over the welfare of those children who grew up in the camps. Their mothers were constantly working, and the children received little discipline or education. Generally, women left the children in urban areas by the time they were of school age.

If the women did not happen to notice an advertisement, they could always place their own:

> A married woman with years of experience wants to come and work at a lumber camp. A small camp is preferrable. My primary objective is cleanliness. Notice! I will not bring children with me.

In addition to the high wages, cooks usually had a separate bedroom. Some stayed on the camps for months at a time. One woman from

South Porcupine recalls that the longest stretch she stayed at a camp was nine months, "then I had to see a dentist and I spent a day in town and was back again in the bush."

If months of endless work at a remote lumber camp did not seem attractive, Finnish women could also find work in the numerous cooperatively or privately run restaurants and *poika-talot* (boarding-houses). Newspapers might have several ads per issue, trying to entice women to come. Once again the great attraction was the ability to accumulate some savings since room and board were often included. In 1924, forty men from the Cobalt cooperative rooming-house were offering $60 a month plus room (including heat and electricity) to a woman who would manage the cooking. Some of the boarding-houses had one hundred and fifty to two hundred men for meals daily, and the number of female staff could be as high as fifteen. The largest cooperative restaurants were in Port Arthur, Fort William, Timmins, and Sudbury, all of which handled over one hundred men a day. The women who were in charge had to control the purchasing of the food and organizing the staff in addition to cooking. Thus the men from Timmins reminded prospective employees that they "must have enough knowledge of English to do shopping."

Not all Finnish women were accepted in the lumber camps or in the cooperative boarding-houses. The Timmins restaurant was looking for a new dishwasher because "we had to fire the last one as we suspected she was a *lahtari* (white)." One class-conscious Finnish woman complained, however, that women sometimes got away with their conservative political opinions, even in lumber camps, if they were good cooks. She was pleased to report, however, that just recently they had fired an experienced camp cook "because she had cooked for the white army in Finland."[2]

Private restaurants and boarding-houses also competed for Finnish women, offering food as an incentive. Many of these restaurants, cafes, and boarding-houses were actually owned by enterprising Finnish women, who took pride in their good food, clean premises, and discipline. Mauri Jalava has noted that among the business licences granted in Sudbury for the year 1929 were four to women who received licences for lodging or boarding houses – Fannie Puska, Mrs. Niemi, Mrs. G. Walli, and Mrs. O. Kauhanen – and one woman, Hilja Pulkki, who received a restaurant licence. Few women ever started lumbering operations of their own, although in 1922 one Finnish woman advertised in *Vapaus* for "twenty men to cut cordwood." She guaranteed, "satisfaction as far as the food is concerned."[3] Women also set up private businesses as grocers and masseuses.

All these enterprises gave women a high degree of independence, relatively good wages, and an opportunity to save money. But even women who only worked as dishwashers, cook's helpers, or as cleaning staff in the restaurants and rooming-houses could expect wages of $30 to $40 a month, including food and sometimes board. Women who worked as cleaners on a daily basis earned between 35 and 50 cents an hour. For immigrant women the combination of employment and housing was attractive. This kind of work could also be done by married women. In fact, many of the Finnish businesses which were registered in the husband's name were actually run by women while the men worked in the mines or went away to the lumber camps.[4]

Domestic service attracted Finnish women for similar reasons. Many indicated that they took the job because the salary was good. While there were great regional variations within Canada and wide salary ranges for different kinds of domestic service, even the "greenhorn" could expect at least $12 a month. The average salary by the late 1920s for Finnish domestics was about $25, but could be as high as $50. At first sight, this seems low, but when food, board, and sometimes uniform are also added, the wages become more attractive; and Finnish women happily reported that they were able to save money. Compared to the salaries in Finland, the earnings of Canadian domestics were excellent.

Why then, the Finnish women asked, should they work for $12 a week in a factory and barely survive, when they could receive the same wages plus additional benefits by working with Finnish men or in Canadian homes? Thus many women went, with the same spirit of independence which had enabled them to leave Finland, and sought their fortunes in the resource towns of northern Ontario and British Columbia. The majority, however, worked as domestics.

The Pros and Cons of Domestic Service

SUPPLY AND DEMAND

Canadian women viewed domestic service as a low status, temporary occupation. Yet Finnish immigrant women went willingly to be maids. Salary is one explanation, but considering the many negative aspects of the occupation, there must have been other factors which made domestic service a particularly suitable occupation for Finnish women. It is important to examine all aspects, including the immigrant's and her community's point of view. As the following notice indicates, the occupation did have serious drawbacks:

> It is with deep sorrow and longing that I inform you of the death of my beloved daughter Siiri Mary who became the victim of a terrible death in her place of employment in Nanaimo, B.C. on the first of May at 04:00 in the morning. As she was lighting the

fire in the kitchen stove with kerosene it exploded and the fire ignited her clothes and she burnt so badly that on the fifth of May she died in the Nanaimo hospital at 11:30 in the evening. She was born on January 1, 1906 and died on May 5, 1922 at the age of 16 years 4 months and 4 days. Father remembers you with bitter sadness and longing.

This emotional funeral notice reveals some of the dark realities of domestic service in Canada. Why did the sixteen-year-old girl have to start her work day at 4 A.M.? What knowledge did she have of kerosene? And what protection in case of accident? Who could she turn to for advice, or what avenues for complaint did she have? While the domestic servant looked after all the members and guests of the household, who looked after her? These questions were hotly debated in the various Finnish organizations in North America established for maids.

The University of Toronto probe into the conditions of female labour in Ontario in 1889 noted that the demand for domestic servants exceeded the supply and that it was necessary to import domestic servants from the British Isles.[5] Young girls, often orphans, were brought to Canada through benevolent agencies and ended up as domestics, and the chronic shortage of domestic servants has continued until the present day. There have, of course, been periodic fluctuations in demand, and some communities felt the shortage of domestic workers more severely than others. In general, however, the supply of maids did not meet the demand.

The federal government bent immigration regulations, created special categories and made easier travel arrangements for women who promised to work as domestic servants. In some respects, they were successful as thousands of domestics arrived annually. But while women poured in from one end, they filtered out from the other into different occupations. Instead of alleviating some of the difficulties which made domestic service such an unpopular occupation, the emphasis was always on replacement, finding unsuspecting new immigrants willing to put up with the old problems, at least for a short period of time.

After the turn of the century, Finnish domestics were enticed to immigrate. In fact, it was the only category, in addition to farm work, in which single women from Finland during the 1920s were allowed to enter Canada.[6] Like the British, they too were welcome. The following riddle by Arvo Lindewall in a Finnish paper, *Toveritar,* illustrates the point:

I am not beautiful,
Yet, I am the most wanted woman.

I am not rich,
Yet I am worth my weight in gold.
I might be dull, stupid,
Dirty and mean,
Yet, all the doors are open for me.
I am a welcome guest
All of the elite compete for me.
I am a maid.

The largest proportion of foreign domestic workers still came from the British Isles, 75 per cent before World War One and 60 per cent during the 1920s. Among the other ethnic groups, Scandinavians and Finns showed an exceptionally high propensity for domestic work. In Finnish jargon, "going to work in America" became synonymous with *piikomaan Amerikkaan* (going to be a domestic servant in America). During the 1920s the Finnish domestic servants made up 7 to 8 per cent of all female immigrants classified as "female domestics." In the fiscal year ending March 31, 1929, for example, 1,288 Finnish women arrived in Canada under this category out of a total of 1,618 adult female immigrants from Finland.

This does not necessarily mean that all women actually settled into their declared occupations in Canada. We have noted that other more lucrative opportunities existed for women once in the country. In fact, the Finnish Immigrant Home Records indicate that there was considerable diversity of skills among these "excellent domestic servants." Letters of recommendation from Finland often included revealing additions such as, "she is also an experienced seamstress," or "this woman is a skilful masseuse." The domestic service category was simply the most convenient for immigration purposes.

Nevertheless, the vast majority of working women in Finnish communities were maids. Calculations, based on the two largest urban centres, indicate that of all the Finnish immigrant women employed outside the home during the 1920s, at least 66 per cent were maids in Toronto and Montreal. This does not necessarily mean that they were all live-in domestics, as the terminology describing the work is often vague in both English and Finnish. Toronto and Montreal were not unique. Except for a handful to women who worked in restaurants, "all Finnish women in Winnipeg were maids." A woman from Windsor reported that "there are about 200 Finnish maids here and the married women, without exception are *päivätöissä* ([doing] day work)." This single, overpowering concentration of Finnish women in domestic work had a great impact on organized activity in the Finnish community, which had to adapt to the life patterns of the maids. Just as mining, lumbering and construction work affected the life of Finnish men, influenced their economic status, settlement location and political thinking, domestic work shaped the world-views of the Finnish women.

By the 1920s, also, the nature of domestic service was changing. Whereas live-in maids predominated around the turn of the century, "day workers" were in the majority by the Depression. For example, the percentage of laundresses in the service occupations doubled between 1901 and 1911. It was becoming increasingly difficult to find women willing to live in and, consequently, more of this work was left to the newly arrived immigrants whose choice of occupation was more limited. Finnish women knew upon arrival that there would be no problem in finding a job. One man shamefully recollected:

> There was no work for me, nothing, but my wife was always able to get work as a live-in cook. What to do? I had to take women's work. Oh, I didn't like it. I was to look after the liquor, but in the morning I had to do some dusting too. I hated women's work and the pay was not good either, but we had a place to live and food to eat. As soon as I could get man's work, I left [ROLPH KOSKINEN, Parry Sound].

The consequent role reversal, which heightened during periods of economic slowdown, was a bitter pill for many men to swallow. "My mother worked," remembered a dynamic leader of the Finnish community, "she could always find work in the houses, and my father stayed home with the children." Then she laughed, "He never liked it, but he did a good job!" By 1928 when the Depression had hit the lumbering industry – one of the biggest employers of Finnish men – the frustrated "house-spouse" syndrome spread beyond the urban centres. Women gained in status as "they were the only ones with money to spend." Even in 1937, when all doors to immigration were shut, the government launched a special scheme to bring in "Scandinavian and Finnish Domestics." Most of the maids who came under this plan were Finnish women in their late twenties and early thirties.

The most pressing concerns of newly arrived immigrants included where to live and where to work. As a live-in maid both worries were taken care of at once. Domestics usually lived in middle- and upper-class homes in safe and relatively clean neighbourhoods. No time was spent looking for housing and no initial investment needed to buy furniture or basic kitchen utensils.

The maid's limited free time was carefully monitored by the employers. "The family" was sure to report any unexpected absences or late arrivals. In case of serious trouble or illness at least someone would notice and beware. The stories of unidentified Finnish men found dead by the railroad tracks, lost in the bush, or dying alone from an illness, were not the case for Finnish women. Someone, whether for reasons of moral concern or meanness, was keeping tabs on the maid's whereabouts and routines. For many younger women, the employers became a surrogate family, which disciplined and restricted their social activities. This, of course, was a double-edged sword. One summer evening in 1916 when a Finnish maid in Toronto failed to come home from the local dance at the agreed upon time of eleven, the employers swiftly called the police. In her case the alarm was too late as her beaten body was found on the outskirts of Toronto, but her friend was saved from a similar fate. Genuine concern was appreciated, but many women resented the strict scheduling of their free time. A Port Arthur maid remembers her first evening off in 1910:

> I have been rebellious ever since I was a child. On my only evening off, I was supposed to be back at 10:00 P.M. Well, I went to the hall to see a play and to dance afterwards and didn't get back until one in the morning. I found the door bolted from inside and my blood rushed to my head. They treated me just as if I was a small child incapable of looking after my own affairs. I banged on that door so hard that they finally opened it, and I shouted in my broken English: "I not dog! I Sanni! I sleep inside!"
> [SANNI SALMIJÄRVI].

In addition to a safe "home" the domestics received regular meals. Many farm girls who were used to hearty dinners, however, complained of the small portions served. They had to sneak extra food from the kitchen. Others went to a local Finnish restaurant on their afternoon off "and stuffed themselves with pancakes" so that for at least a day they would not go hungry. One woman noted an ideological difference about eating and explained in a letter to her mother: "Canadians don't give enough food to anybody. They are afraid that if you eat too much you get sick and the Finns are afraid that if you don't eat enough you get sick."

Others complained of the miserly manner in which the mistress checked all food supplies. In one affluent home in Montreal, the maids were not allowed to have cream in their coffee. "When the lady asked for the hundredth time if there was cream in the coffee," explained one frustrated maid, "my friend took the entire cream pitcher and threw it against the wall." With a thoughtful sigh she added, "We Finns, you know, we have such temper – that *sisu* – has caused many a maid to lose her job." On the other hand, many women were fed good balanced diets, were introduced to white bread, various vegetables and fruits unknown in their own country. Not only did they receive regular meals, they learned to "eat the Canadian way."

They also learned to speak some English, usually enough to manage in the kitchen. Jokingly they described their language as *kitsiengelska* (kitchen English). Many were taught by their employers who found communication through a dictionary too cumbersome, others took language classes provided by the Finnish community during their day off.

Along with language skills, the maids were also given an immersion course on Canadian home appliances, customs, and behaviour. On-the-job training included an introduction to vacuum cleaners, washing machines, and the operation of gas ovens. The maids attentively observed the "ladies" and were soon acquiring new role models. In amazement Finnish men complained of the profusion of make-up used by the maids who had started to *playata laidia* (play the lady).[7] Women's clothing reflected the new image; hats, gloves, and silk stockings were among the first items Finnish women purchased. Having obtained these symbols of Canadianization, the maids rushed to the photography studios and sent home pictures of themselves lounging on two-seater velvet sofas, sniffing at a rose and revealing strategically placed silk-stockinged legs. Other pictures showed women with huge hats, the likes of which could only be worn by the nobility or the minister's wife in Finland.[8] We can imagine what effect these photographs had on relatives back home, or on girl-friends who still wore tight scarves and wool stockings. Only one month in Canada, and the photographs showed a total transformation of a poor country woman into a sophisticated "lady" sipping tea from a silver pot, some needlepoint resting on her knee. The reality, of course, was much different.

The main reasons for the unpopularity of domestic service in Canada are the long working hours, hard work, lack of privacy, and low status of the job. The Finnish immigrant women certainly agreed with many of these complaints, but because of their cultural background, their position in the community and their special immigrant circumstances, their view of domestic work was somewhat different.

Historians have suggested that for the young Irish girls in Boston domestic work actually represented upward mobility, since they had been unable to obtain any kind of work in Ireland. A study of Swedes in Chicago indicates that domestic work was reputable and accepted as the norm for the first generation Swedish women who were almost exclusively working as maids.[9] This trend is evident among the Finnish domestics in Canada. When the immigrant community was so over-whelmingly composed of domestic servants, comparisons with other occupations became irrelevant. Instead the domestics created their own internal hierarchy. Their status came from a job well done and they took pride in their honesty, initiative and ability to work hard "to do what previously had taken two women." Together they strove to create a sound collective image and to improve their working opportunities. Any deviance from this norm, any Finnish woman perceived as "lazy" or dishonest, was severely chastised in the Finnish-Canadian press for ruining the reputation of Finns as the "most desirable and highly paid domestic servants."[10]

On an individual level, pride in their work – in their profession – is reflected in the comments of the domestics interviewed for this project. "My floors were the cleanest on the street," or "my laundry was out the earliest every morning" are typical of the self-congratulatory mood. Comparisons with other women were used to illustrate these points:

> Nobody had scrubbed that dirt off, did they look at me when I took off my only pair of shoes, got on my knees and scrubbed that muck till you could have eaten from the floor. Women weren't supposed to show their naked ankles, but heck, I wasn't about to ruin my shoes. Another Finlander, they thought! [IDA TOIVONEN, Thunder Bay].

They worked hard to gain the trust of their employers, and then they boasted, "If I said the sky was green, then the sky was green." Finnish women often showed a strange mixture of an inferiority and superiority complex. While they might have respected the position of the "Missis," they often felt great disdain for "her inability to do anything right." Helmi Vanhatalo, who worked for a wealthy family in Sault Ste Marie during the early 1920s, is a prime example of the confidence and control that shines through from many of the stories told by domestics:

> When that Mrs. noticed that I could take care of all the cleaning, all the dishes and all the cooking, in fact, I ran the entire household, she became so lazy that she started to demand her breakfast in bed. Healthy woman! Just lying there and I had to carry the food to bed. Oh boy, that hurt the Finlander's *sisu*, that a woman makes herself so shamefully helpless. What to do, what to come up with, when there was no point to *kikkiä* [kick back]. So I started making the most delicious old country pancakes, plenty of them and thick, and I added lots of butter and whipped cream. Every morning I carried to the Mrs. a huge plateful, and the Mrs. ate until she was as round as my pancakes. The Mr. ordered her to go on a diet, and Helmi no longer had to take breakfast to bed!

When Nellie McClung chose to make a Finnish domestic the heroine of her novel *Painted Fires*, she agreed with the image that Finnish domestics had of themselves. Having had a Finnish maid, she was familiar with their manners, pride, temper, and customs. The Finns, on the other hand, greeted the book with exalted praise as it showed the Finnish maids "exactly as we like to think we are."[11] The novel was translated into Finnish and sold thousands of copies. The heroine, whose name was also Helmi, was honest to a fault, loyal, extremely clean, and hard-working. She was also strong, stubborn, and defiant. For example, in one scene Helmi slams the dishtray on the head of another domestic who had not pre-rinsed the greasy plates. In the ensuing chaos the employer asks, "Ain't that just like a Finn, Maggie, clean and neat, but high tempered?"

McClung's portrait of a spirited Finnish domestic finds many counterparts in the literary tradition of Finland and of Finns in North America. Because of the Finnish women's love of theatre, of acting and performing, they were often in a position to choose and even write plays for the stage. Invariably the maid was portrayed as "intelligent and honest," constantly involved in her self-improvement, while the masters were corrupt, lazy, and often stupid. In the Finnish-Canadian socialist literature, the class struggle is depicted through scenes of superior servants suffering under less capable masters. The poems of Aku Päiviö, the best-loved Finnish-Canadian socialist writer, reinforced the superiority of the victim. One woman confided:

> Every time I read the poem "Woman's Day" I just cried. It was so true that I could feel it in my bones. The book, you know, was censored by the government, so I removed a tile from the kitchen floor and hid it. When I was in the kitchen by myself, early in the morning, I would read the poem over and over again. It was my private source of strength [ELINA SYTELÄ].

Another woman, Sanni Salmijärvi, describes Finnish domestics by taking examples from the writings of Minna Canth and Juhani Tervapää. The latter's play, *Juurakon Hulda* (Hulda from the Rootstock District) gave Salmijärvi her inspiration and role model. Hulda was a poor farm girl who found employment as a domestic servant. Through hard work and persistent study, she eventually outshone her employers in wit, intelligence, and honesty. "You might be a servant," said Salmijärvi, "but it doesn't mean you are dumb":

> When you can read, a whole new world opens up for you. It doesn't matter where you live, how far from the civilization, or in what poverty. Once I got started, I read everything I could get my hands on....Finnish women are like that Juurakon Hulda, they come from such poor circumstances with nothing in their name, but through hard work and self-education they try to get ahead, find dignity, learn to see beyond their own neighbourhood.

Of course, not all Finnish domestics fit this collective image. Many a woman quietly cried herself to sleep, "too tired to get up to get a handkerchief." The image, however, did create a role model of a domestic for Finnish women to emulate; and if they reached this goal, if they convinced their friends that they had earned the respect of their employers, they also gained the support and respect of the Finnish community. Many bizarre stories came to light when Finnish women explained that really they were the ones in control in such families as the Molsons, Otises, and Masseys. Perhaps the most incredible came from Ida Toivonen, who served the widow of a former lieutenant-governor in Quebec. She discovered that her living quarters on the first floor of the house were infested with rats. Having spent an entire night catching them, she laid the seven fat specimens on the breakfast table.

Within the social hierarchy of the domestics, those who specialized and worked for the "millionaires" had the highest status within the community. They were also the first to acquire $50 a month salaries. Cooks were also at the top of the hierarchy within domestic service occupations and so too were nursemaids and companions. Chambermaids, kitchen helpers and "generals" following, in that order. As can be seen, for women with a Finnish cultural background, domestic service was not necessarily a "low status occupation."

"WHEN YOU ARE A DOMESTIC YOU ARE NOTHING BUT A SLAVE"

The most serious and persistent complaints of Finnish women in domestic service were the lack of privacy, loss of individuality, the sense of being totally controlled by a strange family. Domestics who stayed with the same family for a long period lost their chance to have a family of their own; children and husbands were seldom tolerated by the employers. Those lucky couples who were able to hire themselves out as butler-maid teams were rare exceptions.[12] Not many husbands were satisfied to have a part-time wife who was available only every other Sunday and one afternoon a week, although such "hidden" marriages did exist. More often, the maid became an extension of somebody else's family and an integral part of their daily routine, but not necessarily part of their emotional life. As years went by and the maid aged, the chance of having a family of her own receded. The exceptionally high age of the women giving birth in Montreal to illegitimate children – 37.6 in 1936-39 – suggests that some women made a deliberate decision to have a child of their own while it was still biologically possible.

The employers of most domestics did not provide pensions, nor take much interest in the whereabouts of a retired maid. To make matters worse, the maid had no family, no home, no life of her own. "All my life, I just worked and worked, I seldom went anywhere or met anybody," remembers one resident of an old-age home, "and now I know nobody, I am just wondering why God keeps me alive?" The tremendous personal sacrifices demanded from a reliable domestic, the willingness to become a shadow, a quiet figure in the corner tending to the household tasks, was described by one maid as "equal to being buried alive."

This sad fate befell some Finnish domestics, but many others fought against it vigorously. Any free time, the precious Wednesday or Thursday afternoon off, when the maid was allowed to do as she wished and meet people of her choice, was carefully planned in advance. Here the Finnish community was of special help and support.

COMMUNITY SUPPORT

The Finnish communities quickly adjusted to the maid's unusual time schedules in order to enable her to have some social activity. Finnish organizations, which until the 1930s were largely socialist locals of the Finnish Organization of Canada (FOC), arranged social occasions, gymnastics practices, theatre rehearsals, and dances during "the maid's day." The halls kept their doors open so that the maids could relax after their weekly pilgrimage to Eaton's. They could go and have coffee, meet each other, discuss the work situation, find out about new job opportunities, and for a few brief hours escape from their employers. The FOC locals were not the only groups vying for the maid's attention. Finnish congregations, especially in Toronto and Montreal, also catered to them. They scheduled their services for Wednesday and Sunday evenings and provided social coffee gatherings and reading rooms for the maids.

When the Finnish consul to Canada, Akseli Rauanheimo, tried to convince Canadian industry, railroads, and the government to contribute to the building of a Finnish immigrant home in Montreal, one of his chief concerns was the welfare of the maids. "Many of them have nothing to do on their afternoons off except sit alone on park benches." The home was not only to be used for entertainment, but also to function as a refuge for those women who were mistreated by their employers and who had no other "home" to go to then. Similarly, such temporary shelters for maids in other major Finnish communities were usually provided by those women who ran maids' employment services. Almost exclusively, the Finnish women relied and trusted only people from their own culture. For example, the Women's National Immigration Society in Montreal reports only nine Finnish women among over one thousand women who visited the home before the First World War. Vancouver's YMCA traveller's aid, which sought out stranded immigrant women from the docks and railway stations, only found three Finnish women during the busy immigration year of 1923. Similarly, the Women's Welcome Hostel in Toronto did not find a single Finn among the thousand women it assisted in 1911.[13]

This attitude of mutual help in the Finnish community added to the bargaining power of those domestics who knew that their services were in demand and who had the means to contact new employers. Most Finnish maids did take advantage of their ability, "to slam the

door so that the chandeliers were shaking," or alternately to "sneak
out of the backdoor so that nobody would notice." During their first
year as domestics in Canada, the women changed jobs frequently. For
example, the Finnish Immigrant Home in Montreal accommodated
women who were seeking new positions for the sixth time in one
year.[14]

The Finnish employment agencies were the key to the domestic's
flexibility. They were quick to advise the women not to accept intolerable conditions. Many enterprising women kept rooms for just such
a purpose, keeping close watch on the greenhorns who were most
vulnerable to exploitation. Still, even with a helpful Finnish woman,
the hiring was a harrowing experience. Elli Mäki remembered it vividly:

> The first lady who came picked me because I was obviously the
> cheapest and strongest one, she wanted a greenhorn who would
> work like a dog....I cried and washed her floors and I was always
> hungry, but I stayed there for four months until I went back to
> Mrs. Engman....She got me a new job right away, but this time I
> quit after one crazy day, sneaked out secretly....In my third place
> I stayed for seven and a half months and was able to demand
> $35.00 a month, but I quit that place too...because I had to be
> home at eleven o'clock and it broke my heart to leave the dances
> during the intermission and see my good looking boy-friend stay
> behind.

As the maids gained confidence in their own ability to do the job,
they became more defiant in the work place and often refused to be
treated like slaves. Hilja Sihvola explained:

> In one place where I worked the lady started to shout at me
> because I hadn't got up early enough to do the washing at 6:00
> A.M. I told her that nobody shouts at me and I quit. I decided to
> take that day off and went to stay at Ilomäki's [home for maids]
> but as soon as I got there the phone rang for me. It was the
> employment office calling, they figured that I had quit because
> my lady had called for a new maid. They phoned me to let me
> know that a new job was already waiting for me. Next day I was
> working again.

In addition to the private agencies who received payment for every
maid they placed, the Finnish Immigrant Home and many churches
arranged employment for the maids. The system was the same kind
of "cattle auction." Ida Toivonen remembers that "the women just
stood in a line and the ladies came to pick which one they wanted."
While most Finnish-Canadian sources claim that the Finnish maids
were sought-after workers, there are also examples to the contrary:
"There were places that would take only Finns, but there were also

places that wouldn't take a Finn for any money. Once I was told bluntly that, 'We won't hire Finns because they are all red and stubborn.' "

One woman remembers being told to quit singing the "International" while washing the kitchen floor. "I'll sing what I want," she replied and with that lost her job. Nellie McClung also referred to the reputation of Finnish maids as socialists and trouble-makers. But on the whole, the employers were not interested in the private lives of their maids, not to speak of their political opinions, as long as the floors were scrubbed, the laundry washed, and the family fed.

THE CLASS-CONSCIOUS MAID

To some Finnish domestics, the wages, the availability of work, and the supportive networks within the community were not enough. Instead they sought a more elusive goal – a strong collective class consciousness.

Unlike such characteristics as temper or shyness, class consciousness is acquired through experience, cultivated by self-study, and cemented by daily injustice. We have noted earlier that Finland was swept by a socialist fervour during the first two decades of the nineteenth century and the domestic question was hotly debated both in the legislature and media. Special homes for maids were established where women could acquire domestic skills. A newspaper, *Palvelijatar* (Maid), discussed at length the "maid's rights" and suggested protective measures. The paper's editor, Miina Sillanpää, a Social Democrat member of Parliament since 1907, raised the grievances in the Finnish legislature. Thus it is highly probable that many maids who arrived in North America had already learnt to accept the socialist world-view.

Because domestic service was the major occupation for Finnish women, it received much attention from the Finnish socialists in North America. Unlike North American socialists who were focusing on women in factories, Finnish socialist leaders were worried that the live-in domestics would adopt the "capitalist outlook of their employers when they are clearly an indistinguishable part of the working class." They were baffled as to how to organize the domestics who were serving thousands of different "bosses" all over Canada. In the end, the main impetus was placed on raising individual awareness, making each maid fight for her own rights within her particular place of employment, while the community would provide her with the best possible support: knowledge, training, cooperative housing, and minimum guidelines for wages and working hours. Unsuccessful efforts at unionizing the maids were also made in major urban areas.

The key to bringing the maids into the socialist fold was to give them hope of improved working conditions by frankly discussing the problems and solutions in the Finnish North American press. In this, the socialist women's newpaper, *Toveritar,* which had over three thousand subscribers in Canada in 1929, played a vital role.[15] In a special issue for the maids, on May 9, 1916, the editor, Selma Jokela-McClone, analysed the situation:

1 While the factory worker is seldom in direct contact with her employer, the maid has personally to face her boss on a daily basis and negotiate her undefined work.

2 A maid is a highly skilled worker, yet she has no possibility to learn her trade before she starts working.

3 Maids do not necessarily work for the big capitalists, many serve the middle class and even the more prosperous working class, which can confuse the issue of class struggle.

To deal with these problems Jokela-McClone suggested that:

1 Because the maid meets her employer as a human being she must have the self-confidence and the sense of self-worth to demand decent human treatment.

2 Maids must become professionals by improving their skills to the utmost of their ability. The key to successful bargaining is the ability to perform well.

3 They must organize maids' clubs, cooperative homes, employment exchanges and raise the class-consciousness of the maids before they can put forth strong demands.

These guidelines were adopted by Finnish socialist women's groups in Canada, but not without a debate. Many questioned "the need for special skills," or the argument that a maid was a professional, or a highly trained worker. There were those who saw the maid as "an appendix to the parasite class" and not a trustworthy member of the working class. Maids themselves asked what good training centres or clubs were when the maids didn't have the free time to attend them. Despite the skepticism, attempts were made to implement the plan.

In New York and San Francisco well-organized and highly effective maids' cooperative homes were established. These were a model for other communities to emulate. In Canada the cooperative maids' home movement among the Finns had sporadic support at best. The need for such homes was partially met by private establishments which provided temporary housing when necessary. The employment exchange for Finnish maids was also in the hands of Finnish women who were generally trusted and reliable, unlike the situation in Manhattan, for example, where several large American agencies competed for Finnish maids. Besides, in 1916, both the United States and Canada were experiencing shortages of domestic servants, "giving the maids great opportunities to be selective." A 1922 article in *Vapaus* concluded that obtaining work was not the problem, but rather the exhaustingly long working days.

By the mid-1920s, when Finnish socialist activity had taken a more radical turn toward communism, the question of maids' unions and organizations rose again. This time, the response was at best luke-warm. The first *Palvelijatar Yhdistys* (Maids' Organization) was founded in Toronto on December 6, 1925. Prior to this, the Finnish Organi-zation of Canada's Toronto local had given their Don Hall free of charge for the maids to use on their afternoons off. In 1926 the orga-nization placed a permanent advertisement in the *Telegram* and set up a job exchange at the hall. Later the advertisement was only placed in the paper if someone was in need of work. At times the organization had over twenty paying members. Eventually it became inactive, only coming to life briefly again on January 6, 1929, under the name of the Finnish Domestic Club. A year earlier the Chinese community of Toronto had established a union of domestic workers at 87 Elizabeth Street complete with an employment exchange. Among the Toronto Finns a cooperative home for the maids was discussed, but it never materialized.

In 1927 Vancouver women also decided to establish a cooperative home and employment exchange for maids. They established a fund for this purpose, but by the end of 1928 gave up the idea. Instead, they decided to investigate the possibility of joining the existing Domestic Servants' Union (the majority of whose members were Chinese). Nothing came of this joint venture.

The largest Finnish maids' organization was established in Montreal in 1928, where the need for protection was greatest since the city was the immediate recipient of all newly arrived maids disembarking from transatlantic steamers. Here a cooperative home was established in 1930, only to be dissolved within two years by the Depression. This home and job exchange was in competition with the Finnish Immi-grant Home established by the consul of Finland and the Seamen's Mission in 1927. From the beginning the housing coop had over thirty members. In 1928 an article in *Vapaus* pointed out that the city had about five hundred Finnish women of whom less than 2 per cent were housewives, the rest were all working as maids or in the service indus-tries.

Similar maids' groups were established in Sudbury in 1928, in Sault Ste Marie in 1929 and more sporadically in Port Arthur and Timmins during 1928-30. Common to all these maids' organizations was the desire to achieve a minimum wage level. The women in Sault Ste Marie all swore that they would not "scab" for lower wages. In Sudbury the maids were keen to establish insurance schemes for the sick and unemployed. In all locations great emphasis was placed on self-education, not in domestic skills – on class consciousness and understanding the role of women in a communist society.

In total, a rough estimate would suggest that about two hundred Finnish domestics belonged to the organizations designed for the specific purpose of promoting maids' interests. The small numbers suggest that domestic servants did not have the time or will to give their only afternoon off to attend meetings, especially since other Finnish women's groups could carry on the task. In northern Ontario the Timmins domestics suggested a complete integration of women's organizations instead of splintering women into small interest groups. Finnish men "did not take the organizations seriously," and the groups were not strong enough to have any influence on wages. "Despite this," concludes a published assessment of the maids' organizations, "they had great impact in making the maids realize that they too were part of the working class and most welcome in socialist circles."

Bootleggers and Tavern Maids: the Spirit of Free Enterprise

Some Finnish women did not wish to be domestic servants, lumber camp cooks, rooming-house keepers, dishwashers or waitresses. Instead, they were looking for even faster ways of making money and more lucrative business opportunities. These women were not afraid to break the law to achieve their goals.

Koiratorpparit (the "doghouse keepers" [keepers of blind pigs]) were at once the most respected and despised women in the Finnish communities. They were women of power, property, and control over men. The most successful owned sophisticated taverns complete with gambling saloons, dance halls, and rooms for rent. The success of female bootleggers is directly linked to the abnormalities of Finnish immigrant life in Canada. They flourished in all resource towns where men were longing for diversion, starving for the company of women, or just lonely for any camaraderie. They also existed in urban areas where the strict liquor laws and dress codes of "official" taverns alienated immigrants. As prohibition crept in, bootleggers expanded and diversified their business.

Tavern culture and the abundance of bootleggers is not unique to Finnish immigrants. Joe Beef's canteen in Montreal is but one example of the type of service that could be obtained in a working-class tavern.[16] What is quite exceptional, however, is the fact that in Finnish communities women began to dominate the business, setting the standards, prices, and their own code of operating ethics. Basically, there were three types of operators: those who sold bottles or home brew on the street, at work sites, or near the docks; those who opened their homes to customers; and those who ran more sophisticated businesses with a variety of entertainment, food, and drink.

Finnish women were attracted to the bootlegging business for many reasons. It was "independent" work, it allowed the women to work with Finnish men, and most of all, it paid well. Many married women with children found other work opportunities difficult to obtain. For them live-in domestic work was out of the question. The other alternatives preferred by Finnish women all demanded great physical strength, hard work, and long hours. The wages were enough to sustain a single woman, but were hardly adequate to support children too. Thus, women with children, especially if single parents, found bootlegging attractive. The other vulnerable group were older single women, often widows who found it more difficult to find work. When these women tried to find alternative ways to make money they discovered that bootlegging was one of the most lucrative. The initial investment was not great, and there seemed to be no shortage of customers.

Several questions emerge from this practice. Why did bootlegging become "a woman's job?" What kind of women kept *koiratorppia*, and why were these illegal establishments so popular? The following information on the illegal operations was gathered from oral interviews conducted with the bootleggers, their customers, and their critics, supplemented by information from written sources, particularly the newspapers of the time.

Lydia Punni arrived in Vancouver in 1924. She came from the countryside in Finland and was horrified with what she found in Vancouver: bootleggers, prostitutes, and all variety of vice. "Women," she said, "Finnish women selling booze and deceiving men!" So shocked was Punni that she began her own private investigation into the matter, carefully recording the names and family circumstances of the Vancouver *koiratorpparit* operating in 1924. "One day, nobody will believe what life has been like," she reasoned, "so I decided to write it all down." She stumbled on the subject having been innocently hired by a "restaurant" which turned out to be an unlicensed tavern. "They liked it when an old country fool came to sell booze, she was sure to attract in new customers...they [the tavern keepers] knew all the tricks." Sixty years later, Punni pulled from her drawer in the Vancouver old-age home her extraordinary document and highlighted its contents on tape. The following are extracts from the written material and interviews which allow us to reconstruct a dozen Finnish bootlegging operations in Vancouver in 1924. Surnames have been deleted.

> Hanna: an old maid from Karelia who lived with her sister, but when she [the sister] moved to Toronto, Hanna started to sell liquor out of her home. She also performed abortions. She married late in life and stopped bootlegging.

Emma: a widow with one daughter.

A: a widow with one daughter.

"Bear": "an old widowed hag" with two daughters who ran an illegal tavern, stopped selling liquor when she got married.

A & A: two sisters who ran a lucrative tavern, married (or had many men) several times.

Eeva: a widow with two sons whom she brought up by selling liquor out of her home.

Impi: divorced (left her husband in the east) with two boys in Canada and supported one son in Finland. She was alone in Vancouver and sold alcohol by the bottle.

"Dirty Maija": middle-aged single woman, bootlegger and a prostitute.

Manta: biggest operator in Vancouver, met lumberjacks at the docks and took them to her *koiratorppa,* sold them drinks and herself. She had a husband and two children living somewhere else, and she supported them with her business. Finally she went back to her husband.

Mrs. T: her husband left her and went back to Finland. Mrs. T. supported herself by bootlegging from her home until she found a permanent male partner.

J & O & V: the operations of these three sauna owners included bootlegging and prostitution. They were family-run, husband and wife teams where men took care of the sauna and bootlegging and the women of all the "extra services."[17]

From this sample it seems that older, single, or widowed women with children were most likely to be found in the bootlegging business. For many of them it was a temporary solution to sudden economic difficulties. One recently widowed woman, who was crying for help in her desperation and worried about her survival and the fate of her two children, soon found her problem solved by a man of action: "'Start selling booze,' he said, and then bought the first bottle for me. He unscrewed the top and took a gulp from the bottle he had just brought. 'There, you have just served your first customer,' he said."

In addition to the bootleggers who sold bottles or single drinks, there were women who opened their homes to thirsty men looking for a drink and a "living room." Men who lived in crowded rooming-houses, or who spent months in bunkhouses in lumber camps, had no opportunity for a home-like atmosphere, privacy, or the company of women. The simple "doghouses" did not pretend to be taverns or elaborate social clubs. Instead the woman would serve drinks, and one or two, sometimes more, men would sit around her kitchen table or on the couch in the front room. They would drink, play cards, and chat. Often the discussions shifted from the old country, to women, to politics. The atmosphere was friendly and congenial and the clientele steady. Men soon began to identify with their doghouse, seeing it as an extension of their life, their living room. The women who opened their homes were much admired and spoken of with warmth and respect. Sanni Salmijärvi explains what an ideal doghouse was like in Thunder Bay:

> They had to be pleasant and comfortable and the women, often it was the women or the wife of a couple, had to be specially wonderful people. The main reason was that these men had no home of their own, so it [doghouse] was their substitute home. If the women were also beautiful, then all men could admire them, not touch, just admire and talk.

Certain mystery surrounded some of the most successful bootleggers. They were at once despised and spoken of with awe. An autobiography of a Timmins woman describes one bootlegger of mythical proportions.

> The Queen of Hearts, it was said, kept a spotless house, and no fault could be found with her morals. She was a business woman – for drinks only and no funny business – but she did not have any friends among the Finnish housewives, nor did she take part in any of the various social activities.

The author further explains the many stories about the Queen of Hearts. It was told that she had two sons in Finland whom she was putting through university and that, "she had bought a lovely home for her aged mother in Helsinki." She had avoided being arrested for years, but when she found herself behind bars one day, she sent a Finnish baker to fetch the $400 to pay the fine. How much more money was hidden in her house, wondered the curious community?[18]

Women controlled Finnish bootlegging establishments in Vancouver, Winnipeg, Toronto, and all the northern Ontario resource towns. A female missionary, Lahja Söderberg, who travelled among the Finns in Cochrane, Hearst, Timmins, and Kirkland Lake, explained how women could operate the *koiratorpat*. She remembers Hilda, who had the "biggest bootlegging joint in Hearst," as a religious person, "real good-hearted woman, never charged me for room and board, wanted me to stay at her house." Hilda was a mother of three and had a husband who worked outside. The police knew all about her operations and the husband paid the nominal fines. Another, formerly religious woman had become a bootlegger at the insistence of her husband, but soon became a "successful hard-nosed business woman" and left her husband and started her own unlicensed tavern. According to this missionary, all of the eight to ten Finnish bootleggers in Hearst in the 1920s were women.

One customer who tramped across Canada gives the following account:

> The doghouses in Thunder Bay, Sudbury and Toronto were almost all run by women, older women in their forties and fifties, some married. They were strong and big "mammas." There were at least forty illegal Finnish taverns in "Artturi" [Port Arthur] and "Viljami" [Fort William], another 20 in Sudbury and in Toronto there were two dozen just within a walking distance from Widmer Street [SULO ÄIJÖ, Parry Sound].

Two former customers drew a map of downtown Toronto where they marked all those doghouses that they had visited "at the beginning of the depression." They came up with eighteen separate businesses all within four city blocks. The owners were remembered as Silver Mamma, "the biggest woman you had ever seen," or "Darling," who was big and strong, so strong that nobody went near her. In addition, the men commented that alcohol could be bought by the bottle from just about every Finnish home on Widmer Street. The common denominator, according to these customers, was that the women were mature, strong, and untouchable: "They were not afraid of men, they could throw them out like straws if the men were too noisy. The women knew how to keep order and the men could not touch them if they wished to come back again." Another man nostalgically recalls Big Selma from Kirkland Lake who became legendary for her frequent "flying lessons to men" as she threw the rabble-rousers out of her doghouse.

An expanded version of the living-room type of establishment was a place that also served meals and sometimes offered rooms for rent. In the politically torn Finnish communities, the most astute doghouse keepers had separate rooms for the various factions, "red room for the communists – white room for the [conservatives] – and a yellow room for the IWW gang." A safer set-up, however, was to patronize separate doghouses.

The largest establishments had women customers, music, dance floors, gambling, and restaurants. To run such operations illegally required the cooperation of the local police. The "dance-hall" in Sudbury, for example, received its weekly routine visits from the officer who collected his "pay." This custom was common; there were even instances when women who ran these large unlicensed taverns asked the police to help them collect money owed them by their customers. A man who made the beer deliveries with his horse and buggy in Sudbury explained:

I delivered more beer to the bootleggers than to the licensed joints. The brewery often paid whatever fines the bootleggers collected and they also helped bribe the police, who in turn gave protection to the women who ran the doghouses [J.T.].

The *koiratorppas* were clearly a well-established part of urban and frontier life and their popularity relied on many factors. First, the illegal establishments were not governed by any specified hours. Miners who were thirsty after their evening shift could wander over to see a "mamma" for a nightcap without having to worry about his appearance. Sundays, when other drinking establishments closed down, were the busiest for bootleggers. After all, Sunday was the only free day workers had. Secondly, the owners knew their customers well, and there was an element of mutual trust. The client would not inform the police of the operation, and the owner, in turn, gave credit to her clients. It was customary that men brought their entire pay cheques to the mammas with the instructions that they be told before the money ran out. When the money was gone, they packed their bags and went back to a work camp, often using the doghouse as their permanent mailing address. And thirdly, the *koiratorppa* was like a private club, meeting the social needs of lonely men. Competition kept the prices reasonable and the owners, who relied on repeat customers, relatively "honest," although some complaints were heard over the size of a drink, diluting, and even "cleaning out" itinerant drunks.

There seemed to be little ethnic mixing among customers. Finnish clubs usually only had Finnish clients. So when trouble arose, when fights ensued over gambling irregularities, or when drunken men vented their frustrations, the victims of the attack were also Finns. This contributed to the Finns' reputation for being quick to use a knife and to aim it at another Finn. The female owners were rarely the target of the attack.

While most men who relied on the services of the *koiratorppa* spoke with admiration and respect for the women who ran them, and while some women reluctantly conceded the necessity for such establishments, the Finnish organizations, churches, and press waged an endless battle against this kind of illegal activity. The socialist and religious Finns were at loggerheads over most issues, but they were united in their efforts to stop alcohol abuse among Finns. Female voices were often heard the loudest in the cry for temperance, and their attacks on the bootleggers were most virulent. While the women's press depicted alcohol as a "male problem," it conveniently ignored the fact that within Finnish communities women contributed significantly by providing the distribution network. In Toronto three of the identifiable mammas were also members of the socialist women's club which protested against drinking, one was a well-known agent for *Toveritar*, and two were identified as members of the Finnish United Church. The double standard around this issue clearly extended to women. Nor were men the only alcohol abusers. In 1918, when Ontario was relatively "dry," forty-year-old Mrs. P. died of alcohol poisoning in Sault Ste Marie.

In February 1919, when *Canadan Uutiset* was forced by the War Measures Act to publish in English as well as Finnish, the following article from Port Arthur appeared in the paper:

> [Many] are suffering from the loathsome consequences of the blind pigging, for they are operated even now charging for the whiskey mixed with dope and water from 8 to 15 "plunks" a bottle...you have been dragging our people under disrespect. Or is it good to you, if all will be classed as outlaws because some of us are doing things that are against the law?

This worry over the collective national image of Finns in Canada was reflected in other articles. A man from Sudbury complained that, "The national honour of Finns is at rock bottom, because one can find countless numbers of *koiratorppas*." A "Hoobo" from Timmins observes that although Finns are not the only ones keeping doghouses, in comparison to their numbers there are "shamefully many of them." *Canadan Uutiset* fuelled the complaint by pointing out that there were more wholesale and retail Finnish bootleggers in both Fort William and Port Arthur than of any other nationality. The main concern here was not the drinking or the visitations to the bootleggers, but rather what other people would think of this habit. Surprisingly enough, women were seldom mentioned; the critical finger was pointed at the men.

The one aspect of bootlegging apparently not controlled by the women was the actual brewing of the moonshine, and it is here that the authorities seemed to crack down most severely. Women, however, did brew home-made beer, as they had done for centuries in Finland. At times they sold the beer to their customers, but this did not create a major concern. The manufacturers of stronger spirits were frequently arrested, fined, even given prison terms, but the women who helped them and sold the drinks were left in peace. At times it seemed that because of the reluctance to arrest women, they could get away with "almost murder":

> Mrs. Signe Niemi, the wife of a Finnish farmer who was convicted of illegal manufacture of alcohol, was released because of insufficient evidence. Mrs. Niemi was initially arrested for shooting three times with a Winchester rifle at the provincial police who came to arrest her husband Walter from home early on the 19th of August.

Women were arrested occasionally. A correspondent from Timmins reported that finally, after having been able to run their blind pigs peacefully, "and sell their brews," two Finnish mammas were jailed and fined $300 each. Immediately their customers, the Timmins mine workers, paid the fines. This kind of double standard of morality bothered the organized socialists. "Eva," a Timmins correspondent for *Toveritar*, concluded that "there will be *koiratorppas* like there are mushrooms during the rainy season," and that they will not disappear as long as organized, class-conscious people continue to support them. In Canada women were seldom seen as customers at the blind pigs unless they were accompanied by men. No study has been made of this phenomenon among the Finns in the United States, but it appears that at least in New York, women also patronized the illegal taverns. An article in *Toveritar* described New York's *koiratorppas:* "Now there are in Harlem about two hundred Finnish *koiratorppas* and all of them have a booming business... they attract recently arrived girls from Finland as bait, to sit and entice male customers." The New York operations were started at first by women. As word spread, couples made lucrative full-time businesses out of them.

There is no question that these illegal activities were tolerated by the authorities without whose support the women could not have continued to run their establishments. The initial secrecy soon gave way to only "half-clandestine" operations. In Thunder Bay the boldest put out a sign, "Welcome – *Koiratorppa*," and hoped that the police-man's English was better than his Finnish. The taverns were not hard to spot with "drunken men sleeping on the stairs as sign posts." In rural areas where the police were quick to sniff out every illegally hunted moose, they seemed blind to bootlegging. The inconsistency was also evident when women were arrested for other crimes their husbands committed, such as avoiding the draft. In 1920 Alma Nygård wrote from Sellars, Ontario:

> I too have had all kinds of sorrow and worry during the last two years so that at times I was at a loss what to do when first Hilma died and left me her week-old daughter so that I now had eight children all together and then a year later Etu got an order to go to the army but he didn't go and then the police came to get him but he ran to the forest and they shot after him several times but didn't get him so they took me instead and transported me into the city and they put me in the jail and I only got out by paying bail and then they put me to court and fined me over hundred dollars and Etu has been gone over a year.

Running a doghouse was simply not seen as such a serious crime as hiding a draft-dodger, even if he was your own husband. After all, as one customer noted, "Where could the police go for a drink after late night shift?" In the meanwhile, in the 1920s at least three hundred Finnish women in Canada lived, or supplemented their income, by what can be classified as "criminal activity." Operating blind pigs gave many an elderly person, a widowed mother, or an enterprising couple an alternative, an independent way of making a living. Moreover, it gave the women status, as matrons, mammas, bankers, and bouncers. These were defiant women, women who refused to obey the laws of the land when they did not seem to meet the workers' needs, women who were not afraid of the police or their male customers, women who were very much in control.

Prostitution

The *koiratorppa* mamma was usually an untouchable, respectable matron, but there were also bootleggers who ran "cat-houses" – the illegal saloons which combined "all possible vices":

> It seems to be just the same today [1922 in Timmins] as it was ten years ago, wherever there are a considerable number of Finns, the three vices emerge: gambling, bootlegging and prostitution. These vices flourish semi-openly and are generally well tolerated.

Lydia Punni's list of bootleggers in Vancouver also included several prostitutes who, with one exception, were married. It appears that *koiratorppas* run by couples sometimes evolved into a more definite division of labour where the man looked after the bootlegging while the woman served the clientele and prostituted herself. The largest cat-houses might be operated by several couples, as was the case in Vancouver at the Sauna-Saloon-Cathouse owned by J & O & V. Men took care of the business aspect of the operation while women "massaged all the money from the men." Hilda Lähde, from Sault Ste Marie, gossips in a letter to her friend:

> Mrs. S. built a new house for herself with her husband's life insurance money near the CPR tracks on John Street towards North Street and there in the house with her live several women the same kind as herself and her boy-friend A. and the K. couple are renting there. [Mr.] K. is also a bootlegger and has other women but still lives with his wife who also chases men.

Among the organized Finnish women, there was not much sympathy for the big-time operators, the professional prostitutes who owned property, often lived with a man, were bootleggers and did not seem to have economic necessity as a reason for continuing their sordid lifestyle. The opposite was true of the single women, "driven to prostitution" because of tragic personal or economic circumstances, practising their trade as a last alternative. These women received an enormous amount of official sympathy from socialist women's groups and the press. To them, the prostitute was but another victim of the capitalist system. They exposed the vulnerability of women and the double standards which existed in the male-dominated, competitive social order. Theorizing and sympathizing was easy enough on paper or from the distance of a speakers' platform. Stories about their more downtrodden sisters were touching; poems and plays about daughters who sold themselves on the street to support a family brought tears to the eyes of the audience. But the reality in a face-to-face encounter with a prostitute was harsher. A progressive socialist activist discovered this for herself when a well-known Finnish prostitute moved into a house across the street from her Port Arthur home. She explained that Hurja Hilma was a prostitute, but "nobody could tell by looking at her." According to Hilma's neighbour, "She was so well dressed and beautiful, even her body shape, and the way she walked, she could have worn a crown fit for a Queen." One morning Hilma broke the traditional code of silence of her peers and invited her neighbour from across the street in for a cup of coffee. "I am too busy," blurted Sanni Salmijärvi immediately. "Maybe later," she added to soften her initial harsh reaction. Salmijärvi hurried inside to hide, ashamed of her reaction, amazed by her own inflexibility:

> I went in and I sat down to really think. I remember the morning so vividly, and I sat and thought for a long time, asking myself, "Who was I to cast the first stone at her?" She was a lonely woman, maybe she didn't have a single person that she could call a friend. And then I asked myself, "What do I know of the reasons why she is a prostitute?" For a long time I tried to understand myself, and then I decided that I would not be a worse person if I visited Hilma....When I went to her house she had laid out such a beautiful table with cakes and *pulla*. Her place was sparkling clean and her daughter was wearing an immaculately starched dress... from her conversation you could tell she came from a good family....Still, I never visited her again or asked her to my house. She asked me a few times, but I just made some excuse. I just couldn't force myself.... Finally she moved to Nipigon and got married.

This incident plagued Salmijärvi for the next sixty years, and to this day she still asks herself why she, a woman who has always been a rebel, progressive and open-minded, would "turn her back to another woman in need of a friend." Finnish prostitutes, no matter how well behaved, were doomed to a life of loneliness and ostracism by their own community, even its most progressive elements, including those women who failed to practise the social gospel they preached.

By listening to descriptions of the Finnish prostitutes given by clients, well-meaning social workers, and casual, often disgruntled, observers, it is possible to piece together a common profile of the prostitute who operated alone. She usually had a better than average education; some had finished high school. Physically, she was described as frail but attractive, often as the "most beautiful woman in town"; and many noted that she walked with her head held high, almost as though she belonged to a class – perhaps a very misunderstood class – of her own. She seldom spoke to anyone, was discreet about who her clients were, and lived alone. Some women operated out of rooming-houses, where Finnish men lived, others would get referrals from the *koiratorppas*, but usually the women were not directly linked to either. Privacy, their own room or even a house, was a most sought after pleasure in an environment where men lived packed together, "like herrings in the salt barrel." Cleanliness was another trademark:

> I always used a Finnish prostitute, you know, they were clean and they didn't swear like some others. I really learned to like some, you know, when there are no other women around the prostitute becomes almost like a girl-friend, you know, and even when you understand that she is as nice to other men, for that one night she was mine. I almost married one, but she got TB and died.

A woman who spent many hours at the bedside of three Finnish prostitutes who were dying of syphilis, offering spiritual comfort, recalls their tragic story: "They were all women who had good education in Finland, but in Canada they could not find their own kind of work." Being frail and unaccustomed to hard physical labour, they became prostitutes. The money was good, they could continue to buy attractive clothes, and all of them had nice homes. It is difficult to estimate the monthly salaries of the average Finnish prostitutes. Customers recall that they paid anywhere from $2 to $5. During "high season" when the lumberjacks returned from the camps, the fee could be as high as $10. Three prostitutes who operated during the late twenties and early thirties in the Timmins-Porcupine area died of syphilis, and "two of them died praying," while one was "such a hard boiled communist that nothing would touch her." Their deaths can be confirmed in the newspapers, but interestingly enough no cause of death is given. In fact, venereal disease was not once mentioned in the obituaries, church or funeral home records as the cause of death for anyone. Surely it must have claimed many victims. "You can figure out what happened to the men when both Finnish prostitutes in Cochrane got syphilis," exclaimed one angry woman.

Prostitutes have always been a part of society, and there have always been men who use them. However, in immigrant enclaves, with an acute shortage of women, reliance on prostitutes, "on sharing women," increased. "Even immigrant men are men, not machines, and men need women – simple as that. Often the prostitutes were the only women available." When asked about the fear of venereal disease, the philosophical answer was: "Life is a gamble, every day I went down into the mine I wondered if it was my turn to die that day. We gambled with women too, we had no choice, had to get wages and had to live too."

These lonely Finnish prostitutes received very little negative press in the two Finnish-Canadian newspapers and were treated rather patronizingly and sympathetically in the socialist women's newspaper, *Toveritar*. When the commentary was negative, the criticism usually focused on the circumstances rather than the individual. A man in Niagara Falls objected that the Finnish prostitute there "had to carry on in the presence of her young son." The rowdy bootlegger-cum-prostitute who worked in collusion with a man, sometimes even a husband, was the recipient of most of the media scorn.

Prostitution, then, was accepted in the Finnish communities. It was a practice which offered financial rewards to a few women who refused to do housework or heavy labour and who were unable, because of language barriers or discrimination, to find more respectable alternate employment. The single prostitutes managed to create a collective image which added to their popularity and allowed them to charge more. "I would surely pay twice as much for a Finnish woman!" exclaimed one man. The ethnic exclusiveness of Finns seemed to extend even to the bedrooms of the prostitutes. By insisting on fine dress – "the Finnish prostitutes were the most stylish women in town" – and cleanliness, they built an aura of respectability around their work.

The Finnish immigrant prostitutes do not seem to fit the standard profile of the "wayward worker." Lori Rotenberg's study of turn-of-the-century Toronto prostitutes indicates that most were between the ages of fourteen and twenty-five because "youth was a highly market-able commodity for which men could pay well." Finnish prostitutes, however, were mature women often in their thirties and forties.[19] Furthermore, Rotenberg's comparison of the ethnic breakdown of the inmates in Institutes for Delinquent Women in Toronto in 1911 shows only 6 per cent classified as "foreign-born," while the remainder were British- and Canadian-born. Of the immigrant prostitutes, the British-born were greatly over-represented compared to their proportion of the Toronto population, while the foreign-born were under-represented.

These statistics raise many questions: Were there indeed less foreign-born prostitutes? Were foreign-born women not deemed worthy of saving and hence not institutionalized? Or were foreign-born prostitutes simply not caught? The last seems to be true of the Finnish prostitutes who were not street-walkers who solicited in public. Instead the mature women worked in the relative comfort of their own homes or rented rooms – sometimes they were given a bedroom in a rooming-house or *koiratorppa* – and they enjoyed the protection of their clientele. The community also shielded them from the authorities. Community women grudgingly admitted both the need for prostitutes and the necessity to hide their existence in order to maintain a positive image of Finns in Canada. Still, the prostitutes were outcasts, they knew their boundaries. They did not attend church or social organizations, and they were doomed to a life without female companionship.

Bootlegging and prostitution were two extreme examples of the entrepreneurial spirit of Finnish women, both made possible by the great demand for women and socializing in the male-dominated Finnish communities. The lack of stable structures and other alternatives for Finnish men further increased the demand for such illegal activity. On the other hand, the vulnerability of single immigrant mothers and older widows in Canada channelled many women into these occupations, which they might have shunned in their home village in Finland. Bootlegging and prostitution were natural outgrowths of the immigrant life, and further examples of the heavy social cost of the immigration experience. The *koiratorppari* (doghouse keeper) of Canada did not have her counterpart in Finland. Prostitutes did exist but they were not as much in demand in a country that had an excess of women.

Finnish women and the communities they lived in tried to accommodate to the new economic and social structures and the changes in employment opportunities. Many were able to take advantage of the uneven sex ratio and demand good wages as cooks, cleaners, and rooming-house keepers. The very high percentage of domestic workers among Finnish immigrant women and the visible addition of bootleggers and prostitutes were also part of this accommodation process. Women's relative independence, coupled with the propensity of Finnish men to seek employment in the remote resource regions of the country, directed some Finnish women into the bush. Here once again, ethnicity played an important role in the decision-making process. Overall, the Finnish immigrant women felt that in Canada they did achieve their primary goals; they were able to find or create steady work for themselves at a decent wage.

CHAPTER 6

Women in the Immigrant Church

At first glance the Finns in Canada seem to be a very religious and homogeneous group; as late as 1931, 88.3 per cent declared that they were Lutheran. At the same time, many held bitter, anti-religious sentiments. Furthermore, a mere 3 per cent of the Finns who claimed to be Lutheran in the census report had actually bothered to join the church in Canada. In direct contrast, Finland claimed at least 90 per cent of its inhabitants as members of the church. Clearly immigrant conditions had greatly altered Finnish religious practices and convictions.[1]

Many factors shaped Finnish immigrant women's attitudes to organized religion in Canada. The roots of some of the strong anti-clerical sentiments were in Finland, where the Finnish Lutheran Church enjoyed legal, financial, and political privileges. Moreover, Finnish Lutherans in Canada faced new problems when they tried to reconstruct the familiar, authoritarian, patriarchal Lutheran Church in the new world. For one thing, they had to combat the threat posed by the competing religious alternatives such as the Presbyterian Church and the United Church of Canada and their missionary work among Finnish women.

Several new religious movements gained strength among Finnish immigrants in Canada during the late 1920s, but because their major development and growth occurred in the following decade, they will not be discussed extensively here. Most notable of these is the Pentecostal movement which has since become a powerful religious force within the Finnish-Canadian communities. It is also important to note that at this time the Lutheran Church was in a most dismal state. The 1930s witnessed a rigorous reorganization and remoulding of the church to serve better the immigrant needs. The many strong Finnish Lutheran congregations in Canada today are a result of this later development. The focus of this chapter, however, is on the early period and the perplexing and resounding failure of the Finnish Lutheran Church to maintain its membership in Canada.[2]

Anti-clericalism and the State Lutheran Church in Finland

The Finnish Lutheran Church historically has served as the centre of education and political power in Finland. Although some of these civil responsibilities were removed from the direct control of the church in the mid-1870s, membership in the church remained compulsory. Technically, after the 1889 revision of the church laws, it was possible for there to be non-Lutheran Finns in the country, but no separate administrative network was created for them. The Orthodox Finns who lived in Karelia were simply seen as part of the Russian State Church and counted as members of the diocese of St. Petersburg. Legislation to introduce total freedom of religion was debated for over a decade, but when it finally became effective in 1923, the Lutheran Church still enjoyed status as the national State religion. Church laws were still debated in Parliament, the president appointed the archbishop and the bishops, and the state continued to collect taxes for the church. Most significantly, the 1923 act made Lutheran religious education compulsory in the public schools, thus guaranteeing the continuation of the teaching of Christian morals according to Lutheran guidelines.

Thus, during the heavy emigration years of 1890-1923, Finns automatically belonged to their state church. Confirmation and communion were compulsory before marriage. Any personal documents required for emigration had to be obtained from the church. Legally, it was possible to leave the church after 1923, but in reality very few Finns did. It was easier to stay within the familiar religious fabric. The total number of Finnish women who took advantage of the separation of church and state from 1923-29 was slightly over twenty-one thousand out of more than one and a half million Finnish females. In practice, then, all Finnish immigrants were Lutheran.[3]

Because the immigrants were officially Lutheran does not necessarily mean that they supported Lutheran theology or any other Christian teachings. The power of the church was much criticized, particularly by the Finnish socialists. This was not only because of the strict interpretation of the marxist anti-religious theory, but also because of the political developments that were unfolding in Finland at that time. As socialism swept over much of the country, Finns were struggling to gain political independence from Russia. During the great general strike, the state church was seen, at best, as a lukewarm supporter of legislative reform. Ministers who feared the anti-religious developments among the socialists, and who did not want to lose their special estate in Parliament, felt safer within the tsarist regime. When the Finnish Civil War broke out, the church was seen as a staunch supporter of the white army. Some ministers were harassed or murdered by the reds. The Archbishop of Finland had opposed the socialists ever since the foundation of the Social Democratic Party in 1903, when he declared a socialist could not be a Christian. Furthermore, after the white victory in the eyes of the church, the reds were not only its enemies but were traitors to the country.

The socialists' antipathy towards the "white church" sprang, in part, from the fact that some priests took part in the post-civil war vendetta against the reds. Since Finnish religious leaders had traditionally held political power, they continued their activity in politics as elected members of Parliament. They were most visible in the extreme right-wing parties. It was against this turbulent background that the reformation of church law was debated in Parliament.

The image of the church among the left-wing Finns did not improve after 1923, as many pastors were among the visible supporters of the growing fascist movements. They were active participants in the *Akateeminen Karjala-seura* (Academic Karelia Society), which was characterized by its *ryssä viha* (hatred for Russians) and by its scorn for *petturit* (traitors). In 1933, of the fourteen members of Parliament of the fascist party in Finland, *Isänmaallinen kansanliike* (Patriotic People's Movement), five were Lutheran ministers. In the eyes of the socialists the strong right-wing movements of the late twenties were *sini-musta-pappiliike* (blue-black-priest's movement).

There were some who encouraged more understanding of social issues. Among the workers were some who did not support the vehemently anti-religious stance of the Finnish Social Democratic Party. Immediately after the 1905 general strike, they formed Christian Socialist movements and their own political party. It is significant that the impetus for this movement came from the people, not from the church. However, once initiated a few Finnish Lutheran ministers lent their support to the Christian socialists. In the 1907 elections, however, they were able to elect only two representatives to Parliament; and by the time of the civil war, in 1918, had lost those two seats. Unlike many other western European countries where Christian socialism was a strong political force and an alternative forum for people in support of working-class goals, in Finland, the Christian socialist political movement was a failure.

The Lutheran Church was extremely patriarchal. The 1923 reforms, did not extend to women, who were barred from the ministry and from the church councils. They could, however, take part in admin-istrative duties, and increasingly served as deaconesses, mainly as volunteers. Ironically, the same women who were not only members of Parliament, but cabinet ministers, could not sit on the church coun-cils, a fact that was not overlooked by the feminist, socialist women of Finland. This religious background, a mix of politics and patriotism, was the Lutheran heritage which was to become the foundation of the Finnish immigrant churches in Canada.

The Finnish Lutheran Churches in Canada

In Canada the religious atmosphere was quite different. Here several factors contributed to a dramatic change in the religious life of the immigrants. First, and perhaps most important, Canada had no state church and hence no compulsory religious taxation, no clearly struc-tured church hierarchy or monopoly, no trained Finnish-speaking Lutheran ministers, and no resources for church construction. Secondly, the timing of Finnish immigration to Canada coincided with the strong reform impulse in Finnish political and religious life. The late nineteenth-century reformist groups that could be contained under the umbrella of the state church in Finland had no such disciplinary structures in Canada. In addition, many of the immigrants who had adopted socialism could freely discard any traditional religious trap-pings in Canada. Thirdly, immigrants were mainly young adults with optimistic economic objectives, highly mobile, and not necessarily interested in their own spiritual well-being, especially if it involved monetary sacrifices. In 1932 in the midst of a reorganization of Finnish Lutherans in Canada, Reverend Pennanen lamented to his colleague: "Love for pleasure and worldly-mindedness are very common among the people, who sleep in a happy-go-lucky dream on the road of damnation."[4]

The clergy in Finland were quick to criticize the "godless" Finnish Canadians. They raged against emigration to a country that demor-alized the people and delivered them to the lap of Satan. But when it came to providing concrete support for the religious life of the Finns in Canada, the mother church turned its back. Bishop Johansson lamented in 1903 that, "Finland could send trained pastors to North America only after its own needs were first met."[5] The church was as good as its word, and, with one exception, not one cent was spent on the spiritual well-being of Finnish-Canadian immigrants. This forced the fledgling religious communities to spend much of their time and effort in fund-raising activities. Years later, one Finnish Lutheran minister commented in his personal correspondence that, "the great-est weakness of American congregational work is the fact that money is the most important element in it."[6]

It was, therefore, with great trepidation that many religious Finns embarked on their voyage to Canada. A group of women, waiting for their ship in Hanko harbour, broke into a spontaneous hymn only to be told by returning immigrants to forget such nonsense. "There is no God in Canada!" What a relief it was when the long voyage was at an end, and the ship slid past Quebec City and into Montreal harbour. "Church towers everywhere, and a huge cross on the hill to boot, ah God was in Canada after all."[7] But this God was worshipped in strange ways, in unfamiliar languages, even the beloved hymns were different. The choice of religions was confusing, and the often glittering and imposing churches were intimidating to the Finns who were dedicated to simplicity and modesty.

The only alternative for those who wished to continue their traditional religious practices in Canada was to become self-sufficient: to build their own churches, give their own sermons, sing their own songs. With these goals in mind, the first Finnish Lutheran Church was established by the coal-miners in Nanaimo, British Columbia, sometime in 1893. This church never had a long-term resident pastor and was greatly dependent on the local membership and the church elders. Occasionally the members pooled their funds to obtain the services of a Finnish pastor. Ten years after the church's founding, its total annual budget was $73.58, of which the pastors' fees were $60.80. Despite many obstacles, the congregation raised its own building, which was completed in 1899. All members were obligated to give one free day a week to its construction and provide the necessary financial resources out of their own pocket. Around the turn of the century the church could claim a congregation of about a hundred. By 1910, however, church membership seemed to wither. Socialist activity claimed many of the former church supporters, and the rest moved away from Nanaimo in search of work.[8]

This first attempt to establish a Finnish church illustrates the difficulties and changes in religious practice. The church was called Lutheran, but it was in fact totally independent and had no official ties with Finland. It was built and maintained by the parishioners, and its welfare was directly linked to the devotion, stability, and financial contributions of its members. Finns were used to taking their church for granted, trained pastors and beautiful churches being provided through state-collected church taxes. Direct dues were a new phenomenon. In this way, if the congregation did not have enough money, the pastor was not paid. If it did not like his personality, he was replaced.

This situation offered women a new and important role in the church. While the Finnish Lutherans were strictly patriarchal, women were needed to raise the money. No money, no church! Women's auxiliaries, sewing circles, and other traditional religious social gatherings gained new meaning and momentum. Instead of collecting money for missionary work among unknown people in foreign lands, or lending a helping hand to the needy, women were now directly contributing to the maintenance of their own church. Their contributions saw immediate results: a new roof, a paid Sunday school teacher, an organ, or a pot-bellied stove. Shortage of funds was a chronic and depressing problem for the immigrant church, and the women's efforts to alleviate it were crucial.

Immigrant conditions also altered women's roles as Sunday school teachers. In Canada it was necessary to teach not only the traditional Lutheran practices, but also the Finnish culture. The immigrants could not rely on the Canadian public school system to teach their children Finnish Lutheranism. It was also the women's task to inculcate Finnish nationalism in the children to maintain a religious bridge between the old and new country. Language instruction in Finnish – in effect, teaching the children to read and write – became an important part of church activity.

Shortly after the founding of the Nanaimo Finnish Lutheran Church, the prairie farmers of New Finland, Saskatchewan, organized their own congregation. In its first meeting on 1 November, 1893 the members decided to join with a larger Finnish-American Lutheran Church body called the Suomi (Finland) Synod. This umbrella organization was officially founded in Calumet, Michigan, in 1890 to improve communication, standardize practices, supply trained pastors, and assist the missionary efforts among Finnish immigrants in North America. It took its model and traditions from the state church in Finland and tried to uphold its elitist structures in the new environment. The New Finland congregation was its first Canadian member. The families agreed to pay 25 cents a month to the Synod on the condition that, "it will send us a pastor once a year to give sermons . . . for other ministerial duties such as baptisms, confirmation classes and weddings we would pay separately." All names entered in the minute books as founding members of the New Finland congregation were male.

Deeply devoted Christians were not satisfied to see the pastor only once a year. Therefore, much of the religious instruction on a day-to-day basis took place in the home. In keeping with Finnish tradition, reading and religious teaching was combined. John Hawkes has recorded a rare glimpse of this method of self-study. He describes two little Finnish girls in New Finland in 1895-96:

> I noticed sometimes on coming in from the outfit, that the two children would be leaning on the bed with a little book before them. The elder would gabble in Finn and the younger would gabble after her...I found that the elder, not yet six, knew the Finnish catechism by heart and was teaching it to her younger sister, not yet five.[9]

The Suomi Synod helped this young congregation, but the monthly fee proved too hefty a sum for the pioneering families. In 1898 the dues were reduced by half, and "all poor and sick could receive the pastor's blessings free of charge." Church services were held every other Sunday at the New Finland school, erected in 1896. Until 1906, when the community decided to raise funds for a church building, women were not mentioned in the minutes and they did not appear to have had any role in the church administration. With the increased demand for funds, women's participation became visible. In February 1909 the women of New Finland were formally organized into the New Finland Sewing Society. Instrumental in gathering the women together was Mrs. L. Luoma, who travelled by horse and buggy around the twenty-mile radius of the Finnish settlement, urging and encouraging women to join. This society was "to assist the New Finland Finnish Lutheran Church both financially and materially." It met with tremendous enthusiasm, and fifty-nine women joined at its founding meeting. Here was a sorely needed opportunity for prairie women to socialize in a manner acceptable to the religious community and, at the same time, to contribute financially to the church.

The practices of the sewing circles varied slightly from community to community, but basically they followed the same format. Initially the organization would raise funds through membership fees or coffee evenings to purchase materials such as thread, wool, and cloth. These were distributed among the members who would take the materials home and bring back finished products which could then be sold. After only two months, the New Finland women held their first bazaar, which netted $49. The most popular items were practical clothing, but larger handicrafts, such as quilts, which could be raffled or auctioned off for a good price, were also welcome. Often the women who prepared the items for sale ended up buying them from each other, as their isolated communities did not attract many outside customers. In addition, these sewing circles organized community picnics, "fishing for prizes," and promoted the ever-popular "flower baskets" or "lunch baskets" which were sold to single men. The maker of the basket, a single or widowed woman whose identity was kept hidden, would agree to have lunch with the purchaser of the basket. The sewing circle then filled a social as well as a monetary need.

These organizational efforts can be seen as mere extensions of women's traditional roles as coffee-makers and knitters of socks, but nobody can doubt the importance of their financial success. In less than a year the New Finland women had made over $425, of which $350 was given to the men. Of this money, $200 went to decorate the church interior and $50 to pay off the church loan. That first year they also donated $100 to paint the church and $10 to a Finnish religious college in the United States. In January 1910 the importance of the women's activities was recognized and the sewing group was officially linked to the church as the Congregational Sewing Society.

This did not limit the women's outward goals. The following year they raised funds for the construction of a temperance hall and established the only money-lending institution in the community, charging 8 per cent interest. During the First World War the women donated a further $179 for the temperance hall on the condition that they could use the building, free of charge, for their social gatherings, meetings, and bazaars. In 1918 they bought a $300 organ for the church. As was the case in British Columbia, temperance organizations were a high priority for Finnish women's group in Saskatchewan. John Hawkes describes his meeting with a Finnish Lutheran pastor who had come to New Finland in 1897 to attend to a wedding:

> He [the minister] told me that there were two kinds of Finns of two different faiths and dispositions and character. The one kind were Catholics [Orthodox], pacific and lacking in energy. The others were Lutherans, he said; "fierce, fight, drink, but honest" – and he added "These my people." ...I did not know one of them [Finns] who was a total abstainer.

Until the First World War, the sewing circle had been purely a social and fund-raising institution, but in 1919 the women decided to attend to their own spiritual needs by incorporating the singing of hymns and reading of scriptures and prayers in their meetings. Some women were thus able to satisfy their desire to spread the gospel as long as they did not dangerously encroach on male authority within the church. In a few short years the sewing circle's membership had soared to over one hundred women. The attraction of the sewing circle seems to have been greater than that of the church itself. In 1915, for example, the congregational registers show only seventy-five women, one hundred men and one hundred and fifty children as members of the church.

The popularity of the women's group also stemmed from the lack of other alternatives for organized activity in their isolated bloc settlement. In an independent women's group the members could demonstrate their organizational skills, openly share their daily complaints and concerns and, with their financial success, gain a sense of self-worth denied them by the patriarchal church, which was more than willing to take and spend their money but not to give them any voice in religious services or church affairs. These were to remain an exclusive male preserve.

Church life was not as harmonious as might be expected. Even in New Finland ideological splits and divisions threatened the unity of the congregation. In a lay organization, personality conflicts among powerful families could be enough to create new congregations. This small rural community was no exception: in 1897-98 disputes within the church split the membership, some establishing themselves within a National Finnish Lutheran Organization. This group was formed in the United States in 1898 from the independent Lutheran churches that had refused to join the Suomi Synod. The main disagreement between the two centred around the dominant role of ministers within the Synod. The National Lutherans claimed to be more democratic – a people's church – and hence more suited to immigrant conditions, where memberships and lay preachers played an important role. According to the National Lutheran Church organization's by-laws, women could vote in the church councils if the individual congregation so decided. This was a significant departure from tradition and an acknowledgment of the importance of the role of women in the immigrant church. Much to the horror of the traditional Suomi Synod, the new National Lutherans went even further and in 1897 ordained a "woman named Erika Rantanen as a deacon with preaching privileges." In 1902 Professor Hjelt drew the following scornful portrait of her, leaving no doubt as to the position of the traditional Lutherans:

> In Conneaut in the first row of the audience sat a certain peculiar person *(kummallinen ihmisolento)*, who, when you first looked, was hard to identify as either a man or a woman. She was dressed entirely in black; high on her head was some sort of a bishop's or priest's hat, and atop that a kind of protective covering. She wore heavy eyeglasses on her nose, and bushy hair flowed down onto her shoulders. All she lacked was a beard; otherwise, you would have thought that she looked just like a Russian priest. . . . She was that woman who still roamed around the American Finnish communities in order to preach and do other priestly functions, even though it was generally known that she needed care in a mental hospital.[10]

The worst insult to a nationalistic Finn was to be called a "Russian," and, furthermore, according to this author, a woman must be crazy to think that she had the ability to preach. The "women's issue" in North American Lutheran churches refused to go away. By 1909 the Suomi Synod had to relent enough to allow women some rights within the church councils.

The religious rift in New Finland between the traditional Suomi Synod and the National Lutherans did not, however, seem to have any basis on dogma; it was purely a family feud. The disputes were healed briefly when church construction united the Finns, but the congregation split once again in 1919, and in 1924 the splinter group officially joined the National Lutherans. The ease of establishing new congregations in the new world proved too enticing to immigrants thrilled with a new sense of religious freedom and power in directing their own spiritual life.

New Finland is an exceptional community among the Finns in Canada because it is the only place where religious life triumphed over secular institutions. New Finland's churchgoers were left relatively untouched by the ridicule and disruption caused by anti-clerical Finns in other communities where Lutheran congregations were established: Copper Cliff (1897), Sault Ste Marie (1905), Port Arthur (1897), and Fort William (1897). The first two congregations joined the Synod and the last two functioned independently until 1908 when they joined the National Lutheran Church. All of these congregations suffered from a lack of pastors, quarrelsome parishioners, and anti-religious outside pressures.

The Port Arthur community managed to erect a fine church building within a year of its founding meeting, which was attended by fifteen couples. But socialist harassment was so persistent and severe that, "the city had to send police to stand guard during the divine service and to hinder anyone from attempts to defile the church."[11] The brief church history published on its fiftieth anniversary makes only a minor mention of the Ladies Aid Society, founded sometime before 1909 by Pastor Heimonen. The women were praised for their effectiveness and strength. From the few surviving minutes, it is clear that the Port Arthur women were the financial backbone of the church. They met every other Thursday evening at one another's homes to allow the live-in domestics to attend the coffee parties and to avoid any confrontation with the socialists. By the 1920s they too had incorporated hymns and bible reading into their meetings; and they often invited the resident pastor to speak to their group.

Much less is known of the Fort William congregation as it was very much under the wing of the Port Arthur church. Its difficulties with the hostile environment were even more pronounced than in Port Arthur. A year after the church was founded, the congregation decided to construct a joint building with the local Finnish temperance organization. Soon after the temperance society acquired new members with socialist beliefs who were able to take over the organization and its property. Undeterred, the Lutheran congregation built its own church in 1900, but lost this one to a few energetic and persuasive fundamentalist members of the congregation who changed it to a Laestadian sect.[12] In 1902 the Finns built their third meeting place in Fort William, which they had to sell in 1910 because church members had moved to another part of the city. While no information is available on the activities of the women, no doubt they were busy financing the construction of all three buildings.[13]

In addition to the Port Arthur and Fort William congregations, the National Lutherans founded small congregations in Toronto (1926), Elma, Manitoba (1915), Dunblane, Saskatchewan (1914), and Manyberries, Alberta (1922). Except for the Toronto congregation, very little information exists on their activities. The Toronto group, mainly made up of domestics, seemed to host an endless number of coffee parties for their sewing circle meetings, the actual sewing being done at home.

The Copper Cliff "Wuoristo" congregation, which joined the Synod immediately upon its founding in 1897, did not list any women as its founding members, nor did they hold any prominent positions in the church council. From the official minutes and the brief history, it would appear as if there were almost no women at all in the congregation.

Yet despite the lack of women in the official record, the Copper Cliff sewing circle had a long and important history. It was founded in 1897, the same year as the church, by one "enthusiastic and glowing person, Mrs. Greta Koski." The women were not accustomed to proper meeting procedures nor interested in personal glory, so they did not keep official minutes until 1923 nor elect officers until the late thirties. But this did not deter their work; "We were just a bunch of old-country women who worked as we knew how." The Copper Cliff women organized social gatherings, "often having to work in great secrecy so that the socialists did not find out the intended date and organize a competing event for the same evening."[14] Meetings at the church were hindered because of lack of cooking facilities and poor water supply. Women, who refused to meet without their coffee, carried full and ready-to-serve coffee-pots from home. More often, the Copper Cliff women gathered in each other's homes. According to Reverend Pikkusaari's calculations, over one hundred women opened their homes for the sewing circle coffee sessions between 1914 and 1947. Their amazing organizational vigour and success were evident in the treasurer's book for 1910, the year the women decided to pay off the church debt. They succeeded in collecting the $1,154.52 by holding numerous social evenings in Copper Cliff, Creighton Mine, Crean Hill, and Garson. They travelled to each by horse and buggy and continued to prepare the delicious foods and entertainment until the debt was paid.

In addition to paying for the church building, the women were called upon to wash the dishes and make the coffee for all church meetings. For all their copious meetings and crucial financial contributions, the Copper Cliff women's sewing society is dismissed by one sentence in the congregation's official fortieth anniversary publication: "The oldest [church organization] is the women's sewing circle which has, throughout the decades, worked diligently and supported the congregation financially." For the pastors who wrote the church history, women were always only secondary, their work necessary, but not comparable to that of the men who were the real spiritual communicants and decision-makers.

The situation was the same in Sault Ste Marie where the church officers were all men. The first woman appeared in the record in 1907, as the dues collector, and by 1910 three women were named as collectors. Women were also used as Sunday school teachers; and when the congregation was wealthy enough to hire a teacher for summer Confirmation classes, it decided to "look for a suitable woman who could be had for less money than a man." At summer school the students were taught, in addition to Bible studies, to read and write Finnish, and to study the history and culture of Finland with special emphasis on religious history.

When it was time to organize a fund-raising committee, congregation women filled six of the nine posts in 1912. The situation did not change much over the years. In 1918 one woman became second secretary. Both of the money collectors were women as were all "church servants." The Sault Ste Marie congregation did not build its own church until late 1923, at which time the women's sewing society handed over one thousand dollars for this purpose. A year later, women organized a regular sewing circle to pay off the rest of the church debt.

One Finnish Lutheran Church, the Finnish Seamen's Mission in Montreal (later known as St. Michael's Lutheran Church), stands apart from the other immigrant congregations: it received funding and a pastor from Finland. Montreal was an exceptional Finnish community; its Finnish population was more recent than in the rest of Canada, and it was the site of the Finnish consulate. When the newly appointed consul, Akseli Rauanheimo, arrived in Montreal in February 1923, he found only thirty Finns living in the city. They had no organizational framework and no means to help the expected mass of immigrants to arrive in Montreal, now that the United States was restricting entry. During the eight years between 1923 and 1930, nearly thirty-five thousand Finnish immigrants landed in Canada, most of them in Montreal.

Rauanheimo was a determined and diligent man, and in 1925 he began to bombard the Seamen's Mission in Finland with letters seeking assistance to set up a Finnish Immigrant Home in Montreal and to obtain a pastor to look after "Finland's children" in the city. On 18 November 1926 the Seamen's Mission relented and agreed to send Reverend Frithiof Pennanen to Montreal in the early winter of 1927 and to pay his salary. In the late fall of 1926, prior to the arrival of Reverend Pennanen, a visiting Finnish Lutheran pastor from the United States held a service in the Wetmount Redeemer Lutheran Church, located in the vicinity of the homes where Finnish domestics were employed. At this meeting the importance of the congregation and the immigrant home were stressed, and funds were solicited from the audience. Most of the donors, according to Rauanheimo, were Finnish maids whose monthly salaries ranged from $25 to $35, yet together in one evening they pledged $968. One woman later recalled:

I was so poor, oh how poor I was. I had not paid all of my passage money, I had promised to help my brother, and my wages were small, and I couldn't even speak English, but still I promised $25, because I thought that the others would have a nicer experience in landing than I had – oh that feeling of longing and loneliness.[15]

Reverend Pennanen arrived on 17 April 1927 and at his first sermon sixty people joined the congregation, the majority of whom were single women. Initially the congregation prospered because of its enthusiasm, but soon dissension between the old-country pastor and the new-country women, "who wanted to run the church their way," emerged. Financial difficulties during the 1930s increased the tension and, to fuel the problems further, Finland decided to stop paying the pastor's monthly salary of $150. Reverend Pennanen, never happy with his position in Montreal, wanted to go home. He was unable and unwilling to adapt to the new conditions which demanded flexibility, humility and "democracy" within the church. The congregation, on the other hand, complained that the pastor was too arrogant, too rigid and unwilling to listen to their requests. After the women were called upon to pay the pastor's salary, they were no longer willing to employ a man they didn't like. Five years after leaving Montreal, he wrote bitterly: "The more than six years that I spent over there in ever darkening situation were strange years of education in suffering . . . after returning from Canada, I suffered for a long time great spiritual anguish."

Despite the financial chaos and loss of the pastor, the women were determined to carry on. Feverish activity followed as all avenues for continuation were explored. The immigrants were not particular; they just wanted to maintain a Finnish congregation. One possibility was to join the United Church of Canada, which offered to set up a Finnish-language congregation in Montreal. Another was to join the United Lutheran Congress of America (ULCA), which was willing to provide financial assistance. In the end they chose the ULCA. The replacement for the old-country pastor was Reverend Juho Yrttimaa who was anything but a traditional Lutheran. In fact, he was not a Lutheran at all, nor a "properly trained" pastor, but had served as a minister of the United Church in Sault Ste Marie and spent several years as a missionary for the Congregationalist Church in Tibet. At first it was suggested that Yrttimaa be retrained, but the adoring Montreal female congregation strongly objected. Reverend Yrttimaa served the congregation for thirty-three years with all the flexibility (sometimes foregoing his salary) required of a successful immigrant pastor.

Montreal's Finnish Lutherans were not alone in their struggle to support a congregation. After the initial spurt of church organization around the turn of the century, the Lutherans in Canada went into a decline until the late twenties and early thirties when new congregations were once again founded. Much of the organizational effort fell on Reverend John F. Saarinen who, thanks to the assistance of Suomi Synod and ULCA, was a paid church organizer in Canada. Reverend Saarinen was truly an immigrant pastor, born in Massachusetts and trained in Hancock, Michigan. When Suomi Synod recognized that the financial burden of providing pastors to the remote Canadian settlements was too difficult to bear, it worked out an agreement with the ULCA in 1928 which transferred Canadian Finnish Lutheran work into their hands. This treaty was ratified in 1931, and the new organizational spirit revitalized religious life within the parent, non-Finnish ULCA.

After three years of vigorous organization, Saarinen was able to report that the ULCA's Finnish congregations contained 1,259 baptized members. Between 1931 and 1935 the following new Finnish Lutheran congregations joined the ULCA: Kirkland Lake, Sudbury, Timmins–South Porcupine, Toronto, and Windsor in Ontario; Montreal in Qubec; Sylvan Lake and Manyberries in Alberta; and Vancouver in British Columbia. Significantly, the anti-clerical environment of such large Finnish centres as Timmins and Sudbury kept the Lutheran congregations – traditional and nationalist – out until the 1930s. In the rest of Canada less than four hundred Finns had bothered to join their branch of the Lutheran Church which most closely resembled the traditional church in Finland.

A partial explanation for the decline in religious involvement is that the community's religious people were defeated by the strength of the socialists. One marvellous travel diary of a Finnish pastor who made several attempts to preach the word of God is a telling reminder of the difficulties facing immigrant pastors. Moreover, the reminiscences also shed light on the power of women in the resource communities and their decision to leave the church. The pastor recalls how he managed to secure a room at the home of an elderly woman who allowed him to hold a service, but only three people came:

> The next day again, I spent going from house to house urging people to come. In many places I was met with derision, distrust and hostility. . . . The owner of a boarding-house did not allow me to put my advertisement on her wall. I asked "Don't you fear God at all?" "He never did me any good," she laughed . . . a few years before, I was told, she had been a God-fearing woman.

In South Porcupine the pastor was more successful:

> In South Porcupine I met the keeper of a boarding-house who had opened her heart to the word of God and she placed her house at my disposal. About 50 people greeted me at the first meeting. Many of these were young men, recently arrived from Finland and quite a number had brought hymn books from the

old country. Only ten women were present. I was told that the women in this place are "wilder" than the men.[16]

In his summation, the pastor recorded that, "nowhere have I witnessed such a coarseness as in Timmins and Porcupine. Drunkenness is the rule, marriage is not holy." The pastor wondered why this "sinful mob" was able to assimilate the newcomers, many of whom were God-fearing people on arrival, into the "red communist" mould. He was especially taken aback by the hostile, anti-religious attitude of many of the women.

The women's reaction is not so surprising if the immigrant situation is taken into consideration. Even though the Finnish Lutheran churches in Canada gave women more power within the congregation, they continued to downplay the role of women in society and glorified the self-sacrificing mother who devoted her life to her husband and children. In Canada the church leaders found it convenient to promote this country's Victorian image of women which coincided with their own patriarchal beliefs, and a lifestyle which had never been a reality for women in Finland. Many women did not agree. In Canada they had even less time to devote to their families, if they had any. Daily material needs were more pressing; threatening strikes, fear of accidents, and low wages occupied their concerns. It is no wonder then that the membership lists of the women's auxiliaries show, for the most part, married women; those who were single directed their interests elsewhere.

By 1930 Finnish women in Canada were refusing to accept the traditional role assigned to them by the Lutheran Church and did not renew their membership pledges. What good was a church that failed to offer them anything, but instead constantly asked for money and free labour? Reverend Pennanen must have received quite a shock when the women rebelled against his letter demanding they pay their church dues during the early depression years. This step was necessary, according to the pastor, because his salary was no longer paid from Finland. One woman simply replied: "Please wipe my name off the church register as if it had never been entered at all because I will not now or in future pay the congregation's dues." Others tried to justify their actions with longer explanations. A desperate woman who kept a rooming-house in Montreal replied:

Honoured Pastor!

I thank you for your letter which arrived yesterday. I beg to inform you that it is impossible for us to pay our church fees because my son alone is supporting the whole family, father can't get work, and receives no benefits like some others with more money than us, our rooms are empty, as people are out of work they can't pay rent. Now our rent is in arrears as is the gas and water bills. We can't even sell the furniture, who would buy anything these days. My health is in ruins in every way and I am worried about the daily bread. I can't receive any help from the doctor as I have no money. My youngest son has tried to get some work after school finished, but can't get any. At times my life seems very miserable. . . . I ask you to wipe off my name from the membership list.[17]

This does not mean that the women necessarily gave up their religious beliefs; they merely discarded the traditional church which had failed to meet their expectations. The church which was supposed to be the strength of the community, the guiding light for morality and the provider of sound leadership, turned out to be a constant financial headache, disorganized and unable to help its parishioners. Some women simply continued their religious practices in the privacy of their own homes. Others sought new Canadian alternatives.

Canadianization: the Presbyterians and the United Church of Canada

The increasing number of foreigners who arrived to Canada after the turn of the century from non-Anglo-Saxon countries created great concern among Canadians who believed in Anglo-conformist assimilation. While the public educational system was seen as the greatest agent of Canadianization – stripping immigrants, or at least their children, of their culture and language – the Protestant churches also felt impelled to act. At the forefront of immigrant work in the social gospel movement were the Methodists, Congregationalists, and Presbyterians (and later the United Church of Canada); but the Baptists and Anglicans were also involved. The Methodist Church was especially active because it saw itself as a national church and viewed its responsibility in national terms: "Its mission was to Christianize, that is Protestantize, and Canadianize the immigrants." Much of the converting efforts were aimed at the various Catholic and Orthodox religions brought to Canada by eastern, central, and southern Europeans – religions which the Methodists equated with "superstition, ignorance, and autocracy" as opposed to the Anglo-Saxon virtues of "initiative, industry, freedom and democracy."[18] The Finns, despite their Protestant religion and nordic background, were suspect because of their nationalism, drinking habits, and radicalism. As one frustrated commissioner of the Department of Mines lamented, "they do not become British."[19] While claiming to be Protestant and Lutheran, they had not shown any great desire or success in organizing religious communities. Encouraged by the social gospel movement, the Presbyterian Church in Canada decided to fill in the spiritual gaps within the Finnish communities. Initially it focused on the areas where no Finnish Lutheran Church existed and where radicalism, or at least an increasingly secular world view, had taken a strong hold. In Canada the Presbyterian Church, and later the United Church, assumed some of the responsibility which the mother church in Finland had avoided: they provided Finnish-speaking pastors and financial support.

While the basic motives of the missionaries might have been self-serving and encouraged by a desire for social control, it appears that for the Finns the Presbyterian Church satisfied an important need for religious involvement. Besides, the Lutherans and Presbyterians had much in common. The Presbyterian Church accepted Lutheran infant baptism, and the latter converts were able to take communion immediately in their new church. Within the Presbyterian Church women could be full missionaries, and the church councils were democratically organized. All the clergymen the Presbyterian church sent to the communities were Finnish-speaking, and the primary Canadianizing that took place was most welcome: free English lessons. Within the communities, the Finnish Presbyterian branches functioned with great autonomy. While they did not focus on Finland with the same spirit of intense nationalism and patriotism, they did, nevertheless, uphold and promote the cultural values of the Finns. Most important, the Canadian churches offered more room for the women to operate in and, in the interests of their growing congregations, catered to their particular needs. Their emphasis was on what the church could do to help the immigrants instead of how the immigrants could help the church. Help for the immigrants, however, was also believed to help Canada become a stronger, more unified nation.

It appears that the earliest attempt to offer assistance to the Finns took place in the Port Arthur–Fort William district around 1898. A Finnish Lutheran minister, Reverend J. Heimonen, appealed to "the Presbyterian minister at Port Arthur and Convener of the Home Mission Committee of the Superior Presbytery." Subsequently, in 1899 the Finnish Lutheran congregation began to receive an annual grant, while Reverend Heimonen did not have to "identify himself with the Presbyterian church." Reverend S.C. Murray explained this extraordinary generosity: "The plea for assistance that I presented was simply that these were Protestant people who needed pastoral care, and unless they received attention would drift away from religion and from the Church, eventually becoming a menace to the community."[20] The aim, then, was to maintain the Christian influence rather than convert the Finns away from Lutheranism.

Perhaps because of this early plea by the Finns of Port Arthur to the Presbyterian Church, Finns elsewhere in Canada started to receive assistance from the same source. Two of the largest Finnish Presbyterian congregations were founded in Toronto and in Copper Cliff. These, however, were no longer identified as "Lutheran" but as Presbyterian (after church union, United Church of Canada) congregations.

The usual political divisions which existed in the Finnish communities were also present in Toronto. Before the First World War the membership registers of Finnish organizations reveal that the socialists outnumbered the Christians by four to one.[21] Despite these odds, determined Christians sought the word of God. At first they went to the Christian Workers' Mission where they listened to the English sermons, translated for them by a Mr. Morland. Four married women organized themselves into a sewing circle sometime before 1902 and gave their support to the King Street Mission. At the same time, the Heinonens' home, which was also a boarding-house with a restaurant, housed a regular Sunday school. While these Toronto women were busily organizing religious events, their tailoring husbands (except for Mr. Heinonen) were organizing the first Finnish local of the Socialist Party of Canada. In June 1905 when the executive of the Finnish Society of Toronto and the temperance society Taimi decided to merge forces and to alter their constitutions to reflect more clearly a socialist ideology, some members walked out. These dissatisfied Finns founded a second temperance society, *Sarastus* (Dawn), in November 1905. They purchased property at 44 Mitchell Avenue and proceeded to transform it into a hall that could accommodate one hundred and fifty people. This temperance society, only lasted for two years, but in 1910 the hall was purchased by the Presbyterian Church and became known as the Mitchell Avenue Church.

The Finns in Toronto had been receiving visits from the Congregationalist ministers who had been coming up from the United States since 1906. Some of their meetings were held in the Jewish Baptist Mission, but in 1907 the Finns applied for assistance from Knox Presbyterian Church. The congregation did not become truly active until 1909, when Reverend Matti Hirvonen, newly graduated from Boston's Congregationalist Seminary, arrived in Toronto. The religious Finns did not seem to worry about whether they belonged to a Lutheran, Congregationalist, or Presbyterian Church. In fact, when the official transfer to the Presbyterian Church took place and some of the members were asked for their approval, they answered instead: "Let's continue to be Lutheran," seemingly oblivious to the fact that no Finnish Lutheran church existed in Toronto until 1926.

Reverend Matti Hirvonen was faced with the same hostility as his Lutheran counterparts in other Finnish communities. In a private letter he explained:

The opposition to religion was so bitter that many couldn't stand even to look at a pastor. Thus it happened one day, when I was eating in a Finnish boardinghouse, that after a few spoonfuls of soup, I began to feel sick, and had burning sensations in my insides. I had been poisoned.

Despite this hostility, a small group of religious Finns persisted. Mrs. Matilda Ranta was described as a pillar of the church; Miss Alma Könni gave considerable financial support and travelled to Cleveland in search of a pastor. She, too, remembers the constant ridicule, the broken church windows, and the police who had to escort women out of the church. In June 1909 this sole Finnish church in Toronto registered just twenty-nine members; of these the majority (nineteen) were women. In addition, the membership registers revealed that between 1907 and 1909, fifteen single women had joined and then "moved away." These were domestic servants who were moving to New York, Cleveland, and Chicago in search of better salaries. Not only did Reverend Hirvonen have to be concerned about the socialists but also about the fluid population of the community.

While the parishioners did not seem to mind, or even notice, too many differences between the Presbyterian and Lutheran traditions, two major changes were undertaken. First, the Presbyterian Church put great emphasis on seeking new parishioners, providing interesting and enlightening programs for the young and English lessons for the adults. They did not take the immigrant parishioners for granted but were willing to compete for their allegiance by offering them alternatives. After the new minister arrived in 1909, the Presbyterians organized the first youth club, *Johto tähti* (The Leading Star), later known as *Toivon tähti* (the Star of Hope). Immediately twelve girls and six boys joined. The surviving minutes and membership lists for 1913-14 indicate that forty-six young people attended the youth meetings; three-quarters of them were girls. By this time the minutes were written in English, and the program encompassed mainly social activity within a religious environment. The motto of Reverend Hirvonen was: "If young people do not have good company they will stay in bad company!"

Having attracted the youth, many of whom were Toronto-born and could not identify with their parents' radical political beliefs, the church had guaranteed its future. The women's auxiliary minutes from 1915 to 1925 reveal vigorous activity. The women did their best to facilitate and help Finns in distress, especially the Toronto maids. They received guidance and help from the Presbyterian Women's Missionary Society for Immigration. In 1925 this Presbyterian congregation merged with the United Church of Canada, and two years later moved into the newly constructed Church of All Nations building on Queen Street

West. The United Church's Department of Strangers continued the work begun with the Finnish domestics in Toronto. In the church's third annual report of the Women's Missionary Society, the women recorded 113 Finnish girls in English classes and over 400 in night school.

In the poly-ethnic church the Finnish pastors also continued the Toronto congregation's tradition of catering to the women. Reverend W. Leeman organized meeting rooms for the lonely immigrants, and reading material in Finnish. He also expanded one important service by offering mail-box facilities to Finnish domestics. Many did not wish to give out the address of their employer, anticipating frequent job changes. At the height of Finnish immigration to Canada in the late 1920s, nearly one thousand Finns, mostly live-in domestics, had reserved a mail-box at *Queenin kirkko* (the Queen Street Church). There, while collecting their precious letters from home, they sat and chatted with other women, read their mail and drank coffee. The mail service proved to be very effective in attracting Finns to the United Church during their day off. The same domestics who had shied away from other Canadian women's institutions and who had refused to seek help from Canadian hostels, gave their whole-hearted support to the United Church. The sermons were also directed at the women, and services were held during convenient hours for the domestics. "The church became our second home, it was friendly, you could just drop in and rest, never feeling as an intruder. You know, the doors were never locked," remembered one thankful domestic.

The Presbyterians not only paid increasing attention to women and children, they also allowed women to spread the gospel and encouraged them to participate in social work. Two women, Matilda Ranta and Mrs. Rinne, left a strong impression on many from their early years in Toronto as "lay preachers and spiritual leaders." For the more ambitious, it was possible to shake off the lay title and become qualified missionaries. Women were also told to aim beyond the narrow confines of nationalistic goals and to work towards Canadianizing all immigrants. A former Finnish pastor described the benefits of the United Church:

> Within this church we have been brought up to understand more deeply that the work of the congregation must not centre around sermons and the programmes surrounding them, but that social service, the care needed for the non-spiritual well-being of the people is very important, especially among immigrants who do not speak the English language. Social work became an important component of our church work . . . the old country prejudices were shaken off and we started to view the world through Canadian glasses, we started to get rid of that stubborn feeling that we Finns were somehow better than others . . . in our church we

learned to melt together, we knew our own situation, but we also learned to appreciate the others.[22]

Thus the doors of the Church of All Nations remained open to newly arrived immigrants. Some were brought straight there from the train station, others were "rescued in the middle of the night from hotels where they were left by taxi drivers," and all received a warm welcome to the Canadian church.

The origin of the Finnish Presbyterian congregation in Copper Cliff differs from Toronto in one vital aspect: there the Presbyterians were competing with an existing Finnish Lutheran congregation. The Lutherans, however, were suffering from a chronic shortage of ministers, and during an especially long void in 1913, Reverend Arvi I. Heinonen moved to Copper Cliff at the request of the Presbytery of Sudbury. Reverend Heinonen was very active and travelled all over New Ontario. The Copper Cliff congregation was officially founded on 6 January 1914 and held its meetings in the Lutheran Church until Heinonen obtained an office building from the local mining company.

Heinonen was a complex person. Mauri A. Jalava has called him a "zealot." The long-time Lutheran minister in Copper Cliff, Reverend Y. Raivio, has accused Heinonen of embellishing his own success stories.[23] Nevertheless, the ideological differences in the church's stance on education and women were vividly demonstrated in Copper Cliff. To serve the Finnish community and to attract members to the Presbyterian Church, Heinonen immediately organized a Finnish People's Institute *(Suomalainen Kansan-opisto)* and appointed himself its principal. An advertisement for this "only Finnish learning institution in Canada," placed in *Canadan Uutiset* in 1918, lists the following courses: English, Finnish, music, needlework, embroidery, home economics, and folk games. This college, which was obviously structured to attract women and youth, conveniently held its classes on the maid's day off in Copper Cliff (Wednesday) and on Saturday afternoons. The institute was quite a success; in addition to the actual lessons, the institute hosted numerous lectures and housed an open reading-room and library.

Heinonen met with initial enthusiasm and "posed a great danger to the Lutherans," some of whom transferred to the Presbyterian Church. He was most successful in attracting women to the church because "it was so much fun." Here too the sewing circle was busy raising funds. In 1917, for example, it gave $357 to the church. Reverend Pikkusaari noted that Heinonen also demonstrated special skills in teaching children. True to the Canadianizing spirit, Heinonen attempted to introduce multicultural festivities and stressed the importance of attending his English classes. His institute was full of activity, there was "something going on at the church every night." The emphasis, once again, was very much on the non-spiritual needs of the immigrants.

Heinonen was especially committed to the fight against socialism among the Finns in the area. With Financial support from the Presbyterian Church and the Copper Company, he was able to procure anti-Bolshevik literature from Finland. According to Mauri A. Jalava: "Heinonen became an important informant about and against the Finns to the Canadian employers and government officials alike . . . the information and pressure he provided . . . led to the banning of numerous socialist newspapers from arriving in Canada."[24]

Amidst some dissension among his own parishioners, Heinonen left Copper Cliff in 1919 to organize Finns in western Canada. The congregation declined rapidly thereafter. In 1926 a renewed, but less successful, attempt to bring the Finns into the fold of the Canadian churches was launched in the area and, as a result, a Finnish United Church was founded in Sudbury. Reverend Thomas D. Jones was the driving force behind the establishment of this congregation. He devoted much of his time to fighting communism, and his keen desire to help the Finns was motivated by his war on radicalism. United Church clergymen working in the Finnish communities also sought to encourage Finns in their religious activities, and at the same time did their best to hamper the socialists, corresponding heavily with the press censors and the RCMP. This kind of political activity was reminiscent of the state Lutheran Church of Finland and gave the Finnish radicals further ammunition to blame their problems on the priests. This later activity of the United Church among the Finns in northern Ontario scared the Finnish Lutherans into action, who, especially after their reorganization in the 1930s, began to compete for the souls of the Finnish Canadians. By the 1940s most of the former Finnish Presbyterians or United Church members had melted back into the Lutheran Church.

The Presbyterians were also active in western Canada where much of the work was done by Heinonen's sister Vieno:

> In 1921 our Church sent Miss V. S. Heinonen, a Finnish deaconess, to take charge of Dunblane District. Within a radius of fifty miles she had several places which she visited on horseback, conducting services and Sabbath schools, and helping the people of Finnish origin in their various needs.[25]

This young woman on horseback must have been quite a novelty to the Finnish Lutherans on the prairies. Prior to her missionary work in Saskatchewan, she was already known for her "efficient and much appreciated service" to the Finns in Alberta, especially in the Eckville-Manyberries region.

It is difficult to measure the actual success of the Canadian Presbyterian and United Church's work among Finns. Once the Lutheran alternative became a viable choice, many Finns rejoined their traditional way of celebrating Christ. Nevertheless, it appears that the traditional Lutheran Church had great initial difficulties in surviving and adapting to the immigrant situation. It had to learn that, in Canada, church-going was voluntary, and parishioners had to be attracted and not coerced into the fold. The Finnish Lutherans clung to their strictly patriarchal structure despite their desperate need for female support.

The void left by the disarray of the Finnish Lutherans was partially filled by Canadian missionary work which emphasized, in particular, the role of women and children. The United Church was most successful in recruiting single women, having agreed that "saving domestics" was a priority.

Most competition offered to traditional Lutheran values came from secular, anti-clerical organizations. In direct contrast to the frustrations of the religious Finnish communities are the flourishing socialist organisations whose halls were overflowing with activity and whose members spred their message with contagious enthusiasm and vigour. For Finns in Canada, the 1920s belonged to the socialists.

CHAPTER 7

Women in Socialist Organizations

"As far as I am concerned, the whole damn lot are red, including women, who are often worse than the men!" exclaimed one exasperated officer in northern Ontario.[1] Indeed, Finnish women were some of the most enthusiastic participants in the socialist movement, even though many of these women were working in relative isolation because of cultural and language-imposed restrictions.

The problem of Finnish socialist women, however, goes far beyond language difficulties into the structure of the society itself. The Finns simply had no academic elite or middle-class women with idle time or resources to participate as full-time leaders in the movement. Jewish women, for example, had "advanced attitudes toward labour, socialism and communal reform," but they also had an increasing number of middle-class women. Finnish socialist women in the urban areas were mainly live-in domestics locked into their place of employment. Domestic service also prevented interaction with women of other culture groups and denied Finnish maids the opportunity to learn labour activism through unions and strikes. In the rural areas the sheer magnitude of their isolation prevented consistent involvement. When Finnish women chose how to spend their few precious free moments, they preferred to go to a Finnish socialist hall where the afternoon and evening events were specifically tailored to their needs and desires and conducted in their native language. Their political involvement was mixed with cultural activity and a desire to make the most of their free time. It is as if Finnish women wanted to "dance through the revolution," commented one upset organizer.

The key difference between immigrant socialist organizations and their Canadian counterparts was that the former became multi-purpose community centres. The socialist locals were usually the only Finnish organizations in a community and had to attempt to serve all the needs of their members. Halls doubled as schools, employment exchanges, cultural centres, gymnasiums, libraries, and counselling centres, and the socialist leaders gave not only political but also social, moral, and economic guidance. Thus Finnish women who joined the socialist organizations did so for a multitude of reasons, political activism being just one important part of the whole.

A study of Finnish socialist women in Canada must examine the nature of socialism in Finland and then turn inward and explain the immigrants' socialist behaviour in the context of their special needs. It must also take into consideration the position of women within the community. Finally, it must explain the development of not only ethnically separated but gender-separated organizations and the role of leadership.

Roots and Early Growth of Finnish-Canadian Women's Socialist Activity

Around the turn of the century the socialist movement in Finland spread rapidly until it became numerically the largest political force in the country and, in relative terms, the strongest socialist party in the world. Unlike many of its neighbouring countries which leaned towards reformism, in 1903 the Social Democratic Party (SDP) of Finland adopted an explicitly marxist platform. Since this decision had an impact on Finnish-Canadian women's interpretation of socialism in Canada, it needs to be explained further. One reason given by Finnish political scientists for the radicalism of Finnish socialists is that, in Finland, industrialism and unionism developed later than in the rest of northern Europe. Hence, the country had not yet developed a "working-class aristocracy." Elsewhere in Europe, trade union movements preceded workers' political activism, but in Finland it was mainly the reverse. Thus the tradition of bargaining for improvements was largely missing.

Significantly, all Finnish workers, both men and women, gained their full political rights in 1906, after which, change through direct political action by the workers was a real possibility. A tradition of cooperation with the bourgeois political parties had not been part of the Finnish tradition. Cooperation was further limited by the fact that the Finnish middle class was relatively small and allied more closely with the elite than with reform liberals. The issue that most polarized political debate in Finland was the question of landless farmers, which, the property owners feared, would infringe on their basic rights. At the same time it endeared the landless rural people to the socialist movement who took up their cause.

Finally, Finnish socialism became strongly opposed to any kind of religious activity, and as the church preferred to side with the elite, no strong Christian socialist movement could develop. Thus the socialism which was part of some Finnish immigrant women's culture involved heavy political participation, shunned liberalism and Bernsteinian reformism, and was vehemently anti-clerical. From the beginning the socialists had involved women, not only as helpers on the sidelines, but as members of Parliament, union leaders, editors, and agitators. The 1905 successful general strike in Finland had confirmed the benefits of quick, decisive, political action. This strike was an excellent, universal, political lesson to Finnish women. Thus when the Finnish socialists were frustrated with their inability to achieve change through Parliament during the First World War, they turned to revolutionary tactics and civil war was the sad result.

When the Finnish immigrants arrived in Canada they were faced with a further structural anomaly: there was no Finnish elite or middle class to speak of and the strong influence of the church was missing. Into this cultural and political vacuum stepped many dissatisfied rural and urban immigrants as well as some capable socialist leaders who continued to agitate on behalf of their particular political ideology. Thus Finnish radicalism was transplanted to Canada at an opportune time and into the most fertile soil. Immigrant women had come to make money and often nurtured optimistic dreams of a happy future. When the reality did not meet their expectations, they sought ways to improve their situation. In Canada, the socialists were further able to recruit and convert Finnish immigrant women, some of whom had never even heard of socialism before.

The first recorded mention of a socialist women's sewing circle appears in North Wellington, British Columbia, in 1894. It was part of the Finnish temperance society Aallotar, which was going through a process of transformation from a religious to a socialist society. In fact, its members did not clearly articulate their socialist beliefs until 1896. The dissatisfied coal miners were the strength behind the temperance society, but the women took an active part in the mutual aid organization. They wrote to the handwritten newspapers, worked as librarians and teachers in the self-study programs, and lived out their dreams on the stage. Sometimes the dreams turned sour, as a curious note in the Aallotar minutes of 21 August 1893 explains: "It was unanimously agreed that Miss Serafiina Mäki will be compensated for her clothes which burned during the performance of last Saturday night's play. She was satisfied with $6.00."

These British Columbia women, then, were helping to create an organization to provide the guidance and encouragement that would have come from dozens of separate institutions in the homeland. They clung to each other for moral support, fined themselves for breaking the temperance pledge, lectured endlessly on the importance of self-help and learning, and tried to enjoy themselves. The minutes reveal that, unlike the church councils, women sat on the socialist temperance society executive, even though they were relegated to the most arduous tasks. Nevertheless, they exercised their right to speak at socialist meetings years before the first Socialist Party in British Columbia was founded.

The Vancouver Island Finnish women were further radicalized as mine disasters claimed husbands and lovers. Women learned activism in union rallies and funerals. For example, on 29 October 1901 the Finns decided to join en masse – women, children, and the brass band – at Bill Bayley's funeral. Women learned further lessons in Canadian working-class vulnerability as they were continually forced to move their families after each mine shutdown. Every time they faithfully dismantled their halls and homes and rebuilt them in a new location. The same year that Bill Bayley was killed, women listened to Matti Kurikka, the socialist intellectual who had arrived in British Columbia to organize a Finnish utopian colony. Since Kurikka's attitudes to women, free love, and birth control have been discussed earlier, suffice it to state here that Finnish women had the opportunity to learn from the teachings of an eloquent, charming, and persuasive socialist.

Fund-raising was also an important part of the Finnish women's activity: for the construction of halls, the purchase of equipment, books and musical instruments, but also to further socialist causes in Finland and, increasingly, to aid victims of strikes all over North America. A secondary role of the socialist sewing circle was to allow the women an opportunity for their own separate socialization and a chance to learn to conduct their own meetings. Thus, a combination of socialist tradition from Finland and dangerous and unstable working conditions in Canada, which revealed the vulnerability of the working class, eventually convinced the British Columbia Finns that socialism would provide the answers to their problems. This community, as we recall, had an alternative source of inspiration, the Lutheran Church in Nanaimo which began enthusiastically in 1893. The church failed to compete with socialist activity and rapidly declined in membership. The church building was left behind in Nanaimo as the Finns moved to Extension (1901) and to Ladysmith (1903), and no new congregation replaced it until the thirties. And so a community that had initially shared religious principles had changed in a decade into a socialist enclave.

Obvious parallels can be drawn between the early activity of Finnish women in British Columbia and Ontario's Finnish communities of Copper Cliff, Port Arthur, and Toronto. In all of these communities, socialist ideas gained acceptance at the expense of religion, and in all organizations women constituted from one-quarter to one-half of the membership. Their role, however, was still articulated in men's terms and their activity was mainly supportive.

Copper Cliff was a company town where the workers' destinies were directly linked to the Copper Company. Here, too, the Finns sought to erect stricter moral guidelines for the community by establishing a temperance society in 1894, *Oikeuden Ohje* (Guide to Justice) and by building a community centre. The same self-punishment and self-improvement methods that were instituted in *Aallotar* two years earlier were also put on the agenda in Copper Cliff. Initially, *Oikeuden Ohje* allied closely with the religious Finns and with the Lutheran congregation after it was founded in 1897. Mauri A. Jalava concluded that, "the temperance society, rather than the struggling congregation, served most of the social and cultural needs of the Finnish community."[3]

The same sexual division of labour occurred in this society. Women can be found as librarians, sick aid committee members, secretaries, and "investigators of the crime committee." In other words, they were to be the social conscience of the society, raiding taverns and bootleggers' premises to spot members who had failed to act according to the society's rules. Women seemed to find it easier to stick to their temperance pledge, although it was not unusual to find some of them expelled for drinking. This society's demand for abstinence was total. Very little compassion was extended to women's particular difficulties. For example, on 20 January 1898 the temperance society declared that a woman who takes alcohol to ease her pains during childbirth is deemed guilty of breaking her temperance pledge. In 1901 the temperance society had eighty-three members, twenty-nine of whom were women.

By 1902 the activities of *Oikeuden Ohje* were disrupted by internal dissension. Those members who were beginning to embrace socialist ideas wanted to change the direction of the temperance society or, failing this, to leave it altogether. Led by John Wirta, they founded *Copper Cliffin Nuorisoseura* (Young People's Organization of Copper Cliff) in February 1903 and the same year constructed a hall, described as one of the finest opera halls in New Ontario. Before the new hall was complete, Matti Kurikka visited Copper Cliff to drum up support for his British Columbian community, Sointula, and to spread his utopian socialist ideas. But he was "denied access to the temperance hall." The division was clearly marked, and no cooperation with the socialists was permitted. The temperance society and the Lutheran congregation joined forces and finally erected a church building in 1908. Soon the same apathy and inactivity that had plagued the church began to afflict temperance society members.

Instead, the focus of activity and excitement was centred around the new Young People's Hall, which became a mandatory stop-off point for Finnish socialist speakers. About one-third of the members were women. At first, the Young People's Club, created by Finnish immigrants with a left-wing world-view, catered directly to their interests and needs. A combination of theatre, library, gymnasium, school, and dance hall, it also attracted Finns from the surrounding area, and it was here that many young Finns were introduced to socialist ideas. When they examined their own dismal circumstances and felt the power of the Copper Company, which "was able to control arbitrarily all residents," they rebelled. Many who had formerly been religious, or belonged to the temperance society, now looked on in disgust as their former organizations sided with the company, maligned socialists, and spied on other Finns. Anti-religious sentiments, already familiar to some from their disregard for the state church in Finland, took on new meaning: pastors were seen as spies of the capitalists and as enemies of the workers.

An almost identical sequence of events took place in Port Arthur, where socialist Finns began to feel constrained within the newly founded temperance society. By 1902 the community was receiving an increasing number of *Helsingin herrat* (gentlemen from Helsinki), the more class-conscious newcomers who had a background of trade union participation, journalistic skills, or political socialist activity. They were impatient with temperance society meetings, which "spent most of the time forgiving fallen members." On February 1903 the first meeting was held to discuss the need for a separate workers' organization, and in May Imatra 9 was officially founded. "Specifically designed to disseminate socialist information," this organization managed to recruit one hundred and thirty members within a few months, thirty of whom were women.

The formation of Imatra 9 signalled the beginning of the end of the temperance society. Religious Finns deserted it because the society allowed "dancing and theatrical performances forbidden by the Port Arthur Lutherans." The socialists joined Imatra 9. Except for the church then, the socialist hall emerged as the centre of all social and political activity. Women were drawn to the dances, they came to see the plays, to sing in the choirs, and to be part of gymnastics groups. Imatra built its own hall, formed a band and performed plays, which were prepared by a paid director. In 1910 the socialists moved to a grandiose labour temple and opened a five-hundred person auditorium with a play called *The Devil's Church*. In both the old and new halls, many Finnish women, who initially went out of curiosity or a desire for social activity, "contracted the red disease" and joined political discussions, meetings, and protests.[4] The executive of Imatra 9 was composed of both men and women. Men, however, held the key positions.

As the previous chapter has indicated, the Toronto community, both religious and socialist, was run by tailors. Originally the small community tried to cooperate and function harmoniously under one roof – the Finnish Society of Toronto. Its constitution, written in 1902, defined its objectives as educational, social, and cultural, all in the interests of "freedom of thought." As in British Columbia, harmonious co-existence did not last long. As new arrivals, mainly domestics and tailors with union experience from Finland and the United States, entered the community, and as the socialist members became the majority within the Finnish Society, the religious Finns began to drop out.

Finnish women were exposed to socialist leaders such as Frans Syrjälä who had attended the founding meeting of the SDP of Finland and was able to articulate the explicitly marxist anti-religious socialist ideology. Here too, social activity was important: "We were quite some sight carrying our backdrops in streetcars and wearing full stage make-up," recalls Aili Piton, one of the early actresses. Education was not neglected either; a library and a reading-room were set up, English classes organized, and an endless number of "enlightening" discussions and debates were held. In 1903 collections were taken up to help the "starving Finns" and victims of strikes.

Women were invited to participate, encouraged to speak, debate, and attend all meetings. Some heeded the call to action and tried to carve out an equal place for women in Finnish socialist activity. Most, however, were satisfied to carry out only their supportive roles. Unlike resource towns in British Columbia and northern Ontario, Toronto women made up nearly half of the society membership. Despite their numbers, only a few were not intimidated by participation in the business meetings and the heated debates when socialist theory was discussed. The men nagged at the women: "'Go to the meetings, go to the meetings,' my husband used to say as he was going out the door leaving me home with a young baby. How do I go when he is attending meetings every night?" [TYYNE LATVA].

Lack of free time because of family obligations or time restraints imposed by domestic service were only some of the reasons for the women's reluctance to participate in the executive. The primary cause was lack of self-confidence, inexperience in meeting procedures, and fear of speaking in public. Women recognized these disadvantages and some battled hard against their sense of inferiority. They forced themselves to speak in public:

I had made up my mind to speak, in my thoughts at home I had practised over and over again what I would say, how I would say it. I went to the meeting determined that this was going to be the night. 'Any questions?' I heard the chairman ask. My heart started racing, beads of perspiration gathered on my forehead, and then a big lump gripped my throat. Not a sound did I utter . . . next time, maybe next time.

Between 1902 and 1904 *Toivo* published numerous articles on "women and socialism." The paper dogmatized that women had to rely on their own initiative to elevate themselves to equal status with men. Women had to show by their work and behaviour that they were able to fulfil those responsibilities that come with equal rights. Before women reached this level of sophistication, so the argument went, it was useless for them to speak of equality with men:

It is the responsibility of every single woman, be they housewives or just girls, to obtain knowledge. . . . It is true that men have noticed how beneficial it is for them to keep women in some kind of state of dependency. The modern, enlightened opinion, however, absolutely rejects this viewpoint and demands the same rights for women that men already enjoy in the society.

Translations provided from Bebel's *Woman and Socialism* and *Woman in Future Society* predicted that in the new society, a woman would be socially and economically independent. "She will no longer be a slave but will stand beside a man, totally free and in charge of her own happiness." Matti Kurikka echoed similar sentiments in *Aika* and tried to free women from the bonds of marriage, sexual obligations, and child rearing.

The journalists and theorists could write encouraging predictions, but reality was another matter. How were the women to change their attitudes, increase their knowledge, and alter their home environment? Women protested that it was absurd to say that all they had to do was change. It was of no use if in practice men continued to lock them out. One woman activist complained:

What about us women who attend the meetings and social evenings at the society. We are often treated like some kinds of "tooth-picks." Little while ago the subject for debate was announced to be: Is a woman equal to a man? The ensuing discussion was hairy, intended to raise laughter . . . these kinds of underhanded compliments and spectacles do nothing to promote women's enthusiasm or increase their involvement.[5]

Yet the promise that a woman could stop being a slave touched a responsive chord. One major problem for these first Finnish women socialists was that they lacked a viable role model in Canada. All Finnish leaders, religious and socialist, were men. Men had years of experience, generations of ingrained confidence, and the will to rule. Socialist women had only recently, and often just partially, shaken off the religious teachings which had clearly spelled out women's supportive roles. Many were still members of a Finnish church in Canada. Yes, the socialist arguments made sense, but if only there was one example to illustrate that it could work. And so women continued to do the dishes after the entertainment evening. In an article to the newspaper *Raivaaja* in 1905, a Port Arthur woman grudgingly asked: "Are women but pieces of furniture," in the corners of the hall? Should they be taken for granted, or worse yet, ignored? Should they be used only for practical purposes and at other times remain mute? Were women themselves to blame for their conditions? In the lively debate which ensued not only the men, but also the "despicably vain" upper-class (Canadian) women were accused. The harshest criticism, however, was reserved for the church. The institution of marriage, as ordained by the church, was declared to be "simply slavery."

These are the earliest recorded debates on the women's question in a Finnish-Canadian socialist context. While the despair of women is disheartening, the fact that these debates took place at all is an indication of the level of awareness of socialist issues among Finnish immigrant women. The encouragement Finnish women were receiving from some articulate men, even if not followed by practical deeds, was in itself an important step forward. A progressive Finnish man could no longer publicly deny women's right to equality, however he might treat his wife privately:

> My husband, you know, was one of the leaders in the community [Toronto] and he used to be a great actor, always on stage. He was handsome and women used to tell me how lucky I was to have such a man. Lucky? I hardly knew him, he was always at the hall and I was working and looking after the two kids. I couldn't even get the time off to see the plays [MARTTA KUJANPÄÄ].

By 1905 the Finnish tailors of Toronto wished to move beyond their immediate community, to break out of their ethnically exclusive activity, and join the Socialist Party of Canada (SPC). Among the first fifteen delegates sent to investigate the SPC were two women, Mimmi Oksanen and Aino Möttönen, both single domestics who had joined the organization in 1904 and worked on the entertainment committee. Their inclusion was of symbolic significance, but not of lasting value, as they both soon moved to the United States. A year later another delegation of ten Finns was dispatched to apply for a charter from the SPC; and on 18 November 1906 two women, Emmi Pasanen and Hanna Kuosmanen, were among the charter members. Emmi Pasanen was a single domestic who was an active participant in the socialist hall and had also served on the entertainment committee. Hanna Kuosmanen was a seamstress and joined the group with her husband who was a tailor.

The immediate goal of the Finnish tailors in Toronto was to encourage the scattered Finnish socialist groups across Canada to join the SPC. In September 1908 the party held its first Ontario-wide convention at the Finnish Society Hall in Toronto. At this meeting were Finnish representatives from South Porcupine, Port Arthur, Cobalt, and Toronto. Once again two Finnish women attended, Aino Suomi and Sanna Kannasto (Kallio). Aino Suomi was a single domestic from Toronto, and Sanna Kannasto travelled from Port Arthur with her common-law husband, J.V. Kannasto. These women, however, refused to accept supportive roles on the socialist stage. Neither stood by quietly. Aino Suomi became known for her strong criticism of male dominance:

> Are men not everyday and every year grinding hundreds even thousands of women to mud? And now as the desire has awakened in women to be progressive they try to show us to the reactionary direction. They know that when the women become totally enlightened, men will lose the sceptre they now carry. We want to discover what our position as women is.

For the first time, Finnish-Canadian women had representatives of their own. Sanna Kannasto was to impress the delegates with her eloquence, confidence, and knowledge of socialist doctrine. She was not merely a temporary figurehead who would disappear after the conference. Finnish socialist women had found their champion, a woman who not only participated on an equal footing with men but who also addressed those issues pertinent to the Finnish immigrant women.

Sanna Kannasto and Socialist Women's Issues before 1920

Despite the initial enthusiasm of Finnish socialist leaders such as Sanna Kannasto, the Finnish connection with the SPC did not last long. On 5 January 1910 the 146 Toronto Finns (about half of whom were women) were ousted, along with ten Italians, twenty-two Britishers, and thirty Jews. The main difficulty had been the willingness of the Finns to take direct political action, a course not acceptable to the largely Anglo-Saxon executive. In May 1911 Finns took their brand of socialism and their nation-wide membership to the Canadian Socialist Federation (CSF) and in December became the majority of members in the SDP. At the same time Finnish-Canadian socialists had attempted to establish a nation-wide Finnish socialist organization. Their conflict with the Socialist Party of Canada only strengthened this desire, and by October 1911, largely due to the efforts of the Toronto socialists, the Finnish Socialist Organization of Canada (FSOC), better known by its later name the Finnish Organization of Canada (FOC), was born. Its growth was nothing short of spectacular. In 1911 the FSOC had nineteen locals with 1,205 members. A year later it had grown to forty locals and 2,218 members. And when the First World War broke out there were sixty-four locals with 3,062 members. All of these also joined the SDP, making the Finns the largest cultural group within the party, while the Ukrainians added 816 members and "others" 1,502.

Women's issues, as clearly articulated by Sanna Kannasto, played a part during these turbulent organizational changes. In the first convention of the Ontario section of the SPC, held at the local Finnish hall in Toronto in 1908 to the tune of brass bands and the taste of freshly baked *pulla* served by the Finnish women, the question of suffrage was raised. The Finnish women's push for this demand gained impetus after women in Finland were granted the right to vote in 1906. In fact, Finnish women did not need to spend any time convincing their own community of the benefits of women's suffrage. This issue, which dominated so much of the discussion in many Canadian women's organizations, temperance associations, or political meetings and which was the *raison d'être* for many middle-class reformist movements, was taken for granted by both Finnish men and women.[6] Even the most conservative Finnish newspaper, *Canadan Uutiset*, founded in Port Arthur in 1915, declared: "This paper stands for equal rights for everyone regardless of their sex. *Canadan Uutiset* will support women's suffrage battles with all its might."

Another thorny issue which was more pertinent for English-speaking women was the question of women in the work force. Women in Finland were expected to work, and this expectation increased in Canada with the added economic pressures placed on immigrant women. While religious leaders still maintained that women's place was in the home, the reality was that immigrant women worked. Even if they had the "luxury" of staying home with young children, they supplemented the family income by taking in boarders. Thus the question of whether women ought to work or not was irrelevant. In the Finnish Society of Toronto, 55 per cent of the female members were single wage-earners, and many of the remaining married women also indicated that they were "laundresses, seamstresses, waitresses and cleaning women." The debates which sometimes surfaced in *Western Clarion* or *Cotton's Weekly* on women taking away men's jobs at lower salaries did not find their counterparts in the Finnish socialist press. In public, at least, Finnish socialists agreed that women had the equal right and the equal need to work and that efforts should be made to improve their working conditions. The problem was that men seldom made any practical efforts on women's behalf, being too busy organizing their own miners' and lumber workers' unions.

Another issue arose over the ability of women to make independent decisions about marriage, birth control, and their own organizations. Here, too, we have noted that common-law relationships were accepted by both men and women socialists as a sign of progressive attitudes, freedom from religious dictates and traditional social trappings. The fact that pastors were difficult to obtain and that Finns developed anti-clerical feelings helped to fortify this form of revolt. Immigrant living conditions, and the lack of self-disciplining family or social rules, made it easier for immigrant women to discard old traditions and to rise to the forefront of the new. It was this kind of independence, this seemingly outrageous rejection of traditions by Finnish socialist (and many non-socialist) women, that attracted the attention of the Canadian press. *Daily News* of Port Arthur in 1913 attacked three of the most prevalent Finnish traits: socialism, atheism, and free love. Finnish socialists were able to assemble, at a moment's notice, 461 people to counter-argue the accusations. In a paid advertisement they declared that Canada was supposed to have freedom of religion, "and as we understand it every person in Canada has a perfect right to care for his soul according to the dictates of his own conscience." They avoided the issue of free love by stating that Finns have always been against prostitution, against the practice, so prevalent in Port Arthur, of men paying for love; and finally, they proudly declared that, "Yes, we are socialists." They also pointed out to the editors of *Daily News* that socialism was not illegal in Canada.

While the dividing issues between the SPC and the SDP were far more complex than the women's question alone, it did play a part in the discussions. The SDP accepted the importance of women's independent organizations within the party structure, a practice which Finnish women supported wholeheartedly.

Throughout these formative years and the period of FSOC's most dramatic growth, Sanna Kannasto was one of the key organizers for the Finnish socialists. She provided a powerful role model and was tireless in her coaxing of women to join the organization and to form their own independent women's groups. She became a household word, respected by both men and women and praised by the English-speaking socialists until she achieved almost legendary status. Ultimately, like all legends, she fell into disfavour, but not before her lasting mark was imprinted on the consciousness of Finnish immigrants in Canada. Because she was such an important spokesperson for the Finnish socialist woman, we must examine her image of women and socialism in more detail.

Sanna Kallio was born in Yli-Härmä, Ostrobothnia, Finland, in 1878. She moved to the United States in 1899 when she was twenty-one years old. She probably came alone, and not much is known of her political associations in Finland. In the United States she attended the Finnish People's College, and in 1905 joined the Socialist Party of America. She quickly established a reputation as a writer and public speaker, and there she began to organize Finns.[7] She moved to Canada sometime before 1907, probably with J.V. Kannasto, whose name she adopted. The couple, true to the radical Finnish tradition, were never legally married. In 1908, the year she attended the Ontario convention of the Socialist Party, she was selected to become the first paid political organizer for the Finnish socialists. She was dispatched to northern Ontario to increase membership in the party. With a few exceptions, Sanna Kannasto was instrumental in bringing the remote mining towns, rural villages, even temporary lumber camps, into the FSOC. She criss-crossed Canada at least five times and made "countless shorter journeys." Whenever possible she held additional meetings for women, guiding them in organizational questions, on women's role in socialist society, but also discussing the more intimate issues of marriage and birth control. In the summer of 1913, the organization reported 562 women members.[8]

Canadian authorities viewed Sanna Kannasto as one of the most "dangerous radicals," and the RCMP wanted to deport her. They shadowed her movements, attended her speaking engagements, and in April 1920 concluded: "In her speeches as organizer for the Finnish Socialist Democratic Party [she] had shown herself to be a person coming within the provisions of Section 41 of the Immigration Act."[9]

The authorities tried to catch up with Sanna's gruelling pace. Her travelling expenses were paid by collections taken during the speeches or by sale of reading materials, books and memberships, the remainder being covered by the central organization. Therefore, Sanna had to be frugal in her expenditures, not giving herself adequate rest or comfort. In April 1914, she wrote apologetically to the FSOC headquarters in Toronto: "I travelled for the first time in my life in a sleeping compartment as otherwise I would have been too tired even to speak." This was most unusual. Her tours consisted of hours of trekking through uninhabited forests. She often suffered from exhaustion, cold, and lack of shelter, but she carried on. Her monthly expenditures in 1914 were around $150, of which $80 to $90 came from donations. To save money on longer trips she tried to have local socialists give her lifts in their horse and buggy and later in their cars. When roads didn't exist there was no other way but to walk.[10]

In her actions and in her self-image, Sanna Kannasto typified the radical Finnish heroine. After an especially demanding speaking tour in western Canada in 1920, she was arrested by the RCMP while travelling by train to Manyberries, Alberta. Her surviving letters from the small prairie jail illuminate some of her strengths. On 6 February

1920, Sanna wrote that she had "charmed her captors" to the point that she had been left alone to use the warden's typewriter. She also revealed that her language skills in English were "short," and she could hardly understand the substance of the eleven cross-examinations conducted thus far. While she was not pleased with her language skills she was proud of her strength of character, claiming to possess inner fortitude and a defiant trait which Finnish women tried to emulate:

> What makes them [police] most upset is that they don't succeed in making me angry or nervous and thereby in making me cry and confess. I am as if made of iron, I never knew how much I could endure. . . . God help the people when I can once again be in the middle of a crowd. This is agitation at its best.

Five days later she echoed her earlier report:

> I am not nervous, I am a woman made of iron, I have not yet shed a single tear, although I have been in cruel cross-examinations. Despite everything, I am happy and I try to joke and keep up the humour with my prison guards.

What also surfaced in Sanna Kannasto's writings was her attitude to men and marriage. Part of the RCMP investigation focused on her personal life, on her "free" marriage to J.V. Kannasto, which was over by 1920. Bitterly she asked the FSOC's chairman to "send a note to that man of mine whom I so deeply hate, and tell him I have said nothing about his bitch whom he trails behind him . . . after all he does belong to the party." To be a travelling agitator, a radical woman, and at the same time to have a successful marital union seemed impossible. One terse note in the 1914 annual report of the FSOC indicates some of her troubles: "Sanna Kannasto would be the ideal person to send for these agitation tours but J.V. Kannasto strictly forbids it."

To please this man, much less a political activist than his partner, Kannasto kept a low profile for a couple of years and became a mother. She was desperately missed. Aino Pelander wrote in 1916 from Toronto that, "during the international woman's day we couldn't find a woman speaker even though we searched with a needle." This constraint could only last a few years until Kannasto broke loose and was once again free to promote socialism. Her talents were unique, but her life story was not. Children restricted women's ability to organize and travel. Studies of Jewish radical women in the United States indicate that, "virtually the only nineteenth century Jewish women in America who left their mark upon history were spinsters or occasionally, childless wives."[11]

Sanna Kannasto had no equal among Finnish-Canadian women. When her work was made impossible by the police, no woman stepped in to fill her shoes: "It is a great pity that we [FOC] can't use the services of Sanna Kannasto these days [1930] because the bourgeois are so hot on her heals . . . we know of no other [Finnish] woman speaker."[12]

Many of Sanna Kannasto's speeches and articles have disappeared. She reported that she burnt her correspondence because of her fear of the police. Later, when she had been forced to retire from politics, more of her files were destroyed. The results of her teaching, however, have been more lasting. One of them was the formation of separate Finnish women's organizations.

Finnish Women's Organizations before 1920

Sanna Kannasto was an organizer for all Finns, male and female, but throughout her journeys she tried to meet with socialist women. Most of all, Kannasto sent a clear message to women not to hide behind their womanhood or to use children as an excuse to withdraw from politics; she herself was a single mother. The mushrooming Finnish women's socialist organizations and clubs reflect her independent spirit, her defiance of tradition, and her socialist beliefs. She was fond of publishing "live examples" of the most unlikely candidates for socialist agitation. A caption to a photograph which showed a strong-looking woman with an army of small tots around her read: "This is a poor farmer's wife, Senja Koski, does all the household work, looks after the animals, sews all the clothes for her seven children and still finds the time to be most active in the women's reading circle and who is the socialist reporter for her community."

While there was no other strong national women's spokesperson, the Finnish community did develop literally hundreds of grass-roots organizers who became respected leaders within their own geographically confined communities, ardent writers of editorials, union activists and fund-raisers. It is these women, the uneducated, common workers, who spoke English with difficulty, if at all, who were the strength behind the Finnish socialist women's movement. They were the real workers in a workers' movement. They were not idealists, not doctrinaire theorists, but immigrant women who sought to improve their social conditions and who believed that by uniting with other workers they could best achieve change. To accomplish their goals they formed their own organizations.

It is not clear which Finnish community in Canada can claim to be the first to have a separate women's socialist group that went beyond fund-raising and socializing. The *Aallotar* temperance society's sewing circle, for example, slowly evolved from a religious group of women into a socialist support organization. Sewing circles were traditionally part of all secular and religious Finnish organizations. Women instinctively sought a separate identity from men, feeling more comfortable in each other's company. The term "sewing circle," however, acquired a new meaning. After 1908 it was often replaced by such titles as "study ring," "discussion club," or simply "women's club," which more accurately reflected its ongoing activity. The by-product of these organizations was money, but the main aim was to educate socialist women to be good public speakers, debaters, writers and agitators – to draw women out of their shells so they could go out and fight as equals in the parent Finnish Organization of Canada. Women, having tasted ridicule and derision from Finnish men who rarely practised what they preached in their organizations, were determined to improve their skills.

The oldest surviving minutes of such a sewing circle are from Toronto in 1908. This club, however, had been founded several years earlier and had published a hand-written women's paper. Part of the ritual of the meetings was for every woman to come prepared to give either a speech, recite a poem, or read a well-chosen article. Their performances were judged, and by no means gently: "It [the poem] was too short and recited very sharply . . . it is important to articulate more gently so that you are not hacking away like a lumberjack who is splitting wood . . . there is plenty of room for improvement for Aino."

The performers were not the only people who came under scrutiny. The rotating chairpersons were evaluated for their efficiency, fairness, and ability to conduct the meeting according to the bylaws. The secretaries, who also changed weekly, had to learn how to take minutes in order to prepare themselves for future tasks. Topics for discussion varied from questions of morality, to how religion fools workers, to women's role in a socialist society. The aims of this sewing circle, as written in the minutes of 23 January 1908, say nothing about sewing:

> Let us develop ourselves so that we can perform freely and vigorously, so that the day will yet come when we can show that a woman is not only the type who gets a heart attack when she should tell a story or speak in some public place. Lets be enthusiastic!

This form of women's activity was not confined to Toronto. The hand-written newspaper *Piiskuri*, from the tiny village of Pottsville, Ontario (near Timmins), advertised one week in 1912 a "contest for poetry reading" and the next week, the sewing circle's sale of "clothes, baked goods and beer." In the isolation of Smokey Lake, British Columbia, the handful of women not only organized a sewing circle, but also a separate "reading ring" in 1917. The Fort Frances, Ontario, women hosted an entertainment evening where the guest speaker,

Helmi Mattson, novelist and future editor of *Toveritar*, spoke on the history of socialism, equality of the sexes and the international women's movement. Geographic isolation did not stop the women's inquisitiveness and their desire to understand socialism. A prime example of this is the socialist women's sewing circle in Sointula, British Columbia.

The Sointula sewing circle had two primary goals: fund-raising and education. A separate sub-group, *puhujaseura* (speakers' club), was functioning in 1911, but was founded earlier. The meetings were held twice a month and in every meeting there was a speech, poem, story, and a question for debate. All performances were judged and the minutes reveal that most women had to be content with a "satisfactory" grade. Some of the questions for discussion dealt with women's legal position in British Columbia, celebrations of international women's day, and the support of the women's socialist newspaper, *Toveritar*, founded in 1911 in the United States. Women also read socialist articles that discussed women and then debated the issues. In 1912 these women, geographically isolated in their small fishing village on an island in the Pacific Ocean, decided that the only way women could be heard was if Finnish-Canadian women organized their own nation-wide women's conference and founded an independent women's socialist organization. The Sointula women did not consider themselves cut off by their isolation, but felt very strongly that they were a part of a socialist women's movement in North America. Their literacy, their keen interest in the socialist press, and their ability to benefit from travelling socialist speakers encouraged the women to be part of a larger sisterhood.

The women of Sointula, however, decided during the first world war that time was not yet ripe for a nation-wide women's organization. In fact, Finnish women suffered along with the rest of the Finnish community during the difficult war years. The Finnish socialist newspaper *Työkansa*, which had ambitiously become a daily, went bankrupt in 1915. Women felt this loss not only because it cut off their source of communication but also because many women had invested sizable sum of money in support of the paper. When the last issue of *Työkansa* rolled off the press on 15 June 1915, an article indicated that, "*Työkansa*'s sewing circle had decided to give all its remaining funds to the Finnish Socialist local of Port Arthur." This women's sewing circle might actually have done some sewing, but mainly it raised funds through hosting the ever-popular entertainment evenings. One such began with a speech from Edith Metsola, followed by a poem from Mrs. Liukkonen, a piano solo from Mrs. Koljonen, and a play entitled, *A Happy Surprise*. Then came an intermission and women had a further opportunity to raise funds by selling coffee, *pulla*, and sandwiches.

The evening, however, was far from over. When the audience had to travel long distances from nearby farms and lumber camps, they wanted to get their 15 cents' worth of entertainment. The program continued with "women's singing"; a poem from Mrs. Heikkinen; a short play, *In the Jail;* and finally, the highlight of the evening – dancing. This kind of support activity helped the socialist paper and gave women an opportunity to put the lessons learned in the women's clubs into practice.

Women were also supporting socialist activity on an individual level. One woman, who had heeded the desperate call for funds for *Työkansa,* was bitterly disappointed, as she lost her life's savings. The right-wing newspaper *Canadan Utiset* reported in November 1919:

FORSAKEN COMRADE

Hilja Järvinen lost all of her money in the "*Työkansa* bank" . . . she lived with a man and had children with him, but during the depression the man went insane . . . she is working constantly and would now desperately need her money and a doctor. She used to be an active socialist in Copper Cliff.

Järvinen's case was effectively used as a propaganda tool by the conservatives, but it was not unique. Hundreds of radical Finns lost considerable amounts of money when the paper went bankrupt. The purchase of shares and the comrade loans made amounted to $65,000. Undeterred, the Finns established another socialist newspaper, *Vapaus,* founded in Sudbury in 1917, and once again the call for funds was sent to the Finnish socialists in Canada. During the war years, however, organized Finnish activity suffered. Finns were deemed too radical and their socialist activities banned, including the newly founded *Vapaus.* Among the war victims were also the foreign-language locals of the SDP. The War Measures Act was not revoked until 2 December 1919, by which time the FSOC (which had continued to function as a "purely" cultural organization) had lost further members. The organization plummeted to its lowest point in 1920 when it could register only 1,743 members in forty-six locals.[13]

Activity at the sewing circle level also suffered. The Sointula speaking club, for example, stopped its activities in 1915. Since the early sewing circles were an appendix to the Finnish socialist organizations, their fortunes were closely linked. Women had felt and articulated the need for an independent organization, but the war years gave these aspirations a temporary setback.

The Decade of Women's Organizations, 1920-30

After the First World War, the committed Finnish socialists who had stood by their organizations were ready to ally with the Worker's Party of Canada, and with the change of name became the Finnish Socialist Section of the Communist Party of Canada, once again forming a majority in this Canadian radical organization. Finnish socialist women were transferred along with the men into the communist activity.[14]

The renewed sense of vigour felt by the grass-roots organizers and the graduates of the sewing circles culminated in new calls for separate women's organizations. Now that the suffrage battles were over, some Canadian feminists were also moving to the left. Joan Sangster argues that from the 1920s to the 1950s, "the dynamic debate over women's issues was situated within the socialist and communist movements in Canada." Finnish women actively contributed to this debate. They did so by revitalizing women's discussion clubs and by making full use of the radical, socialist women's paper *Toveritar*. Its Canadian circulation numbers were spectacular – over three thousand in 1930 when the paper was banned in Canada. If three thousand Finnish-Canadian women paid to subscribe to the paper, it can be assumed that at least as many more women (mothers, daughters, friends) had access to it. In addition, *Toveritar* was found in all Finnish halls, reading-rooms, and libraries. According to the Canadian census of 1931, there were 12,361 women of Finnish racial origin in Canada who were twenty years or older. Therefore, at least half of the Finnish women in Canada had regular access to a radical socialist women's weekly, and a quarter of them received their own issue. No women's paper in Canada (popular or political) can claim to have so ably penetrated the market.

An important factor in the paper's success must lie not only in its socialist content, which many women could identify with, but also in the fact that it was a paper especially for women. It discussed women's issues, it was often critical of male dominance, it explained facts relevant not only to women, but especially to Finnish immigrant women in North America. Clearly, women wanted and appreciated their own, independent newspapers. In many Canadian communities *Toveritar*'s readership had reached the saturation point, and its agents could only report: "Sorry, no new subscribers, everyone already gets *Toveritar*." The enthusiasm of the Canadian women was rewarded in 1929 when the Toronto comrades captured the coveted *Toveritar* banner as the victor in the paper's annual subscription drive. *Toveritar* now became an integral part of all Finnish women's socialist activity in Canada.

With the same spirit of independence Finnish women set out to strengthen their own organizations. In the 1920s this movement received some support from Finnish men. The Communist Party was encouraging women to become part of an international women's movement, and its aim was to re-form the loose-knit ethnic women's groups into units of centralized political structure. While the party line on the "women's question" took many turns during the era of the Comintern, in the early twenties it was compatible with Finnish women's desire for sex-segregated activity. *Toveritar* whole-heartedly supported the goal to establish separate women's locals in every community where the Finnish section of the Communist Party operated. The male-dominated Finnish Organization of Canada, on the other hand, was divided on the issue. In some communities women met with resistance, while in others the sewing circles were already in existence and only needed slight reorganization. In Finland, Ontario, women were complaining of the mixed messages they were receiving in 1924:

> As we all know the Workers Party and the Socialist Organization [FOC] has made it the responsibility of the locals that belong to it to establish women's organizations, the purpose being to involve more women, but that is where the issue has been left, in reality nothing has been done to revitalize women's activity, at least not by the organization [FOC] or the district assembly. . . . It is important to do something concrete and not to limit the activity to naked demands.

Since women could not count on Finnish men to further their cause, they had to step up their own educational activities and to train and promote their own leaders. The efforts of the early sewing circles were now praised. *Toveritar* also served as an educational tool. No fewer than one hundred and twenty-two communities across Canada had their female correspondents who diligently wrote to the paper. Writing to the paper was an assigned duty, part of the vigorous self-improvement program. Women must also learn to express themselves in writing. But the ability to speak and write was not enough; women also organized special short, but intensive, courses to train organizers and develop their communist ideology. "Women need women organizers because women can understand each other better than men can understand a woman," wrote Siiri Wiita from Timmins. Helma Laakso described the subjects in an educational course in Sault Ste Marie, attended by seven Finnish women in 1921: the woman's place in society and the communist women's movement, economics, the birth and development of nations, class struggle tactics, the international Workers' Movement, and the history of Finnish class war.

In addition, all over Canada Finnish women were producing several hand-written newspapers, in order to improve their writing skills and to provide a communications network. They found these papers less intimidating and the cost was minimal. Several of the *nyrkkilehti* (fist papers) were circulated among women's clubs and a few were bound.

Some titles alone revealed the educational purpose of the papers: *Opin-Ahjo* (Forge of learning), *Kehitys* (Progress), *Naisten Kehittäjä* (Women's teacher). Having first summoned up the courage to write to a fist paper, many women were later encouraged to write to a "real" newspaper.[15] The stress on education and self-improvement increased the number of capable female organizers, speakers, and writers who could hold their own in their demands for separate organizations.

Some women were confused as to the mandate of the women's local sewing circles: what exactly was to be done within them? One Canadian "Mother" described the traditional activities of the sewing circles as "an absolute waste of time." An Albertan woman responded with an explanation of "why we sew – because even workers' organizations need money." The women of Webster's Corners, British Columbia, vowed to make only workmen's socks for their fund-raising bazaars, no bourgeois decorative items! The extent to which many of the sewing circles were in fact transformed into bolshevik cells is questionable. Typically, Sault Ste Marie women "didn't exactly kill the sewing circle, but the women's local will look after its affairs." This perhaps, was their strength – the flexibility to meet the specific demands of a particular community of women, rather than rigidly following the dictates of the Comintern or the Finnish male comrades. Some women did absorb and articulate the communist platform. All were encouraged to recruit new members and to explain the benefits of communism to working-class women. An article in a 1921 issue of *Vapaus* urged:

> Comrades, women workers . . . let us go as comrades – fortified with the socialist text from the Gospel to even the poorest homes, to the homes that have lost all hope, to the darkest corners of the factories and to the most strictly guarded work place! Let us spread knowledge about communism – socialism – as saviour of working women, which will let the whole world be reborn.

In addition to the clearly stated revolutionary goals, the women's locals continued to take pride in their ability to raise funds. Increasingly, however, these funds were given to international causes. Timmins women reported in 1922 that their bazaar netted $179, of which $150 was sent to the Karelia Commune in the Soviet Union. Similarly women from Cobalt reported:

> The Cobalt women have done their duty towards their European comrades and showed the men that they are capable of other tasks besides looking after the family and they organized an entertainment evening . . . for the benefit of comrades in Karelia.

Women also took pride in purchasing their own advertisements in *Vapaus* and *Toveritar* for greetings during Christmas and International

Woman's Day. No less than one hundred and twenty-seven women signed the Christmas greetings from Timmins which urged "Vigour to the Class War!" In this way women were simultaneously supporting the socialist papers and declaring their separate identity.

All of the Finnish women's locals were ostensibly under the purview of the Communist Party's Women's Bureau, which in 1924 adopted a strategy of broadening its radical ethnic activities. Finnish-Canadian women were now urged to affiliate themselves with the newly formed Canadian Federation of Women's Labour League (WLL), a communist-led organization with locals in a handful of Canadian cities, such as Toronto, Winnipeg, Regina, and Vancouver. The affiliation of at least twenty-seven Finnish women's groups with the League, between 1924 and 1929, and reports of their activities in the English-language radical press, testify to their eagerness to forge links with other Canadian women as well as to promote socialist, feminist solidarity.

Finnish women, however, did not find a comfortable niche within the WLL. They tried to integrate into the English-speaking activity by taking part in WLL-organized marches, international women's day parades, and by inviting members from Ukrainian women's groups to their entertainment evenings. The language barrier was a real obstacle, but so too was the desire for ethnically exclusive cultural activity. In smaller Finnish communities, such as the mining towns of Alberta, Finnish women did report some success. In 1931 Mary North wrote: "There are women here who speak all languages whom we have tried to organize into a Women's Labour League local, and finally were able to put one together in Bellevue last summer." Some of North's earlier disappointments included a lecture night in Blairmore, Alberta, when the guest speaker was Becky Buhay. Only three English-speaking people were in attendance, one Chinese, and the rest were Finns, most of whom couldn't understand a word of the speech.[16]

Part of the feminist solidarity was also the Finnish women's commitment to the *Woman Worker,* the official organ of the WLL published between 1926 and 1929. Finnish women tried to support the paper, which had a small following among trade unionists and intellectuals but virtually no readership among ordinary English-speaking women. Elma Jackson reported from Alberta that many of the subscribers of the *Woman Worker* were Finnish women who could not even read English, "but say that they will give the dollar anyway to support the magazine." Finnish women were quite appalled at their English-speaking sisters' lack of commitment to their own paper. When *Woman Worker* was suspended after the death of its editor, Florence Custance, Finnish women believed that this was only an excuse. The real reason lay in the disorganization among the English-speaking comrades and their unwillingness to work hard or make sacrifices to keep their own paper. Clearly, Finnish women placed much more importance on newspapers as their means of communication. They also observed how the "[English] women's organizations disintegrated, and there was no activity." In contrast, the Finnish women's locals continued to push ahead full steam, "just the same as before," despite the weakness of the WLL. This was possible since, from its inception, Finnish women "made up 95 per cent of the members." Not only feminism and socialism, but also the desire to maintain their own culture united the Finnish women's activities.

The Decline of Finnish Women's Separate Activity

The year 1930 loomed ominously for Finnish-Canadian socialist women. That year they received several blows from the WLL, the Canadian government, the socialist Finnish men, and the economy. To begin with, Finnish women felt insulted that all of them had been by-passed when a new interim executive was selected to revitalize the WLL. The Jewish and English women of Toronto, who made up but a small fragment of the members, "have elected the new executive." No explanation for this overtly discriminatory action against Finnish and Ukrainian women was ever offered. To add insult to injury, T.A. Ewen forbade the Finns to publish a critical letter on the issue. "To put it mildly, this restriction is unusual." The letter demanding explanations was published, nevertheless, and was also critical of the WLL's plans to send a Canadian delegation of women to the Soviet Union. Finnish women strongly protested this squandering of money. Why send a delegation to the other side of the world when the same women in Canada can't even afford their own paper? To add to the troubles, initially no Finnish women were included in the delegation, and when one was chosen she was an obscure Finnish maid.

In light of this treatment, Becky Buhay still had the courage to send a letter to the Finnish women in which she "demanded" funds to help pay for the tour. She suggested $600 from Toronto, $400 from Montreal, $300 from Vancouver, $200 from Timmins and $100 from Sudbury. She concluded tersely, "Send the money immediately!"[17] Finnish women felt bitter. Nothing had changed, not only did they play supportive fund-raising roles in their own community, but also the English-speaking women seemed to be only interested in their money.

A further serious blow was dealt by the Canadian government. In November 1929 *Toveritar* was banned in Canada. The women desperately tried to reverse the order and sent a multitude of telegrams and petitions to Ottawa. They urged the Finnish men to protest this violation of their freedom of speech. They recalled the enthusiasm with

which women had protested, only a year earlier, the conviction of
Arvo Vaara, an editor of *Vapaus*, who was jailed for "seditious libel."
Finnish men did not return the favour. Why do the men now forsake
us, women asked, is it beneath men's dignity to assist women?[18]

Toveritar did not survive the loss of its three thousand Canadian
subscribers. The end of the paper, with which Finnish women in
Canada had closely identified, left a lasting void in the socialist women's
movement. Its successors in the United States included *Työläisnainen*
(Woman Worker) and *Naisten Viiri* (Women's Banner), but none of
these recaptured either the vitality or the popularity of *Toveritar*.
Finnish-Canadian women tried to convince the male-dominated executive of the FOC and *Vapaus* to start a new Canadian women's paper.
"It would be invaluable in agitation work," they argued. The problem
was that Finnish women were defending a separate women's paper
at a time when the Communist Party had decided that women should
integrate back into the movement. Finnish women disagreed: "Women
would feel more responsible to write to their own paper, not to leave
it up to men, but the idea that they must write even if they have poor
writing skills is important . . . this way we would also develop women
writers."[19]

The women tried to entice the men by financial incentives to support
them. They gathered over one thousand subscription pledges for a
new woman's paper, but to no avail. The men did not accept, or even
understand, the urgency for a woman's paper. Instead they instituted
a woman's page in *Vapaus*, which was officially started on 27 February
1930. "This is not enough!" cried the women, but no one heard, and
so ended the first and only adventure into journalism that Finnish-
Canadian women have had.[20]

Thus, the history of Finnish-Canadian socialist women was a constant
struggle to find their place within the larger Finnish organization,
Canadian political parties, or in the women's movement. Ultimately,
the women could only depend on themselves, and historically, were
happiest within their own sexually and ethnically segregated groups.
This does not mean that they lived out their lives in isolation – quite
the opposite. Finnish women felt very much a part of the larger socialist, feminist movement whose goals they supported, not only in spirit
but also financially. For this reason, the Finnish women were very
much shaken when they realized the discriminatory attitudes felt by
the WLL leadership toward the Finns. Language difficulties and cultural
barriers also marred efforts at cooperation.

Ultimately, the Finnish brand of socialism was closely linked to their
culture. Radicalism and anti-religious views were imported from
Finland, but in Canada they flourished with renewed vigour. Here
the socialist activity went far beyond politics and was linked to all the

economic, social, and cultural needs of the women. Finnish women recognized their increased vulnerability as immigrants who did not have family support systems. They agonized over the dangerous working conditions of the men and their own unequal status as workers. They did not accept this passively, but tried to elevate their own position as women, immigrants, and workers by participating in socialist activities and by constant self-improvement. From the very first sewing circles to the WLL locals, they constantly strove to gain equality with Finnish men. Despite many important advances, this goal remained elusive.

Thus, some of the questions raised by the visit to the Finnish rest home have now been answered. The Finnish immigrant women who came to Canada between 1890 and 1930 faced unique challenges caused by their gender, class, and ethnicity. Their distinct cultural heritage, the socio-economic imbalance in their communities, and their often defiant world view determined their strategies in marriage, employment, and social organization. In many respects Finnish women appear to have been exceptional.

The spirited determination that was evident in the eyes of the senior citizens exercising in the Vancouver rest home was a product of lifelong hard work and optimism. The women shared an iron will to improve their material, social, and spiritual life, often by making great personal sacrifices. These senior citizens were the hardy survivors. Many others had long perished, broken down by ill health, loneliness, and hard work.

One of the greatest achievements of cooperation in today's Finnish-Canadian communities has been the successful completion of modern, friendly centres for the seniors. Multi-million dollar rest homes in Toronto, Sudbury, Sault Ste Marie, Thunder Bay, and Vancouver stand as testimony to the mutual dependence of immigrants, but also to a willingness to band together. Unfortunately, many of the political and religious divisions still raise barriers and segregate Finnish activity. Volunteer women, with a few significant exceptions, are still praised mainly for their ability to serve coffee and *pulla*, and to raise funds. Perhaps the one final impact and contribution to the Finnish community by the surviving, tough pioneers, the vast majority of whom are women, will be to help bridge these divisions through the community's common desire to respect the elders and their dreams of a better world. For most women, the journey to the rest home has been a long, arduous struggle, with many disappointments. With a shared spirit of optimistic defiance, however, these women were able to add meaning to this struggle and enjoyment to their lives.

Notes

INTRODUCTION

1. Interview with Sirpa Sallinen, Vancouver, 1982.
2. Irving Abella and Harold Troper, *None Is Too Many* (Toronto, 1982).
   One of the first critical assessments of Canadian immigration policy and
   racism towards Blacks is Harold Troper, *Only Farmers Need Apply* (Toronto,
   1972); on Japanese discrimination, see Ken Adachi, *The Enemy that Never
   Was* (Toronto, 1976), and Ann Gomer Sunahara, *The Politics of Racism:
   The Uprooting of Japanese Canadians during the Second World War* (Toronto,
   1981); on Asians, see Hugh Johnston, *The Voyage of the Komagata Maru:
   Sikh Challenge to Canada's Colour Bar* (Calcutta, 1979); on Ukrainians, see
   Frances Swyripa and John Head Thompson, eds., *Loyalties in Conflict:
   Ukrainians in Canada During the Great War* (Edmonton, 1983).
3. Donald Avery, *'Dangerous Foreigners': European Immigrant Workers and Labour
   Radicalism in Canada, 1896-1932* (Toronto, 1979). On immigrant violence,
   see Jean Morrison, "Ethnicity and Violence: The Lakehead Freight
   Handlers before World War I," *Essays in Canadian Working Class History*,
   eds. Gregory Kealey and P. Warrian (Toronto, 1976), pp. 143-60; Anto-
   nio Pucci, "Canadian Industrialization versus the Italian Contadini in a
   Decade of Brutality, 1902-1912," in *Little Italies in North America*, eds. Robert
   F. Harney and Vincenza Scarpaci (Toronto, 1981), pp. 182-207.
4. Juliet Mitchell, "Four Structures in a Complex Unity," in *Liberating Women's
   History*, ed. B.A. Carroll, pp. 385-99; Joan Kelly, *Women, History, and Theory:
   The Essays of Joan Kelly* (Chicago, 1984), especially pp. 51-64; see also,
   Barrie Thorne and Marilyn Yalom, eds., *Rethinking the Family* (New York,
   1982).
5. Gerda Lerner, "Placing Women in History," in *Liberacing Women's History*,
   ed. B.A. Carroll (Chicago, 1976), p. 359, (original emphasis).
6. Interview with Aina Mackie, Vancouver, 1982.

CHAPTER 1: WOMEN IN FINLAND

1. Tapani Valtonen, "Väkiluvun ja ikärakenteen kehitys," in *Suomalaiset:
   Yhteiskunnan rakenne teollistumisen aikana*, eds. Risto Alapuro *et al.* (Porvoo,
   Finland, 1980), pp. 12-14.
2. The estimates for arable land vary. Jyrki Leskinen, in *Finland Facts and
   Figures* (Helsinki, Finland, 1979), gives the following estimates of land
   use in 1979: 8.6 per cent agricultural land, 87.3 per cent used by forestry
   industries, pp. 86, 16. The figures cited here come from Leskinen's *Facts
   about Finland* (Helsinki, Finland, 1981), pp. 8-9, 37.
3. *Handbook for Travellers in Russia, Poland, and Finland* (London, England,
   1868), p. 383.
4. *Kalevala* was collected by Elias Lönnrot and its first version was published
   by the Finnish Literature Society in 1835. The book is generally credited
   for giving a vital boost to the birth of Finnish national identity.
5. Väinö Voionmaa, *Suomen karjalaisen heimon historiaa* (Helsinki, Finland,
   1915); Matti Sarmela, *Reciprocity Systems of the Rural Society in the Finnish-
   Karelian Culture Area* (Helsinki, Finland, 1969).

6. John Dyke, "Report on Continental Emigration," 1 Dec. 1882, p. 58, Immigration Branch, RG 76, vol. 13, file 77, part II, p. 58, Public Archives of Canada (PAC); cited by Mauri A. Javala, "Scandinavians as a Source of Settlers," in *Scandinavian-Canadian Studies*, ed. Edward W. Laine.

7. The term "urban" is generally used by Finnish scholars to describe those areas which are incorporated as a city *(kaupunki)* regardless of the population. After 1951 incorporated villages *(kauppala)* were also sometimes included.

8. W.F. Kirby (trans.), *Kalevala: The Land of the Heroes* (London, England, 1985), Poem 23, "The Instructing of the Bride," pp. 287-311.

9. Anna-Liisa Sysiharju, *Equality, Home and Work* (Finland, 1960), p. 16.

10. Tuulikki Hosia, "Suomalainen naisihanne," in *50 vuotta Suomen naisten yhteistyötä* (Helsinki, 1961), p. 102.

11. Eino Jutikkala, "Suomen teollistuminen," in *Suomen talous-ja sosiaalihistorian kehityslinjoja*, pp. 208-17. Jutikkala notes that industrialization arrived to Finland relatively late, limiting the work opportunities in the urban areas. On women and wage work, see Riitta Jallinoja, "Naisten palkkatyön yleistyminen," in *Naisnäkökulmia*, eds. Katarina Eskola *et al.* (Helsinki, Finland, 1979), pp. 17-41; for women in the cities before industrialization, see Merja Manninen, "Kaupunkilaisnaisen asema Suomessa Ruotsin vallan aikana," in *Naiskuvista todellisuuteen*, eds. Päivi Setälä, *et al.* (Hämeenlinna, Finland, 1984), pp. 43-67.

12. Riitta Jallinoja, *Suomalaisen naisasialiikkeen taistelukaudet* (Porvoo, Finland, 1983), pp. 80-81. In England, for example, the number of single people among the upper class began to increase in the sixteenth century. Lawrence Stone, *The Family, Sex and Marriage in England 1500-1800* (Bungay, England, 1979), p. 41.

13. Riitta Jallinoja, "Miehet ja naiset," in *Suomalaiset*, p. 223. For example, Jallinoja cites the wages of farm hands as being double those of maids.

14. Ibid., p. 229; Aune Innala, *Suomen naisen alkutaival lainsäätäjänä* (Helsinki, Finland, 1967), p. 39.

15. Eino Murtorinne, "Kirkon seitsemän vuosikymmentä," in *Kirkko suomalaisessa yhteiskunnassa 1900 — luvulla*, eds. Markku Heikkilä and Eino Murtorinne (Hämeenlinna, Finland, 1977), pp. 8-9; Raija Sollamo, "Nainen kirkon palvelijattarena," in *Se on kaikki kotiinpäin*, eds. Sirkka Sinkkonen and Eila Ollikainen (Pieksämäki, Finland, 1985), pp. 76-86. Sollamo explains that while recommendations were made about deaconess work in 1913, it did not become part of church legislation until 1943. Until then this overwhelmingly female occupation was handled mostly by volunteers, as was Sunday school.

16. Jaakko Numminen, "Yhdistymisvapaus ja aatteellinen järjestäytyminen," in *Suomalaisen kansanvallan kehitys*, ed. Pentti Renvall (Porvoo, 1965), p. 110.

17. Riitta Jallinoja, *Suomalaisen naisasialiikkeen taistelukaudet*, pp. 32-52.

18. Jaakko Numminen, "Yhdistysvapaus ja aatteellinen järjestäytyminen," in *Suomalaisen kansanvallan kehitys*, pp. 116-19.

19. Minna Canth, *Työmiehen vaimo*, was first published and performed on Finnish stage in 1885. The play, *The Worker's Wife*, was translated into English by Mary Taanila Lehtinen and published in *Finnish Americana* 4 (1981), pp. 1-73. Much of the controversy which surrounded Canth's radical plays is discussed in V. Tarkiainen, *Minna Canth* (Helsinki, Finland, 1921); Hilja Vilkemaa, *Minna Canth: elämäkerrallisia piirteitä* (Helsinki, Finland, 1931). Canth's letters have been published by Helle Kannila, ed., *Minna Cantin kirjeet* (Helsinki, Finland, 1973).

20. Oma Mäkikossa, *Yhteiskunnalle omistettu elämä: Miina Sillanpään elämän ja työn vaiheita* (Helsinki, Finland, 1947), p. 99. Her pioneering work among maids is described in *Miina Sillanpää 80 vuotta* (Helsinki, Finland, 1946), pp. 7-31.
21. The socialist children's organization *(Ihanneliitto)* was founded in 1902; in 1906 the youth organization was revamped into Social Democratic Youth League *(Sosialidemokraattinen Nuorisoliitto);* by the year 1906, there existed 48 separate workers' gymnastics and sports clubs *(Työväen Voimistelu- ja Urheiluseura)*. The strength of the cooperative movement is reflected in the increase in membership. Between 1906-8, 300 new workers' cooperative stores were founded and the membership of cooperative stores tripled to 95,000. Lauri Haataja *et al.*, eds., *Suomen työväenliikkeen historia*, pp. 62-63.
22. Oskari Tokoi, *Sisu: "Even Through a Stone Wall"* (New York, 1957), pp. 209-23; "Emigration from Finland, 1893-1944," RG 76 C4682-3, vol. 651, part 4, PAC.

CHAPTER 2: GEOGRAPHICAL DISTRIBUTION OF FINNISH WOMEN IN CANADA

1. The 1901 Canadian census, pertaining to Finns, is quite inaccurate. Estimates of the actual number of Finns in Canada are much higher. Akseli Rauanheimo, first consul of Finland, estimated the number of Finns in Canada to be 10,000 at the end of the century, *Kanadan-kirja* (Finland, 1930), p. 204; from calculations using available local information, the actual number was probably around 4,000, of whom about 1,000 were women. For a discussion on the problems of the census figures dealing with Finns, see Mauri A. Jalava, "Radicalism or a 'New Deal'?: The Unfolding World View of the Finnish Immigrants in Sudbury, 1883-1932" (M.A. thesis, Laurentian University, 1983), pp. 11-22.
2. Nanaimo Finnish Evangelical Lutheran Church minute books begin in 1894, but some members had joined late in 1893. The membership books are incomplete and while the congregation did not officially disband until 1930, its active phase was over by 1910; see Yrjö Raivio, *Kanadan suomalaisten historia* I, pp. 208-14. Raivio reprints the membership list of the congregation from 1893-98.
3. Reino Kero, *Suomen siirtolaisuuden historia* (Turku, 1982), p. 60. According to Kero, the initial emigration was overwhelmingly male. In 1873 only 7.4 per cent of the emigrants were family emigrants. By 1882 this figure had risen to 19.6 per cent after which it began to decline.
4. Two Finnish congregations were established in Ontario before the turn of the century. The Copper Cliff Finnish Evangelical Wuoristo Congregation was founded in 1897. Its archives are microfilmed and part of the Multicultural History Society of Ontario collection (MSR 2038 and MSR 8117), housed in the Archives of Ontario under the congregation's present name, St. Timothy's Lutheran Church. The collection is restricted. The other congregation, the National Evangelical Lutheran Church in Port Arthur, was founded in 1897. Its records are extensive and held by the congregation. They have not been microfilmed and are restricted. For the purpose of this work restrictions were lifted for the marriage registers and birth and death records, copies of which are in the author's possession.

5. National Evangelical Lutheran Church (Port Arthur), Marriage Register 1901-1908.
6. *Dominion of Canada Sessional Papers* xxxv, no. 10 (1901), #25, p. 182, cited in *A Chronicle of Finnish Settlements in Rural Thunder Bay* (Thunder Bay, 1976), p. 113. This book is an excellent account of the rural settlements and early development of Thunder Bay, as is Mark Rasmussen, "The Geographic Impact of Finnish Settlement on the Thunder Bay Area of Northern Ontario" (M.A. thesis, University of Alberta, Edmonton, 1978), where the early settlements are discussed on pp. 46-52.
7. *A Chronicle of Finnish Settlements in Rural Thunder Bay*, p. 18.
8. Oiva Saarinen, "Finns in Northeastern Ontario," *Laurentian University Review* 15, no. 1 (1982) p. 42, quotes, "one retired INCO employee," from *Inco Triangle* (October 1956), pp. 41-54.
9. Advertising for a husband, wife or companion was quite common in Finland and is especially prevalent in the immigrant communities of North America.
10. Letter from J.G. Colmer on behalf of the high commissioner, Lord Strathcona, to Lars Krogius, 20 Mar. 1899, "Emigration from Finland, 1899-1903," RG 76 C4683, vol. 25, file 651, part 2, PAC.
11. Matti Halminen, *Sointula*, (Helsinki, 1936), p. 62.
12. Ibid., p. 84.
13. The United States had begun to restrict immigration in 1921, but the full impact was not felt by the Finns until 1924; see Mauri A. Jalava, "Radicalism or a 'New Deal'?" p. 14.
14. Reino Kero, *Suomen siirtolaisuuden historia*, table 6, p. 57. It is interesting to note that twice as many female children were emigrating. Many were brought over to baby-sit, to work in rooming-houses or as maids. Still, overall, the percentage of children in the total emigration remained very low.

CHAPTER 3: QUALITY OF LIFE

1. Ole Edwart Rolvaag, *Giants in the Earth* (New York, 1929).
2. RG 76, vol. 26, file 651, part 5, "Emigration from Finland 1926-1944," Microfilm Reel C-4683, A. Rauanheimo to A. L. Jolliffe, Comissioner of Immigration, 14 Nov. 1928, PAC.
3. Handwritten family history in Finnish by Emil Mustama, no date. Copies are in the possession of the author; a translated and abbreviated version by Anne Mattson is published in Nancy Mattson Schelstraete, ed., *Life in the New Finland Woods: A History of New Finland, Saskatchewan* (Rocanville, Sask., 1982), pp. 93-94, 189.
4. For example, *Vapaus*, 18 July 1922, reports the burial of eighteen-day-old Violet who was buried close to her home without ceremony. Violet's death was at least recorded, but many others were not.
5. Eura: xxi, letter from Aino Norkooli, 27 Oct. 1939, American Letter Collection, University of Turku (ALC). Some examples of death notices: "Our only child died after having suffered the most awful pain, that horrified even us. The pain was caused by scarlet fever and suffocation" (*Vapaus*, 26 Feb. 1921); "Devastated by bitter sorrow we thus notify you that our gently loved, only daughter died accidentally having fallen into a barrel which had three inches of water" (*Vapaus*, 16 Mar. 1921).
6. While women interviewed were quite open to the discussion of intimate matters, such as abortion, no one interviewed for this book admitted any

knowledge of infanticide. Reino Kero, in *Suomen siirtolaisuuden historia I*, p. 57, indicates that a higher proportion of females were under the age of sixteen when immigrating to North America. In 1923 it was 11.8 per cent compared to 6.6 per cent for boys.

7. The most detailed information is given of children who met accidental deaths. It is almost as if parents were trying to exonerate themselves from blame. Usually parents described, to the best of their ability, what seemed to cause the death of their child. For example: five-year-old Oiva Nikkinen died of blood poisoning caused by an infected tooth (*Vapaus*, 19 Jan. 1921); a one-year-old Arvo Mäki died of a toothache and stomach ache (*Vapaus*, 2 Feb. 1921); Gust Markkula fell into a well and died (*Vapaus*, 24 Sept. 1921).

8. RG 10, 30 A I, "Historical Field Work – Rainy River and Thunder Bay Districts," report on summer work in Thunder Bay, 1926, by S.M. Carr-Harris, public health nurse, Archives of Ontario. She reported that, "Miss McKinnon shared the work in those Finn settlements visited this summer." Apparently Miss McKinnon was able to speak Finnish. The reports from the townships of Marks and Lybster are dated January 25, 1926 under a "report of summer work in Thunder Bay District July to December, 1925." It seems that Nipigon was visited between February and June 1925. In addition there are reports with no dates for the Pearson and Lybster townships. All of this information was presumably sent to Dr. J.T. Phair, Director, Child Hygiene Division, Provincial Board of Health in Toronto.

9. Annette Pahkala Phillips, "Delivering Babies: Midwives," in *Life in the New Finland Woods,* p. 45; interviews with Aune Mattson and Mary Polvi (New Finland, Saskatchewan, 1982).

10. RG 10, 30 A I, "Historical Field Work" report "On the way to Forbes and Ware School Number 4," by S. M. Carr-Harris, 27 Oct. 1929, Archives of Ontario (AO).

11. Alcoholic poisonings were often caused by taking huge overdoses of alcohol, drinking methyl alcohol, or less successful home brews; train accident statistics included men found dead on railroad tracks, men who died while jumping off trains or unsuccessfully attempted to jump into a moving train. Work-related train accidents are not included in this category. The accidentally shot category includes men shot by someone else accidentally, hunting accidents and all men found "mysteriously shot" in the forest. The latter possibly include many suicides; all work-related accidents which were specifically described, i.e., mining, lumber camp and construction sites; the "other" category includes those deaths listed simply as "accident."

12. RG 76, vol. 101, file 15197, part I, "Undesirable immigrants," Microfilm Reel C-4776, letter from Commissioner of Immigration, Winnipeg, Manitoba, to W.D. Scott, Superintendent of Immigration, Ottawa, Ontario, 4 Aug. 1903, PAC.

13. Katherine McCuaig, "'From Social Reform to Social Service.' The Changing Role of Volunteers: the Anti-tuberculosis Campaign, 1900-30," *CHR* LXI, no. 4 (December 1980), p. 481.

14. Nancy Mattson Schelstraete, ed., *Life in the New Finland Woods,* p. 189.

15. RG 76, vol. 26, file 651, part 5, "Emigration from Finland, 1926-1944," Microfilm Reel C-4683, from G.E. Buchanan, City Solicitor, Sudbury, Ontario, to Deputy Minister of Immigration, 15 May 1931, PAC; Mauri A. Jalava has suggested that this letter was written to expedite the deportation of Finnish radicals; see "Radicalism or a 'New Deal'?" pp. 240-41.

168   *Defiant Sisters*

16. "Aallotar Minute Books," minutes of the founding meeting, 11 Oct. 1891, North Wellington, British Columbia, and enclosed rules for the "Organization to Aid in case of Injury or Illness," Series C-2, file 1 and file 5, Benefit Society "Revised Constitution 1908," FCHSC/AO.
17. MSR 7389, Reino Kero Collection, AO.
18. This poem was written for Mary Levo from Port Arthur, Ontario, printed in *Vapaus*, 12 Mar. 1921.
19. For example, see Betty Järnefelt-Rauanheimo, *Vierailla veräjillä* (Finland, 1928); interview with Lahja Söderberg (Vancouver, 1982).

CHAPTER 4: "CANADA IS HELL FOR MEN—HEAVEN FOR WOMEN"

1. Aili Grönlund Schneider, *The Finnish Baker's Daughters* (Toronto, 1986), p. 79.
2. Ika: CXC, letter from Linda Maja, Copper Cliff, Ontario, 10 Sept. 1924, American Letter Collection, University of Turku (ALC).
3. Kar: CXXVI, Sylvia Hakola, Schreiber, Ontario, to her friend Toini Talonen in Finland, 5 Sept. 1925, ALC.
4. Kar: CXXV, Nikolai Järvenpää, Port Arthur, to his girl-friend, Toini Talonen, in Finland, 20 Aug. 1925, ALC.
5. The newspapers only reported wife-beating if it was severe and if the wife had the courage to take her case to court. Some examples of convictions in wife beating (and murder as a result of beating) are found in: *Toveritar*, 4 Nov. 1916; *Vapaus* 22 June 1922; *Vapaus*, 29 Nov. 1923; *Vapaus*, 1 July 1924; *Vapaus*, 18 June 1925; *Vapaus*, 18 Oct. 1928.
6. National Finnish Evangelical Lutheran Church in Port Arthur, Marriage Registers. The first Canadian-born bride was married in 1913. The first North American-born male was married in 1904. Between 1904-30, 80 second-generation males were married at an average age of 23, which was much younger than the average age for Finnish-born men. The first time a non-Finnish bride was married in this church to a Finnish groom was in 1923.
7. Aili Grönlund Schneider, *The Finnish Baker's Daughters*, p. 84.
8. "Agricola," *Kulkurina Amerikassa, uutisraivaajana Canadassa* (Duluth, 1952), pp. 114-17.
9. Keijo Virtanen, *Settlement or Return* (Helsinki, 1979), table 18, p. 80 and pp. 128-29. According to Virtanen, of all returned emigrants, 29.4 per cent left within the first two years and an additional 30.2 per cent before their first five years were up; Finnish Immigrant Home Registers for Men and Women 1927-1931, MG 28 V128, vol. 6, files 1-3, PAC.
10. Examples of married women who left their husbands and children can also be found. In most cases the women tried to support the children who were left in the care of some relative. K-VI: L; Muur: V, both in ALC; interview with Ida Toivonen (Thunder Bay, 1984); Briitta Simpson, *Minä menen Amerikkaan* (Helsinki, 1956). In this autobiography (p. 18), Simpson describes why she left:

    I became bored with the little city. Life became stale. Home strangling....To the world! To freshen up! For Adventure! to Freedom! my eternally romantic soul which was thirsty for new experiences was shouting, and protesting against the confines of marriage.

11. *Vapaus*, 1921-25, while only two of these ads came from the western provinces, the practice was also widely used in British Columbia, Alberta and

Saskatchewan (except in New Finland). *Toveritar,* which was published in Oregon, attracted these western Canadian advertisements.

12. Luvia: 1, Albert Bergström writing the history of White Lake, B.C., 30 Dec. 1952, ALC.

13. The *Woman Worker,* Mar. 1928, C.F. of W.L.L. letter, 15 Feb. 1928, signed by Ellen Machin (president) and Florence Custance (secretary). The letter is addressed to the Timmins League.

14. J. Donald Wilson, "A Synoptic view of *Aika,* Canada's First Finnish-Language Newspaper," *Amphora,* 29 (March 1980), pp. 9-14; Arja Pilli, *The Finnish-Language Press in Canada, 1901-1939: A Study in the History of Ethnic Journalism* (Turku, Finland, 1982), pp. 40-57.

15. Matti Kurikka discusses the Oneida colony and the philosophy of John Humphrey Noyes in *Aika,* 15 May 1904.

16. See Angus McLaren and Arlene Tigar McLaren, *The Bedroom and the State* (Toronto, 1986); Dianne Dodd, "The Hamilton Birth Control Clinic in the 1930's," OH LXXV, no. 1 (March 1983).

17. The hundred women were selected from oral interviews conducted for this dissertation. The common criterion was that the women had to belong, at some time in their life, to a socialist organization or subscribe to a socialist newspaper, and they had to be married or living in a common-law relationship for a period longer than two years. The first 100 were picked in alphabetical order. It is noteworthy that 18 of the women had no children at all, and 51 had only 1 child.

18. These ads ran throughout the twenties. The Port Arthur Kaleva Drug Store prices were first advertised in *Canadan Uutiset,* 16 Dec. 1920, for $2.50 a dozen for both men and women. In 1921 the prices rose and remained stable throughout the twenties at $3.50 for women and $3.00 for men, *Vapaus,* 1 Dec. 1921, 11 Feb. 1926 and 17 Oct. 1928. White's Drug Store in Port Arthur was also advertising "birth control devices" for $2.00, but it is not clear exactly what they were selling.

19. KAR: CXXXI, Hilja Rantala, Rosegrove, Ontario, 14 Jan. 1937, ALC.

20. Anna Ruuska is responding to a letter written by another farm woman with a large family in Finland, Ontario, who feels that their problems and work load do not receive adequate attention and that they are made to feel guilty about the large families which they were unable to prevent, *Toveritar,* 22 July 1924.

21. KAR: LVIII, letter from Eero Halli, Port Arthur, 20 Jan. 1933, ALC.

CHAPTER 5: FINNISH WOMEN AT WORK

1. *Vapaus,* 27 Feb. 1930; contemporary observations by Finns in the United States support the thesis that women's earnings compared favourably with those of men. For example, see Akseli Järnefelt-Rauanheimo, *Suomalaiset Amerikassa* (Helsinki, 1899), p. 33; Akseli Järnefelt-Rauanheimo, *Meikä-läisiä merten takana* (Porvoo, 1921), pp. 104-10. Autobiographies written by Finnish domestic servants who moved from Canada to the United States because of higher wages include: Olga S. Fagerlund, *Tarinani lännen ihmemaassa* (Lappeenranta, Finland, 1980); Briitta Simpson, *Minä menen Amerikkaan* (Porvoo, 1956).

2. *Vapaus,* 26 Feb. 1921. This type of persecution of "white" Finns was more common among men.

3. Mauri A. Jalava, "Radicalism or a 'New Deal'?, p. 33, note 39; *Vapaus,* 8 May 1923; interviews with Elina Sytelä (Sudbury, 1974). Keeping

boarding-houses was also typical of other immigrant communities; for example, see Isabel Kaprielian, "Women and Work: the Case of Finnish Domestics and Armenian Boardinghouse Operators," unpublished manuscript, 30 May 1984.

4. For example, the Algoma Hotel in Port Arthur offered $40 a month for a woman to work in the kitchen, (*Canadan Uutiset*, 9 Jan. 1919). A Windsor woman reported that hourly wages for day-workers were 35 cents (*Vapaus*, 10 Oct. 1928), but Toronto women claimed that they were receiving 50 cents.

5. Ramsay Cook and Wendy Mitchinson, eds., *The Proper Sphere: Woman's Place in Canadian Society* (Toronto, 1976), pp. 172-74.

6. RG 76, vol. 651, part 4, Microfilm Reel C 4682, "Emigration from Finland 1921-1926," New Canadian Immigration Regulations concerning emigration from Scandinavia and Finland, 15 June 1922, PAC.

7. Carl Ross, "Finnish American Women in Transition, 1910-1920," in *Finnish Diaspora II*, ed. by Michael G. Karni (Toronto, 1981), p. 244.

8. For example, see Varpu Lindström-Best and Charles M. Sutyla, *Terveisiä Ruusa-tädiltä: Kanadan suomalaisten ensimmäinen sukupolvi* (Helsinki, 1984), especially, pp. 143-56.

9. Ulf Beijbom, *Swedes in Chicago,* Studia Historica Upsaliensia XXXVIII, pp. 197-98; David M. Katzman, *Seven Days a Week* (Chicago, 1981), pp. 66-70.

10. MG 8 G62, vol. 2, file 59, "Consulate of Finland Correspondence," PAC.

11. Nellie L. McClung, *Painted Fires* (Toronto, 1925), translated into Finnish by Väinö Nyman, *Suomalaistyttö Amerikassa* (Helsinki, 1926); review of *Painted Fires* in *Canadan Uutiset,* copies in author's possession courtesy of J. Donald Wilson, n.d.

12. Butler-maid, cook-chauffeur, companion-gardener, combinations were especially popular during the depression when men could not obtain any other work.

13. RG 76, vol. 48, file 1836, parts 1-3, "Women's National Immigration Society, Montreal (Reports) 1892-1914," Microfilm Reel C-4712, PAC; RG 76, vol. 109, file 20765, part 1, "Vancouver Hostel – sponsored by Young Women's Christian Association – Traveller's Aid Reports: Immigration 1919-1925," Microfilm Reel C-4772, PAC; RG 76, vol. 337, file 356358, part 2, "Women's Welcome Hostel, Toronto, Ontario," Annual Report 1911, Microfilm Reel C-10,247, PAC.

14. MG 28 V 128, vol. 6, files 1-3, Immigrant Home Registers for Women list a total of 3,044 women between 1927 and 1931, PAC.

15. See, Varpu Lindström-Best and Allen Seager, "*Toveritar* and the Finnish Canadian Women's Movement 1900-1930," in *The Press of Labour Migrants in Europe and North America 1880s to 1930s,* eds. Christiane Harzig and Dirk Hoerder (Bremen, 1985), p. 255.

16. Peter De Lottinville, "Joe Beef of Montreal: Working Class Culture and the Tavern, 1869-1889," *Labour/Le Travail,* no. 8/9 (Autumn 1981/Spring 1982), pp. 9-40.

17. Interview with Lydia Punni (Vancouver, 1982). Original list is in Punni's possession. For supporting evidence, see interview with Lyyli Kontio (Vancouver, 1982); photographs (courtesy of Dr. Bryan Palmer) of the Hastings Street Finnish area show two-storey frame buildings squeezed together on small lots. According to the interviews, the ill-reputed sauna actually had two entrances, one for men and the other for women, but a door allowed easy access to both sides. Finns were most annoyed by this

"disrespect for sauna," an age-old Finnish institution traditionally associated with health and cleanliness.

18. Aili Grönlund Schneider, *The Finnish Baker's Daughters*, pp. 54-59.
19. Lori Rotenberg, "The Wayward Worker: Toronto's Prostitute at the Turn of the Century," in *Women at Work: Ontario, 1850-1930* (Canadian Women's Educational Press, 1974), p. 36; C.S. Clark, *Toronto the Good* (Montreal, 1898), pp. 134-35. The age structure of New York prostitutes was similar to Toronto; see William W. Sanger, *The History of Prostitution* (New York, 1910), p. 452.

CHAPTER 6: WOMEN IN THE IMMIGRANT CHURCH

1. *Seventh Census of Canada, 1931* IV, table III: "Racial Origin of the Population Showing First, Second, Third and Fourth Largest Percentage of Country of Birth, Religion, Mother Tongue and Race with which Males Tend to Intermarry," pp. 238-39; Rev. Markku Suokonautio, "Reorganization of the Finnish Lutherans in Canada," *Polyphony* 3, no. 2 (Fall 1981), p. 93.
2. For information on the Finnish Canadian Pentecostal movement, see Tellervo Kähärä, *Kansanpappi Toivo Pajala* (Thunder Bay, 1985); *Toronto Saalem-seurakunta 1930-1980* (Vancouver, 1980). An example of the success of later Lutheran work is Veikko Saarela, *Agricola – Ankkuri aallokossa* (Buckhorn, Ontario, 1981).
3. Juha Seppo, "Kansankirkkona uskonnonvapauslain toteuduttua," in *Kirkko suomalaisessa yhteiskunnassa 1900-luvulla*, p. 71. Seppo's statistics indicate that while about 21,000 women applied to leave the church, over 24,000 men did so during the same time period.
4. Rev. Fritiof Pennanen to Rev. John F. Saarinen, 18 August 1932, Series B-10, file 3, FCHSC/AO.
5. A. William Höglund, "Breaking with Religious Tradition: Finnish Immigrant Workers and the Church, 1890-1915," *For the Common Good* (Superior, Wisconsin, 1977), p. 29.
6. Rev. Pennanen to Rev. Juho Yrttimaa, 27 June 1937, MG 8 G62, vol. 13, file 14, PAC.
7. Interview with Aune Tanttu (Montreal, 1981); Sakari Pälsi, *Suuri, kaunis ja ruma maa: kuvia ja kuvauksia Kanadan-matkalta* (Helsinki, 1927), pp. 70-73, Pälsi describes the immigrant's first visit to a Catholic church in Quebec City; Akseli Rauanheimo, *Kanadan-kirja* (Porvoo, 1930), p. 147. Rauanheimo explains how the first sign of life in Canada for most immigrants is the golden cross on Mont St. Anne; on p. 153 he describes the impact of the lit-up cross on Mount Royal in Montreal.
8. Nanaimo Finnish Evangelical Lutheran Church Membership Records 1893-1894 and 1898 and Minute Book, which begins 30 December 1894, but it is clear that the congregation has already functioned for some time. Yrjö Raivio, *Kanadan suomalaisten historia* I (Vancouver, 1975), pp. 208-14.
9. John Hawkes, *The Story of Saskatchewan* (Chicago, 1924), p. 670.
10. K. Marianne Wargelin Brown, "A Closer Look at Finnish American Issues" in *Women Who Dared: The History of Finnish American Women*, eds. Carl Ross and K. Marianne Wargelin Brown (St. Paul, Minnesota, 1986), cites Prof. A. Hjelt in *Teologinen aikakauslehti*, 1902.
11. *50 Vuotta 1897-1947*, the 50th Anniversary of the Port Arthur, Ontario National Ev. Lutheran Church (1947), pp. 13-14; outline of the early

history of Thunder Bay by Alex Langila, Thunder Bay Finnish Canadian Historical Society.

12. Yrjö Raivio states that the Apostolic Lutherans (more commonly known as Laestadians) in Canada have not had a permanent trained minister, but several small congregations were founded and they received visiting ministers from the United States. They met mainly in each other's homes or rented existing Lutheran churches. Yrjö Raivio, *Kanadan suomalaisten historia* I, p. 305.

13. G.A. Aho and J.E. Nopola, *Evankelis-Luterilainen Kansalliskirkko*, pp. 354-55; V. Rautanen explains that one of the first organizers of the Fort William Church was Mrs. Johnson (a hotel owner), who leaned towards Apostolic Lutheranism, and she "denied the congregation entry to the church."

14. Lauri T. Pikkusaari, *Copper Cliffin Suomalaiset ja Copper Cliffin Suomalainen Evankelis-Luterilainen Wuoristo Seurakunta* (Hancock, Michigan, 1947), pp. 125-29.

15. MG 8 G62, vol. 2, file 35, "St. Michael's Finnish Ev. Lutheran Church," 24 p. manuscript of the history of the first decade by Fanny Fältmars, dated Apr. 24, 1937, PAC. The author gave examples of domestics who pledged two months wages.

16. MG 8 G62, vol. 2, file 60, typed four-page manuscript of a "Finnish pastor doing home mission work among his country people in Ontario," n.d.

17. MG 8 G62, vol. 13, file 6, Sanni Laine to Rev. F. Pennanen, 17 Aug. 1932.

18. Marilyn Barber, "an Introduction" to J.S. Woodsworth, *Strangers Within Our Gates* (Toronto, 1977), p. xvii.

19. RG 76, C7369, vol. 219, file 95027, "Activities of Finnish Agitators in Northern Ontario," G.E. Cole to Alex Gillies, Department of Immigration and Colonization, 26 June 1924, PAC.

20. Rev. Arvi I. Heinonen, *Finnish Friends in Canada* (Toronto, 1930), p. 99. This book was prepared for the Board of Home Missions of the United Church of Canada to aid in missionary education. It is part of a series of textbooks which included such culture groups as "Orientals," the Doukhobors and Ukrainians. It was, therefore, in Rev. Heinonen's best interest to glorify his own work and the prospects for future conversions in order to obtain more help (money) from the home mission.

21. The annual report of the Finnish Society of Toronto (the socialist organization for Finns) for 1908 listed 156 paid members while the Presbyterian Finnish Church (the only non-socialist organization among Finns in Toronto) listed merely 29 members in June 1909. For further details, see Varpu Lindström-Best, *The Finnish Community of Toronto, 1887-1913* (Toronto, 1979).

22. *Canadan Viesti* 26, no. 2 (Winnipeg, 1955), p. 5.

23. Yrjö Raivio, *Kanadan suomalaisten historia* I, p. 311; Mauri A. Jalava, "Radicalism or a 'New Deal'?," p. 155.

24. Mauri A. Jalava, "Radicalism or a 'New Deal'?", p. 46.

25. Arvi I. Heinonen, *Finnish Friends in Canada*, p. 102.

CHAPTER 7: WOMEN IN SOCIALIST ORGANIZATIONS

1. RG 76, vol. 219, part 2, Microfilm Reel C7369, file 95027, "Activities of Finnish Agitators in Northern Ontario," letter from RCMP commissioner to Department of Immigration and Colonization, 25 June, 1931, PAC.

2. Joan Sangster, "The Communist Party and the Woman Question, 1922-1929," *Labour/Le Travail*, 15 (Spring, 1985) pp. 25-56; Linda Kealey, "Canadian Socialism and the Woman Question, 1900-1914," *Labour/Le Travail*, 13 (Spring, 1984) pp. 77-100.
3. Mauri A. Jalava, "Radicalism or a 'New Deal'?," p. 38.
4. C. Kouhi, "Labour and Finnish Immigration," p. 30-33; for Finnish participation in pre-World War One Thunder Bay, see Jean Morrison, "Ethnicity and Class Consciousness: British, Finnish and South European Workers at the Canadian Lakehead Before World War I," *The Lakehead University Review* (Spring, 1976), pp. 41-55. Morrison found that the "distinctive feature" of Finns in the labour movement was their radicalism.
5. *Toivo*, 6 Mar. 1904, article by Hetaliisa.
6. Catherine Cleverdon, *The Woman Suffrage Movement in Canada* (Toronto, 1950), reprinted in 1974 with an introduction by Ramsay Cook; Carol Lee Bacci, *Liberation Deferred? The Ideas of the English-Canadian Suffragists, 1877-1918* (Toronto, 1983).
7. Elis Sulkanen, *Amerikan Suomalaisen Työväenliikkeen Historia* (Fitchburg, 1951), p. 491.
8. Aku Päiviö, *Canadan Suomalaisen Sosialistijärjestön Ensimmäisen Edustaja-kokouksen Pöytäkirja, 1914* (Port Arthur, 1914). This first meeting of the Finnish Socialist Organization of Canada was held in Port Arthur, Ontario, 19-23 Mar. 1914. Sanna Kannasto, "the Organization's Agitator," was highly praised at the meeting where she was a major participant.
9. RG 76, vol. 625-27, file 961162, "Agitators 1919-1920," part I, letter from F. C. Blair to Mr. Ireland, 27 Apr. 1920, PAC.
10. MG 28, v46, vol. 3, file 24, letter from Sanna Kannasto, Elma, Manitoba, to J.W. Ahlqvist, 30 May 1914, PAC. Kannasto estimates her monthly expenditures; file 34, Sanna Kannasto's monthly expenditures from her tour of British Columbia from Dec. 1, 1919 to Dec. 31, 1919 are $196.45. Collections taken in her meetings had netted $137.25 and she states that 2,048 people came to hear her during the month.
11. C. Baum, P. Hyman, S. Michael, *The Jewish Woman in America* (New York, 1976), p. 34.
12. MG 28 v46, vol. 16, file 38, "Correspondence: Concerning the Women's Labour League of Canada," letter from John Wirta, Toronto, to Ellen Stenlund, in Sylvan Lake, Alberta, 7 Feb. 1930, PAC.
13. For restrictions on Finnish activity see RG 2 series 1, Records of the Privy Council Office, P.C. 2384, published in the *Canada Gazette*, 30 Sept. 1918 and 5 Oct. 1918, PAC; for an excellent discussion of the repression of Finnish newspapers see Mauri Jalava, "Radicalism or a 'New Deal'?", pp. 69-98; see also P.C. 2381, P.C. 2384, RG 2, vol. 841 and P.C. 2786, RG 2, vol. 850, PAC; for information on *Canadan Uutiset* see RG 6E, vol. 565, Secretary of State: Chief Press Censor 1915-1920, file 237 C-1 and vol. 568, file 237 T 3, PAC; J.W. Ahlqvist, "Muistelmia sosialistilehtien julkaisemisesta" *Vapaus 1917-1934* (Sudbury, 1934); Gregory S. Kealey, "The State, the Foreign-Language Press, and the Canadian Labour Revolt of 1917-1920," in *The Press of Labour Migrants*, pp. 311-45.
14. For information on Finns in the Communist Party, see William Rodney, *Soldiers of the International*, p. 46; Ivan Avakumovic states that "Finns provided over half the members of the CP during the 1920s when the party membership fluctuated between 5,000 and 2,500, but notes that the Finnish numbers were inflated because the FOC was a "social and

cultural" organization, Ivan Avakumovic, *The Communist Party in Canada: A History* (Toronto, 1975), p. 35; Edward W. Laine notes that this is strictly true only for the years 1922-25 when the Finnish section was an integral part of the CP, Edward W. Laine, "Finnish Canadian Radicalism," pp. 97-100 and footnote 14. Ukrainians were the second largest group and together with the Jews and Finns they comprised between 80 and 90 per cent of the party membership. Avakumovic also states that "women were as rare as university graduates in any socialist organization," p. 5, but this was clearly not true of the Finns where women consistently made up 30 to 40 per cent of the paid members. For information on women in the CP, see Joan Sangster, "The Communist Party of Canada and the Woman Question, 1922-1929," pp. 25-88.

15. For information on the tradition of hand-written newspapers see Varpu Lindström-Best, "'Fist Press': A Study of the Finnish-Canadian Hand-written Newspapers," in *Roots and Realities Among Eastern and Central Europeans*, ed. Martin L. Kovacs (Edmonton, 1983), pp. 129-36. There were also bound volumes of fist papers. For example, see an article in *Vapaus*, 19 November 1928, which urges women to "send your fist papers to your district's secretary and we will circulate them forward to the locals (in central Ontario district)." Record of the oldest woman's Fist Press in Canada is from Toronto in 1907 when *Naisen Askel* (Woman's Step) was written.

16. MG 28 v46, vol. 16, file 38, Correspondence: Concerning the Women's Labour League of Canada 1927-1931, letter from Mary North 1 Apr. 1931; *Vapaus*, 9 Feb. and 30 Mar. 1927.

17. Becky Buhay's demands are reprinted in *Vapaus*, 18 Apr. 1930.

18. *Vapaus*, 25 Mar. 1930, article from "Red Deer area" in Alberta is very critical of Finnish men who do nothing to help the women, "the communist locals pretend not to hear that they should send protests together with women [re *Toveritar* ban] as if it was not a 'man's job' to help women in such matters."

19. MG 28 v46, vol. 16, file 38, Correspondence: Concerning the Women's Labour League of Canada, letter from Hilma Pietilä, Kirkland Lake, Ontario, 22 Mar. 1930, PAC.

20. Ibid., letter from Hilma Pietilä, Kirkland Lake, Ontario, 13 May 1930.

21. *Vapaus*, 27 Feb. 1930, announced that it would begin publishing a woman's page instead of the intermittent woman's columns that had appeared earlier.

Bibliography

Primary Sources

Manuscript Sources

Archives of Ontario (Toronto, Ontario)
    The Communist Party of Canada Records (RG 4)
    Department of Health Records (RG 10)
    Department of Labour Records (RG 7)
    Finnish Canadian Historical Society Collection (A 13)
    Jussi Palokangas Papers (MSR 8123)
Archives of the Finland Society (Helsinki, Finland)
Author's Collection (Toronto, Ontario)
Finnish American Historical Archives (Suomi College, Hancock, Michigan)
Finnish National Evangelical Lutheran Church Archives (Thunder Bay, Ontario)
Helsingin Yliopiston kirjasto (University of Helsinki Library) (Helsinki, Finland)
    Amerikan suomalaisten sanomalehdet (Finnish American Newspapers)
Immigration History Research Center (St. Paul, Minnesota)
    The Finnish American Collection
Lakehead University Library (Thunder Bay, Ontario)
    Finlandia Club Collection (MG 3)
    Sillman T. Collection (D 2101)
Laurentian University Library (Sudbury, Ontario)
Migration Institute Archives (Turku, Finland)
Multicultural History Society of Ontario (Toronto, Ontario)
    Hjorth, Jenny Collection (MSR 6887)
    Hormavirta, Irene Collection (MSR 6889)
    Keto, Reino Collection (MSR 7389)
    Kujanpää, Martta Collection (MSR 6886)
    Latva, Tyyne Collection (MSR 6890)
    Oral History Collection
    Päiviö, Jules Collection (MSR 7635)
    Piton, Aili Collection (MSR 6888)
    Siirala, Kaisa Collection (MSR 7633)
    St. Mary's Lutheran Church (MSR 7406)
    St. Matthews Finnish Lutheran Church (MSR 2029)
    St. Timothy's Finnish Lutheran Church (MSR 2038)
    Svensk, Oiva Collection (MSR 7391)
    Tarvainen, Helen Collection (MSR 7397)
    Toronto Finnish Bethlehem Ev. Lutheran Church (MSR 3268)
Museovirasto (National Museum of Finland) (Helsinki, Finland)
    Pälsi, Sakari Collection
The New Finland Historical and Heritage Society (New Finland, Saskatchewan.
Provincial Archives of Alberta (Edmonton, Alberta)
    Subversives, Revolutionaries, Communists (R 75-126)
Provincial Archives of British Columbia (Victoria, British Columbia)
    Aural History Collection

Provincial Archives of Manitoba (Winnipeg, Manitoba)
    Sissler, William James Papers (MG 14)
Public Archives of Canada
    Manuscript Division
    Eklund, William Collection (MG 31 H80)
    Finnish Immigrant Home (MG 28 v128)
    Finnish Organization of Canada (MG 28 v46)
    Kangas, Victor Collection (MG 30 c138)
    Montreal Finnish National Society (MG 28 v102)
    Montreal Suomi Society Inc. (MG 28 v68)
    St. Michael's Finnish Evangelical Lutheran Church (MG 8 G62)
    Federal Archives Division
    Citizenship and Immigration (RG 26)
    Immigration Branch (RG 76)
    Privy Council Office (RG 2)
    Secretary of State (RG 6)
Research Archives for Migration History, University of Turku (Turku, Finland)
    American Letter Collection
    Finnish Migrants Questionnaires
    Finnish Returning Migrants Questionnaires
    Finnish Steamship Company Passenger Lists
    Computerized Statistics of Finnish Migrants
Saskatchewan Archives Board (Regina, Saskatchewan)
    St. John's Ev. Lutheran Church, New Finland (R 82-60)
    New Finland Library (R 82-310)
    Independent Goodwill Temperance Society (R 82-311)
    New Finland School District No 435 (R 82-312)
Suomen Lähetysseura (Finnish Missionary Society) (Helsinki, Finland)
    Montreal Seamen's Mission Records
Thunder Bay Finnish Canadian Historical Society Archives (Thunder Bay, Ontario)
United Church Archives (Toronto, Ontario)
University of British Columbia Library, Special Collections (Vancouver, British Columbia)
    Aural History Collection
Yleisradion arkistot (Archives of the National Broadcasting Company of Finland) (Helsinki, Finland)

Interviews

Author's Collection
    Aho, Arthur (Whitewood, Saskatchewan, 1982)
    Äijö, Aino (Parry Sound, Ontario, 1984)
    Äijö, Sulo (Parry Sound, Ontario, 1983 & 1984)
    Christie, Gayle (Toronto, Ontario, 1982)
    Eklund, William (Sudbury, Ontario, 1973)
    Ermisoff, Martta (Oshawa, Ontario, 1963)
    Erola, Judy (Ottawa, Ontario, 1984)
    Hemming, Arnold (Whitewood, Saskatchewan, 1982)
    Hepolehto, Reino (Toronto, Ontario, 1986)
    Huhtala, Martta (Parry Sound, Ontario, 1983)

Huhtala, Sylvi (Vancouver, British Columbia, 1982)
Huhtala, Walter (Wapella, Saskatchewan, 1982)
Jokela, Aili (Timmins, Ontario, 1982)
K. R. (Toronto, 1985)
Kämäräinen, Kaarlo (Toronto, Ontario, 1974)
Katila, Otto (Toronto, Ontario, 1974)
Keto, Reino (Toronto, Ontario, 1974)
Kivelä, Meeri (Whitewood, Saskatchewan, 1982)
Kiviharju, Arvo (Whitewood, Saskatchewan, 1982)
Kiviharju, Tyyne (Whitewood, Saskatchewan, 1982)
Knutila, Vilhelmina (Timmins, Ontario, 1983)
Knuttila, Alli (New Finland, Saskatchewan, 1982)
Knuttila, Bertha (New Finland, Saskatchewan, 1982)
Knuttila, Charles (New Finland, Saskatchewan, 1982)
Knuttila, Edwin (Rocanville, Saskatchewan, 1982)
Knuttila, Ray (New Finland, Saskatchewan, 1982)
Knuttila, Walter (New Finland, Saskatchewan, 1982)
Kolari, Lasse (Sudbury, Ontario, 1973)
Kontio, Lyyli (Vancouver, British Columbia, 1982)
Kujanpää, Kaarlo (Toronto, Ontario, 1974)
Kujanpää, Martta (Toronto, Ontario, 1974)
Laakso, Frank (Sudbury, Ontario, 1973)
Laamanen, Aileen (South Porcupine, Ontario, 1982)
Lievonen, John (Sudbury, Ontario, 1973)
Lindström, Armas (Oshawa, Ontario, 1964)
M. M. (Cobalt, Ontario, 1978)
Mackie, Aina (Rousseau, Ontario, 1983)
Mackie, Aina (Vancouver, British Columbia, 1982)
Mäki, Albert (Whitewood, Saskatchewan, 1982)
Mäki, Eino (New Finland, Saskatchewan, 1982)
Mäki, Elli (Parry Sound, Ontario, 1984)
Mäkynen, Elvi (Parry Sound, Ontario, 1983)
Mattila, Walter (Whitewood, Saskatchewan, 1982)
Mattson, Aune (New Finland, Saskatchewan, 1982)
Mattson, Einar (Whitewood, Saskatchewan, 1982)
Mustama, Fanni (Whitewood, Saskatchewan, 1981 & 1982)
Norlen, Martta (Winnipeg, Manitoba, 1982)
Norlund, Fred (Whitewood, Saskatchewan, 1982)
Nummi, Alex (Sudbury, Ontario, 1973)
Nummi, Taimi (Toronto, Ontario, 1974)
Peters, Maria (Niagara Falls, Ontario, 1966)
Pihlajamäki, Tyyne (Timmins, Ontario, 1982)
Polvi, Harold (Rocanville, Saskatchewan, 1982)
Polvi, Mary (Rocanville, Saskatchewan, 1982)
Pontio, Sofia (Sudbury, Ontario, 1973)
Punni, Lydia (Vancouver, British Columbia, 1982)
Rasmus, Matti (Parry Sound, Ontario, 1983)
Säilä, Vilho (Toronto, Ontario, 1974)
Saksinen, Emil (Parry Sound, Ontario, 1980)
Sallinen, Sirpa (Vancouver, British Columbia, 1982)
Salmijärvi, Sanni (Thunder Bay, Ontario, 1984)
Sihvola, Hilkka (Parry Sound, Ontario, 1983)
Sihvola, Paavo (Parry Sound, Ontario, 1983)

Söderberg, Lahja (Vancouver, British Columbia, 1982)
Suokonautio, Markku (Montreal, Quebec, 1979)
Syrjälä, Meeri (Winnipeg, Manitoba, 1982)
Syrjälä, Sävel (Toronto, Ontario, 1979)
Sytelä, Elina (Sudbury, Ontario, 1973)
Tanttu, Aune (Montreal, 1981)
Tamminen, Lyyli (Toronto, Ontario, 1983)
Toija, Alma (Toronto, Ontario, 1978)
Toivonen, Ida (Thunder Bay, Ontario, 1983)
Tolvanen, Jussi (Toronto, 1985)
Tynjälä, Urho (Sointula, British Columbia, 1979)
Uitto, Eino (Parry Sound, Ontario, 1982)
Vanhatalo, Helmi (Sault Ste Marie, Ontario, 1980)
Wauhkonen, Saima (Whitewood, Saskatchewan, 1981 & 1982)
Wetton, Aini (Winnipeg, Manitoba, 1982)

Multicultural History Society of Ontario Collection
Finnilä, Ida by A.-M. Lahtinen (Sudbury, 1977)
Flink, Emma by V. Lindström-Best (Toronto, 1978)
Grenon, Helen by L. Sillanpää (Sudbury, 1977)
Gustafson, Aino by V. Lindström-Best (Toronto, 1978)
Hakola, Elli by L. Sillanpää (Timmins, Ontario, 1977)
Halonen, Hilja by H. Vuorimies (Sault Ste. Marie, 1981)
Harju, Miina by V. Lindström-Best (St. Catharines, 1978)
Harju, Uuno by V. Lindström-Best (St. Catharines, 1978)
Hirvi, Tyyne by A.-M. Lahtinen (Sudbury, 1978)
Hjorth, Jenny by V. Lindström-Best (Toronto, 1978)
Holma, Hilja by V. Lindström-Best (Toronto, 1978)
Hormavirta, Irene by V. Lindström-Best (Toronto, 1978)
Hormavirta, Irene by I. Radforth (Toronto, 1979)
Ikonen, Aatu by V. Lindström-Best (Toronto, 1978)
Johnson, Walter by K. Lindström (Parry Sound, 1980)
Kallio, Laina by A.-M. Lahtinen (Walden, 1977)
Kanerva, Impi by L. Sillanpää (Schumacher, 1977)
Kauppi, Anna by H. Vuorimies (Sault Ste Marie, 1981)
Kekki, Martta by A.-M. Lahtinen (Sudbury, 1977)
Keto, Reino by V. Lindström-Best (Toronto, 1978)
Knutila, Vilhelmina by L. Sillanpää (Porcupine, 1977)
Koivisto, Suoma by H. Vuorimies (Sault Ste Marie, 1981)
Korri, Alva by L. Sillanpää (Porcupine, 1977)
Korri, Linne by L. Sillanpää (Timmins, 1977)
Koskinen, Rolph by V. Lindström-Best (Rousseau, 1983)
Kujanpää, Kaarlo by V. Lindström-Best (Toronto, 1978)
Kujanpää, Martta by V. Lindström-Best (Toronto, 1978)
Laakso, Hilma by A.-M. Lahtinen (Sudbury, 1977)
Laamanen, Aileen by L. Sillanpää (South Porcupine, 1977)
Lahti, Helen by A.-M. Lahtinen (Sudbury, 1977)
Luukkonen, Aino by L. Sillanpää (Sudbury, 1977)
Mäki, Mary by V. Lindström-Best (Toronto, 1978)
Mäkynen, Laina by L. Sillanpää (Timmins, 1977)
Nenonen, Impi by H. Vuorimies (Sault Ste Marie, 1980)
Nevala, Hellen by A.-M. Lahtinen (Sudbury, 1977)
Nissilä, Niilo by Allen Seager and V. Lindström-Best (St. Catharines, 1979)

Oksanen, Aino by V. Lindström-Best (Toronto, 1978)
Päiviö, Jules by V. Lindström-Best (Toronto, 1980)
Piton, Aili by V. Lindström-Best (Toronto, 1978)
Pöyhölä, Taimi by S. Repo (Thunder Bay, Ontario, 1979)
Ranta, Liisa by A.-M. Lahtinen (Sudbury, 1978)
Ruohonen, Kaarina by A.-M. Lahtinen (Sudbury, 1978)
Salonen, Charles by K. Lindström (Hamilton, 1983)
Sillanpää, Sylvia by L. Sillanpää (Timmins, 1977)
Suksi, Edwin by I. Radforth and V. Lindström-Best (Sudbury, 1980)
Svensk, Oiva by V. Lindström-Best (Whitefish, Ontario, 1979)
Sytelä, Elina by A.-M. Lahtinen (Sudbury, 1977)
Tahvana, Aino by A.-M. Lahtinen (Sudbury, 1978)
Tarvainen, Helen by V. Lindström-Best (Toronto, 1979)
Vanhatalo, Helmi by H. Vuorimies (Sault Ste Marie, 1980)
Viita, Anna by A.-M. Lahtinen (Sudbury, 1978)

National Broadcasting Company of Finland
Salmela-Järvinen, Martta (Helsinki, 1968)

Thunder Bay Finnish Canadian Historical Society Collection
Anderson, Helen by C. Budner (Thunder Bay, 1978)
Erickson, Mary by R. Nieminen (Nolalu, 1979)
Grönroos, Gertie by H. Doherty (Thunder Bay, 1979)
Jokimäki, Helmi by R. Nikander (Amherstburg, 1980)
Juhala, Annie by R. Nieminen (Finland, Ontario, 1979)
Kaukola, Sylvi by H. Doherty (Thunder Bay, 1979)
Koivuranta, Mary by R. Nieminen (Thunder Bay, 1979)
Lehto, Anna by R. Nieminen (Thunder Bay, 1979)
Matson, Katri by R. Nieminen (Thunder Bay, 1979)
Mikkelä, Julia by C. Kouhi (Thunder Bay, 1974)
Pitkänen, Aino by R. Nieminen (Thunder Bay, 1979)
Salmijärvi, Sanni by R. Nieminen (Thunder Bay, 1979)
Toikko, Lyyli by R. Nieminen (Thunder Bay, 1979)
Tuomi, Eini by R. Nieminen (Thunder Bay, 1979)
Tuomi, Sara by R. Nieminen (Thunder Bay, 1979)
Wickström, Elma by H. Doherty (Thunder Bay, 1979)
Wirta, Miina by R. Nieminen (Thunder Bay, 1979)

University of British Columbia Library
Tynjälä, Urho (Sointula, British Columbia, 1972)

Provincial Archives of British Columbia Aural History Collection
Michelson, Richard (Sointula, British Columbia, 1972)
Tynjälä, Arvo (Sointula, British Columbia, 1972)

Autobiographies, Memoirs, Diaries, Travelogues

UNPUBLISHED – FINNISH

Hännikäinen, Juhani. "Kulkurin matkakirja." n.p., n.d. Author's Collection.
Koski, William. "Muistelmia Porcupinen kulta-alueelta." Timmins, n.d. 1952?,
MSR 7633 (FCHSC/AO).

Mustama, Emil. "Historia – Esiraivaajien historia, muistiin kirjoittanut poikansa Emil Mustama. Alkaan niin aikasilta ajoilta kun he ovat kertoneet." Whitewood, Saskatchewan, 1961. Author's Collection.

Palokangas, Jussi. "Päiväkirjat." Michigan and Sault Ste Marie, Ontario 1906-30. Jussi Palokangas Papers, MSR 8123 (AO).

UNPUBLISHED – ENGLISH

Tiainen, Anna. "This is the beginning of my life story." Cloverdale, British Columbia, n.d. 1952?. Author's Collection.

PUBLISHED – FINNISH

Acricola. *Kulkurina Amerikassa, uutisraivaajana Canadassa.* Duluth, Minnesota, 1952.

Aho, Aili and Antti J. *Amerikassa piikana ja keltanokkana.* Porvoo, Finland, 1929.

Engelmann, Ruth. *Lehtimaja: Suomalaistytön nuoruus Amerikassa.* Porvoo, 1982.

Fagerlund, Olga S. *Tarinani lännen ihmemaassa.* Lappeenranta, Finland, 1980.

Gripenberg, Aleksandra (translator Hilda Asp). *Uudesta Maailmasta. Hajanaisia matkakuvia Ameriikasta.* Helsinki, 1891.

Hedman, E. A. *Amerikan Muistoja.* Brooklyn, New York, 1925.

Hendrikson, Martin. *Muistelmia Kymmenvuotisesta Raivaustyöstäni.* Fitchburg, Massachusetts, 1909.

Järnefelt, Akseli Rauanheimo. *Meikäläisiä merten takana.* Porvoo, 1921.

————. *Suomalaiset Amerikassa.* Helsinki, 1899.

Johnson, Lempi. *Sisulla ja sydämellä.* New York Mills, Minnesota, 1984.

Lindewall, Arvo. *Suomesta Hawaiin.* Sudbury, Ontario, 1941.

Pälsi, Sakari. *Suuri, kaunis ja ruma maa: kuvia ja kuvauksia Kanadan-matkalta.* Helsinki, Finland, 1927.

Rauanheimo, Akseli. *Kanadan-kirja.* Porvoo, 1930.

Savela, Evert. *Suomesta Sointulaan.* Superior, Wisconsin n.d.

Tokoi, Oskari. *Maan-pakolaisen muistelmia.* Helsinki, 1947.

Von Essen, Martha. *Suomen tyttöjä dollarimaassa.* Jyväskylä, Finland, 1945.

Zilliacus, Konni (translator Juhani Aho). *Siirtolaisia. Kertomuksia Ameriikan suomalaisten elämästä.* Porvoo, n.d. [1899?].

PUBLISHED – ENGLISH

Buck, Tim. *Yours in the Struggle: Reminiscences of Tim Buck.* Toronto, 1977.

Goodman, Laura Salverson. *Confessions of an Immigrant's Daughter.* 1939; reprint Toronto, 1981.

Grönlund Schneider, Aili. *The Finnish Baker's Daughters.* Toronto, 1986.

Mansfield, L. D. *Aim for the Broom.* n.p. 1979.

McClung, Nellie. *Clearing in the West: My Own Story.* Toronto, 1976.

Murray's Hand-Book: Russia, Poland and Finland. London, England, 1869.

Tokoi, Oskari. *Sisu 'Even Through a Stone Wall': The Autobiography of Oskari Tokoi.* New York, 1957.

Periodicals, Newspapers

FINNISH

Aika (Sointula, British Columbia)
Airue (Port Arthur, Ontario)
Canadan Uutiset (Port Arthur, Ontario)
Canadan Viesti (Winnipeg, Manitoba)
Koe (North Wellington, British Columbia)
Liekki (Sudbury, Ontario)
Metsätyöläinen (Port Arthur, Ontario)
Moukari (Edmonton, Alberta)
New Yorkin Uutiset (New York, New York)
Piiskuri (Pottsville, Ontario)
Raivaaja (Fitchburg, Massachusetts)
Säde (Extension and Ladysmith, British Columbia)
Säkeniä (Fitchburg, Massachusetts)
Toiwo (Toivo) (Toronto, Ontario)
Toveritar (Astoria, Oregon)
Työkansa (Port Arthur, Ontario)
Työläisnainen (Superior, Wisconsin)
Vapaus (Sudbury, Ontario)

ENGLISH

The Globe (Toronto, Ontario)
Cotton's Weekly (Cowansville, Quebec)
The Sudbury Star (Sudbury, Ontario)
Western Clarion (Vancouver, British Columbia)
The Woman Worker (Toronto, Ontario)
The Worker (Toronto, Ontario)
The Young Worker (Toronto, Ontario)

Government Documents

Census of Canada, 1911. Special Report on the Foreign-Born Population. Ottawa, 1915.
Dominion of Canada. Report of the Department of Immigration and Colonization for the Fiscal Year Ended March 31, 1929. Ottawa, 1930.
Dominion of Canada. Sessional Papers XXXV. Ottawa, 1901.
Fifth Census of Canada, 1911. Areas and Population by Provinces, Districts and Subdistricts I. Ottawa, 1913.
Fifth Census of Canada, 1911. Instructions to Officers, Commissioners and Enumerators. Ottawa, 1911.
Fourth Census of Canada, 1901. Ottawa, 1903.
Seventh Census of Canada, 1931. Instructions to Commissioners and Enumerators. Ottawa, 1931.
Seventh Census of Canada, 1931. Ages of the People III. Ottawa, 1935.
Seventh Census of Canada, 1931. Cross-Classification IV. Ottawa, 1934.
Seventh Census of Canada, 1931. Population by Areas II. Ottawa, 1933.
Seventh Census of Canada, 1931. Summary I. Ottawa, 1936.
Sixth Census of Canada, 1921. Instructions to Commissioners and Enumerators. Ottawa, 1921.

Sixth Census of Canada, 1921. Origin, Birthplace, Nationality and Language of the Canadian People VIII. Ottawa, 1929.
Sixth Census of Canada, 1921. Population I. Ottawa, 1924.
Sixth Census of Canada, 1921. Population II. Ottawa, 1925.

Published Proceedings and Calendars

FINNISH

Kirkollinen Kalenteri. Hancock, Michigan.
Päiviö, Aku, ed. *Canadan Suomalaisen Sosialistijärjestön Ensimmäisen Edustajakokouksen Pöytäkirja.* Port Arthur, Ontario, 1914.
Parras, Eemeli, ed. *Yhdysvaltain Suomalaisen Sosialistijärjestön Neljännen Edustajakokouksen Pöytäkirja, 1914.* Astoria, Oregon, 1915.
Raittiuskansan Kalenteri. Baraga and Hancock, Michigan.
Raittiuskalenteri (also *Raittius – Kalenteri*). Hancock, Michigan.
Siirtokansan Kalenteri. Duluth, Minnesota.
Työväen Taskukalenteri. Duluth, Minnesota.

ENGLISH

Report of a Preliminary and General Social Survey of Port Arthur, Department of Temperance and Moral Reform of Methodist and Presbyterian Churches, 1913.
Third Annual Report of the Woman's Missionary Society of the United Church of Canada, 1927.

Secondary Sources

Books

FINNISH

50 vuotta Suomen naisten yhteistyötä. Helsinki, 1961.
50 vuotta 1897-1947. Port Arthur, Ontario, 1947.
Aho G. A. and Nopola J. E. *Evankelis-Luterilainen, Kansalliskirkko: ensimmäiset 50 vuotta.* Ironwood, Michigan, 1949.
Alapuro, Risto, Alestalo, Matti, Jallinoja, Riitta, Sandlund, Tom and Valkonen, Tapani, eds. *Suomalaiset: Yhteiskunnan rakenne teollistumisen aikana.* Porvoo, 1980.
Canadan Suomalainen Järjestö 25 Vuotta, 1911-1936. Sudbury, Ontario, 1936.
Canth, Minna. *Työmiehen Vaimo.* 1885.
Engelberg, Rafael. *Suomi ja Amerikan suomalaiset.* Helsinki, 1944.
Eklund, William. *Canadan Rakentajia: Canadan Suomalaisen Järjestön Historia vv. 1911-1971.* Toronto, 1983.
Eskola, Katariina, Haavio-Mannila, Elina and Jallinoja, Riitta, eds. *Naisnäkökulmia.* Helsinki, 1979.
Haataja, Lauri, Hentilä, Seppo, Kalela, Jorma, and Turtola, Jussi, eds. *Suomen työväenliikkeen historia.* Joensuu, Finland, 1977.
Haavio-Mannila, Elina. *Kylätappelut: Sosiologinen tutkimus Suomen kylätappeluinstituutiosta.* Porvoo, 1958.

———— and Snicker, Raija. *Päivätanssit.* Porvoo, 1980.
Halminen, Matti. *Sointula: Kalevan Kansan ja Kanadan suomalaisten historiaa.* Helsinki, 1936.
Haltia, Manja. *Marttatoiminta 1899-1949.* Helsinki, 1949.
Heikkilä, Markku and Murtorinne, Eino, eds. *Kirkko suomalaisessa yhteiskunnassa 1900 luvulla.* Hämeenlinna, Finland, 1977.
Hyvämäki, Lauri. *Sinistä ja mustaa. Tutkielma Suomen oikeistoradikalismista.* Helsinki, 1971.
Ilmonen, Ralph S. *Amerikan Suomalaisten Historia.* Hancock, Michigan, 1930.
Innala, Aune. *Suomen naisen alkutaival lainsäätäjänä.* Helsinki, 1967.
Jallinoja, Riitta. *Suomalaisen naisasialiikkeen taistelukaudet.* Porvoo, 1983.
Järnefelt-Rauanheimo, Betty. *Vierailla veräjillä.* Porvoo, 1928.
Juhla-Julkaisu: Copper Cliffin Wuoristo Ev. Lut. Seurakunnan 40-vuotis-Juhlille 1897-1937. 1937.
Jutikkala, Eino ed. *Suomen talous- ja sosiaalihistorian kehityslinjoja.* Helsinki, 1968.
Kähärä, Tellervo. *Kansanpappi Toivo Pajala.* Thunder Bay, 1985.
Kalemaa, Kalevi, *Matti Kurikka, legenda jo eläessään.* Porvoo, 1978.
Kannila, Helle, ed. *Minna Canthin kirjeet.* Helsinki, 1973.
Kansalliskirkon 25-vuotisjulkaisu 1898-1923. Ironwood, Michigan, 1923.
Kero, Reino. *Suomen siirtolaisuuden historia I.* Turku, 1982.
Kirkkomme työvainiolta. Hancock, Michigan, 1930.
Kostiainen, Auvo, ed. *Nainen historiassa.* Turku, 1984.
———— and Pilli, Arja. *Suomen siirtolaisuuden historia II.* Turku, 1983.
Kuparinen, Eero. *Maitten ja merten takaa. Vuosisata suomalaisia siirtolaiskirjeitä.* Tammisaari, Finland, 1985.
Kuusi, Matti, Alapuro, Risto and Klinge, Matti, eds. *Maailmankuvan muutos tutkimuskohteena.* Helsinki, 1977.
Laaksonen, Pekka and Virtaranta, Pertti, eds. *Ulkosuomalaisia.* Helsinki, 1982.
Lindström-Best, Varpu and Sutyla, Charles M. *Terveisiä Ruusa-tädiltä: Kanadan suomalaisten ensimmäinen sukupolvi.* Helsinki, 1984.
Linkola, Martti, Hakamäki, Toivo and Kirkinen Heikki, eds. *Sukupolvien perintö 2. Talonpoikaiskulttuurin, kasvu.* Helsinki, 1985.
Lucina Hagman. Helsinki, 1923.
Mäkikossa, Oma. *Yhteiskunnalle omistettu elämä: Miina Sillanpään elämän ja työn vaiheita.* Helsinki, 1947.
Mäntylä, Ilkka. *Suomalaisen juoppouden juuret, Viinanpoltto vapaudenaikana.* Helsinki, 1985.
McClung, Nellie (translator Väinö Nyman). *Suomalaistyttö Amerikassa.* Helsinki, 1926.
Miina Sillanpää 80 vuotta. Helsinki, 1946.
Nygård, Toivo. *Suur-Suomi vai lähiheimolaisten auttaminen.* Helsinki, 1978.
Päivärinta, Pietari. *Minä ja muut. Sakeus Pyöriän kertomuksia.* Porvoo, 1885.
Päiviö, Aku. *Sara Kivistö.* Astoria, Oregon, 1913.
Pentikäinen, Samuli, ed. *Talonpoikaisperinne kunnan kulttuuripolitiikassa.* Kokkola, Finland, 1974.
Pikkusaari T. *Copper Cliffin Suomalaiset ja Copper Cliffin Suomalainen Evankelis-Luterilainen Wuoristo-Seurakunta.* Hancock, Michigan, 1947.
Raivio, Yrjö. *Kanadan suomalaisten historia I.* Vancouver, 1975.
————. *Kanadan suomalaisten historia II.* Thunder Bay, Ontario, 1979.
Rautanen V. *Amerikan suomalainen kirkko.* Hancock, Michigan, 1911.
Renvall, Pentti, ed. *Suomalaisen kansanvallan kehitys.* Porvoo, 1965.
Saarela, Veikko. *Agricola – Ankkuri aallokossa.* Buckhorn, Ontario, 1981.
Saarisuu, Arvi. *Riemuvuoden virta.* Wapella, Sask., 1943.

184   *Defiant Sisters*

Saarnivaara, Uuras. *Amerikan Laestadiolaisuuden eli Apostolis-Luterilaisuuden Historia.* Ironwood, Michigan, 1947.
Salmela-Järvinen, Martta. *Miina Sillanpää: legenda jo eläessään.* Helsinki, 1973.
Sariola, Sakari. *Amerikan kultalaan.* Helsinki, 1982.
Setälä, Päivi; Korppi-Tommola, Aura; Jallinoja, Riitta; Kurki, Hannele, Laisi, Helena; Mannila-Kaipainen, Johanna; Manninen, Merja; Pekkola, Jaana; Perttilä, Mikko and Pylkkänen, Anu, eds. *Naiskuvista todellisuuteen.* Hämeenlinna, Finland, 1984.
Sinkkonen, Sirkka and Ollikainen, Eila, eds. *Se on kaikki kotiinpäin.* Pieksämäki, Finland, 1985.
_____ and Ollikainen, Eila, eds. *Toisenlainen tasa-arvo.* Picksämäki, Finland, 1982.
Sulkanen, Elis. *Amerikan Suomalaisen Työväenliikkeen Historia.* Fitchburg, Massachusettes, 1951.
Sulkunen, Irma, *Raittius Kansalaisuskontona.* Helsinki, 1986.
Syrjälä, F. J. *Historia-aiheita Ameriikan Suomalaisesta Työväenliikkeestä.* Fitchburg, Massachusettes, n.d. [1925?].
Taisteleva seurakunta. Sudbury, Ontario, 1952.
Tarkiainen, V. *Minna Canth.* Helsinki, 1921.
Tervapää, Juhani [Hella Wuolijoki]. *Juurakon Hulda.* Helsinki, 1937.
Toivonen, Anna-Leena. *Etelä-Pohjanmaan valtamerentakainen siirtolaisuus, 1867-1930.* Helsinki, 1968.
Tommila, Päiviö, ed. *Kaksi vuosikymmentä Suomen sisäpolitiikkaa 1919-1930.* Helsinki, 1964.
Toronton Saalem-seurakunta 1930-1980. Vancouver, 1980.
Toronton Suomalainen Bethlehem Ev. Lut. Seurakunta. Toronto, 1976.
Toveritar kymmenvuotias 1911-1921. Astoria, Oregon, 1921.
Utrio, Kaari. *Eevan tyttäret.* Helsinki, 1985.
Vilkemaa, Hilja. *Minna Canth: elämänkerrallisia piirteitä.* Helsinki, 1931.
Virtanen, Keijo, Pilli, Arja and Kostiainen, Auvo. *Suomen siirtolaisuuden historia III.* Turku, 1986.
Voionmaa, Väinö. *Suomen Karjalaisen heimon historiaa.* Helsinki, 1915.

ENGLISH

A Woman in Finland. Helsinki, 1984.
Aaltio, Tauri, Koivukangas, Olavi and Niitemaa, Vilho, eds. *Old Friends – Strong Ties.* Vaasa, Finland, 1976.
Abella, Irving and Troper, Harold. *None Is Too Many.* Toronto, 1982.
Acton, Janice, Goldsmith, Penny and Sheppard Bonnie, eds. *Women at Work, 1850-1930.* Toronto, 1974.
Adachi, Ken. *The Enemy that Never Was.* Toronto, 1976.
Akenson, Donald H. *The Irish in Ontario: A Study in Rural History.* Kingston, 1984.
Anderson, Aili. *History of Sointula.* 1969.
Anderson, J. T. M. *The Education of the New Canadian. A Treatise on Canada's Greatest Educational Problem.* Toronto, 1918.
Anderson, Michael. *Family Structure in Nineteenth Century Lancashire.* London, England, 1971.
Angus, Ian. *Canadian Bolsheviks: The Early Years of the Communist Party of Canada.* Montreal, 1981.
Ariès, Philippe. *Centuries of Childhood: A Social History of Family Life.* New York, 1962.

Avakumovic, Ivan. *The Communist Party in Canada: A History*. Toronto, 1975.

Avery, Donald. *"Dangerous Foreigners": European Immigrant Workers and Labour Radicalism in Canada, 1896-1932*. Toronto, 1979.

Bacci, Carol Lee. *Liberation Deferred? The Ideas of English-Canadian Suffragists, 1877-1918*. Toronto, 1983.

Bagnell, Kenneth. *Little Immigrants*. Toronto, 1980.

Baum, Charlotte, Hyman, Paula and Michael, Sonya, eds. *The Jewish Woman in America*. New York, 1976.

Bebel, August. *Woman and Socialism*. New York, 1910.

Beijbom, Ulf. *Swedes in Chicago*. Vaxsjö, Sweden, 1971.

Blegen, Theodore C. *Norwegian Migration to America*. Northfield, Minnesota, 1955.

The Book of Forms: The Presbyterian Church of Canada. Don Mills, Ontario, 1981.

Bradwin, Edmund. *The Bunkhouse Man*. Toronto, 1972.

Brown, Robert Craig and Cook, Ramsay. *Canada 1896-1921*. Toronto, 1978.

Buck, Tim. *Thirty Years: The Story of the Communist Movement in Canada, 1922-1952*. Toronto, 1952.

Buhle, Mari Jo. *Women in American Socialism, 1870-1920*. Chicago, 1983.

Burnet, Jean, ed. *Looking into My Sister's Eyes: An Exploration in Women's History*. Toronto, 1986.

Caroli, Betty Boyd, Harney, Robert F. and Tomasi, Lydio F., eds. *The Italian Immigrant Woman in North America*. Toronto, 1978.

Carroll, Bernice A., ed. *Liberating Women's History: Theoretical and Critical Essays*. Chicago, 1976.

Clark C. S. *Toronto the Good*. Montreal, 1898.

Cleverdon, Catherine. *The Woman Suffrage Movement in Canada*. Toronto, 1950.

Connor Ralph. *The Foreigner*. Toronto, 1909.

Cook, Ramsay and Mitchinson, Wendy, eds. *The Proper Sphere: Woman's Place in Canadian Society*. Toronto, 1976.

Corbett, Gail H. *Barnardo Children in Canada*. Woodview, Ontario, 1981.

Cross, Michael S. and Kealey, Gregory S., eds. *The Consolidation of Capitalism 1896-1929*. Toronto, 1983.

Dahlie, Joergen and Fernando, Tissa, eds. *Ethnicity, Power and Politics in Canada*. Toronto, 1981.

Davy, Shirley, ed. *Women, Work and Worship in the United Church of Canada*. 1983.

deMausse, Lloyd, ed. *The History of Childhood*. New York, 1974.

Dreisziger N. F., ed. *Struggle and Hope: The Hungarian-Canadian Experience*. Toronto, 1982.

For the Common Good: Finnish Immigrants and the Radical Response to Industrial America. Superior, Wisconsin, 1977.

Ehrenreich, Barbara and English, Deidre. *Witches, Midwives and Nurses: A History of Women Healers*. Old Westbury, New York, 1973.

England, R. *The Central European Immigrant in Canada*. Toronto, 1929.

Evans, Richard. *The Feminists: Women's Emancipation Movements in Europe, America and Australasia 1840-1920*. London, England, 1977.

Flandrin, Jean-Louis. *Families in Former Times: Kinship, Household and Sexuality*. London, England, 1979.

Friends in Need: The WBA Story a Canadian Epic in Fraternalism. Winnipeg, 1972.

Fish, Gordon. *Dreams of Freedom: Bella Coola, 'Cape Scott, Sointula*. Victoria, 1982.

Greene, S. *The Curious History of Contraception*. London, England, 1971.

Gronow, Pekka. *Studies in Scandinavian-American Discography I and II*. Helsinki, 1977.

Haavio-Mannila *et al.*, eds. *Unfinished Democracy: Women in Nordic Politics.* Elmsford, New York, 1985.

Hall D. J. *Clifford Sifton: Volume I, The Young Napoleon 1861-1900.* Vancouver, 1981.

Handlin, Oscar. *The Uprooted: The Epic Story of the Great Migrations That Made the American People.* New York, 1951.

Harney, Robert F., ed. *Gathering Place: Peoples and Neighbourhoods of Toronto, 1834-1945.* Toronto, 1985.

_____ . *Oral Testimony and Ethnic Studies.* Toronto, 1977.

_____ and Scarpachi, Vincenza, eds. *Little Italies in North America* (Toronto, 1981).

Harzig, Christiane and Hoerder, Dirk, eds. *The Press of Labour Migrants in Europe and North America 1880's to 1930's.* Bremen, 1985.

Hawkes, John. *The Story of Saskatchewan.* Chicago, 1924.

Hedges, James B. *Building the Canadian West: The Land and Colonization Policies of the Canadian Pacific Railway.* New York, 1939.

Heikkilä, Ritva, ed. *Sanoi Minna Canth Pioneer Reformer: Extracts from Minna Canth's Works and Letters.* Porvoo, 1987.

Heinonen, Arvi I. *Finnish Friends in Canada.* Toronto, 1930.

Howard, Irene. *Vancouver's Svenskar: A History of the Swedish Community in Vancouver.* Vancouver, 1970.

Jalkanen, Ralph J., ed. *Faith of the Finns.* East Lansing, Michigan, 1972.

Jensen, Joan M. and Davidson, Sue, eds. *A Needle, A Bobbin, A Strike: Women Needleworkers in America.* Philadelphia, 1984.

Johnston, Hugh. *The Voyage of the Komagata Maru: Sikh Challenge to Canada's Colour Bar.* Calcutta, 1979.

Karni, Michael G., ed. *Finnish Diaspora I: Canada, South America, Africa, Australia and Sweden.* Toronto, 1981.

_____ , ed. *Finnish Diaspora II: United States.* Toronto, 1981.

Karni, Michael G., Kaups, Matti E. and Ollila, Douglas J. Jr., eds. *The Finnish Experience in the Western Great Lakes Region: New Perspectives.* Turku, 1975.

Katzman, David M. *Seven Days a Week: Women and Domestic Service in Industrializing America.* Chicago, 1981.

Kealey, Gregory and Warrian P., eds. *Essays in Canadian Working Class History.* Toronto, 1976.

Kealey, Linda, ed. *A Not Unreasonable Claim: Women and Reform in Canada 1880s-1920s.* Toronto, 1979.

Kelly, Joan. *Women, History, and Theory: The Essays of Joan Kelly.* Chicago, 1984.

Kero, Reino. *Migration from Finland to North America in the Years between the United States Civil War and the First World War.* Turku, 1974.

Kirby, W. F. (translator). *Kalevala: The Land of the Heroes.* London, England, 1985.

Kolasky, John. *The Shattered Illusion: The History of Ukrainian Pro-Communist Organizations in Canada.* Toronto, 1979.

Kostash, Myrna. *All of Baba's Children.* Edmonton, 1977.

Kostiainen, Auvo. *The Forging of Finnish-American Communism, 1917-1924. A Study in Ethnic Radicalism.* Turku, 1978.

Kouhi, Chris, ed. *A Chronicle of Finnish Settlement in Rural Thunder Bay.* Thunder Bay, 1976.

Kovacs, Martin, ed. *Roots and Realities Among Eastern and Central Europeans.* Edmonton, 1983.

Kraut, Alan M. *The Huddled Masses: The Immigration in American Society, 1880-1921.* Arlington Heights, Illinois, 1982.

Krawchuck, Peter. *The Ukrainian Socialist Movement in Canada (1907-1918)*. Toronto, 1979.

Laine, Edward, W., ed. *Scandinavian-Canadian Studies*. Ottawa, 1983.

Latham, Barbara and Pazdro, Roberta, J., eds. *Not Just for Pin Money*. Victoria, 1984.

Leskinen, Jyrki. *Finland Facts and Figures*. Helsinki, 1979.

———. *Facts about Finland*. Helsinki, 1981.

Levine, Louis. *The Women's Garment Workers, 1909-1910*. New York, 1924.

Lindström-Best, Varpu. *The Finns in Canada*. Ottawa, 1985.

———. *The Finnish Immigrant Community of Toronto, 1887-1913*. Toronto, 1979.

Lupul, Manoly R., ed. *A Heritage in Transition: Essays in the History of Ukrainians in Canada*. Toronto, 1982.

Matheson, Gwen, ed. *Women in the Canadian Mosaic*. Toronto, 1976.

Mattson, Schelstraete, Nancy, ed. *Life in the New Finland Woods*. Rocanville, Saskatchewan, 1982.

McClung, Nellie. *Painted Fires*. Toronto, 1925.

McCormack, Ross A. *Reformers, Rebels, and Revolutionaries: The Western Canadian Radical Movement 1899-1919*. Toronto, 1977.

McLaren, Angus and McLaren, Arlene Tigar, *The Bedroom and the State*. Toronto, 1986.

McLeod, Sheila Arnapolous. *Problems of Immigrant Women in the Canadian Labour Force*. Ottawa, 1979.

Mill, John Stuart. *The Subjection of Women*. 1869; reprint Cambridge, Massachusetts, 1982.

Neidle, Cecyle S. *America's Immigrant Women*. New York, 1975.

Newton, Judith, L., Ryan, Mary, P. and Walkowitz, eds. *Sex and Class in Women's History*. London, England, 1983.

Nopola, J. E. *Our Threescore Years: A Brief History of the National Evangelical Lutheran Church*. Ironwood, Michigan, 1958.

Norcross E. B., ed. *Retrospective: The First Century*. Nanaimo, British Columbia, 1979.

Norris, John, ed. *Strangers Entertained: A History of the Ethnic Groups in British Columbia*. Vancouver, 1971.

Parr, Joy. *Labouring Children*. London, England, 1980.

Penner, Norman. *The Canadian Left: a Critical Analysis*. Scarborough, Ontario, 1977.

Petryshyn, Jaroslav. *Peasants in the Promised Land: Canada and the Ukrainians 1891-1914*. Toronto, 1985.

Pilli, Arja. *The Finnish Language Press in Canada, 1901-1939*. Turku, 1982.

Piniuta, Harry. *Land of Pain Land of Promise: First Person Accounts by Ukrainian Pioneers 1891-1914*. Saskatoon, 1978.

Potrebenko, Helen. *No Streets of Gold: A Social History of Ukrainians in Alberta*. Vancouver, 1977.

Prentice, Alison and Trofimenkoff, Susan Mann, eds. *The Neglected Majority: Essays in Canadian Women's History II*. Toronto, 1985.

Puntila, L. A. *The Political History of Finland, 1809-1966*. Finland, 1975.

Ramirez, Bruno and Del Balso, Michael. *The Italians of Montreal: From Sojourning to Settlement*. Montreal, 1980.

Rodney, William. *Soldiers of the International: A History of the Communist Party of Canada, 1919-1929*. Toronto, 1968.

Rolvaag, Ole Edwart. *Giants in the Earth*. New York, 1929.

Ross, Carl and Wargelin Brown, K. Marianne, eds. *Women Who Dared: The History of Finnish American Women*. St. Paul, Minnesota, 1986.

_____. *The Finn Factor in American Labour, Culture and Society.* New York Mills, Minnesota, 1977.

Runblom, Harold and Norman, Hans. *From Sweden to America.* Minneapolis, Minnesota, 1976.

Saarinen, Oiva. *The Pattern and Impact of Finnish Settlement in Canada with Special Reference to the Sudbury District.* Sudbury, 1967.

Sanger, William W. *The History of Prostitution.* New York, 1910.

Sarmela, Matti. *Reciprocity Systems of the Rural Society in the Finnish-Karelian Culture Area.* Helsinki, 1969.

Shorter, Edward. *The Making of the Modern Family.* New York, 1975.

Silvera, Makeda. *Silenced.* Toronto, 1983.

Silverman, Elaine, Leslau. *The Last Best West: Women on the Alberta Frontier 1880-1930.* Montreal, 1984.

Sinkkonen, Sirkka and Milen, Anneli, eds. *Toward Equality: Proceedings of the American Finnish Workshop on Minna Canth.* Kuopio, Finland, 1986.

Stone, Lawrence. *The Family, Sex and Marriage in England 1500-1800.* Bungay, England, 1979.

Sunahara, Ann Gomer. *The Politics of Racism: The Uprooting of Japanese Canadians during the Second World War.* Toronto, 1981.

Sutherland, Neil. *Children in English-Canadian Society: Framing the Twentieth Century Consensus.* Toronto, 1976.

Sutyla, Charles, M. *The Finnish Sauna in Manitoba.* Ottawa, 1977.

Swyripa, Frances and Thompson, John Head, eds. *Loyalties in Conflict: Ukrainians in Canada during the Great War.* Edmonton, 1983.

Sysiharju, Anna-Liisa. *Equality, Home and Work.* Helsinki, 1960.

Tester, Jim, ed. *Sports Pioneers: A History of the Finnish-Canadian Amateur Sports Federation 1906-1986.* Sudbury, 1986.

Thorne, Barrie and Yalom, Marilyn, eds. *Rethinking the Family.* New York, 1982.

Tolvanen, Ahti. *"Finntown" a Perspective on Urban Integration, Port Arthur Finns in the Inter-War Period: 1918-1939.* Helsinki, 1985.

Tomasi, S. M., ed. *Perspectives in Italian Immigration and Ethnicity.* New York, 1977.

Troper, Harold. *Only Farmers Need Apply.* Toronto, 1972.

Upton, Anthony, F. *The Finnish Revolution.* Minneapolis, Minnesota, 1980.

Virtanen, Keijo. *Settlement or Return: Finnish Emigrants (1860-1930) in the International Overseas Return Migration Movement.* Helsinki, 1979.

_____. *Letters to Finland.* Ann Arbor, Michigan, 1975.

Warwaruk, Larry, *Red Finns on the Coteau.* Saskatoon, 1984.

Welch, Susan and Ulrich, Fred. *The Political Life of American Jewish Women.* New York, 1984.

Wollstonecraft Mary, *Vindication of the Rights of Women.* 1872; reprinted Middlesex, England, 1982.

Woodsworth, J. S. *Strangers Within Our Gates.* 1909; reprinted Toronto, 1977.

_____. *My Neighbour.* 1911; reprinted Toronto, 1972.

Articles

FINNISH

Ahlqvist J. W. "Iso paja," in *Canadan Suomalainen Järjestö 25 vuotta, 1911-1936* (Sudbury, Ontario, 1936), pp. 5-8.

———— . "Järjestömme toiminta vuoteen 1920," in *Canadan Suomalainen Järjestö 25 vuotta, 1911-1936* (Sudbury, Ontario, 1936), pp. 31-36.
Alapuro, Risto. "Uskonto ja poliittinen mobilisoituminen maaseudulla," in *Maailmankuvan muutos tutkimuskohteena,* eds. Matti Kuusi, Risto Alapuro and Matti Klinge (Helsinki, 1977), pp. 121-47.
———— . "Yhteiskuntaluokat ja sosiaaliset kerrostumat 1870-luvulta toiseen maailmansotaan," in *Suomalaiset: Yhteiskunnan rakenne teollistumisen aikana* (Porvoo, 1980), pp. 36-78.
Alestalo, Matti. "Työväenluokan maailmankuva ja työväenliike," in *Maailmankuvan muutos tutkimuskohteena,* eds. Matti Kuusi et. al. (Helsinki, 1977), pp. 98-111.
Aromaa-Koskinen, Vuokko. "Siirtolaishistoria ja naistutkimus; yleisiä kommentteja ja tutkimusesimerkki," in *Nainen historiassa,* ed. Auvo Kostiainen (Turku, 1984), pp. 189-205.
Elovainio, Päivi. "Naisopiskelijat ja akateemiset naiset," *University of Helsinki Studies in Sociology* 95 (1967).
Engman, Max. "Suomalaistyttö Pietarissa – Fiktio ja todellisuus," in *Ulkosuomalaisia,* eds. Pekka Laaksonen and Pertti Virtaranta (Helsinki, 1982), pp. 260-78.
Eskelinen, Katri-Helena. "Minna Canthin näkemys sukupuolten tasa-arvosta," in *Toisenlainen tasa-arvo,* eds. Sirkka Sinkkonen and Eila Ollikainen (Pieksämäki, Finland, 1982), pp. 9-12.
Eskola, Katariina and Haavio-Mannila, Elina. "Naiset luovan kulttuurityön tekijöinä," *Kanava* 8 (1982), pp. 468-75.
Heinonen, Reijo E. "Kirkko ja oikeistoradikalismi Suomessa 1930 luvulla," in *Kirkko suomalaisessa yhteiskunnassa 1900-luvulla,* eds. Markku Heikkilä and Eino Murtorinne (Hämeenlinna, Finland, 1977), pp. 82-92.
Hosia, Tuulikki. "Suomalainen naisihanne," in *50 vuotta Suomen naisten yhteistyötä* (Helsinki, 1961), pp. 101-106.
Isomäki, Veli-Pekka. "Likat lähti lännelle," *Siirtolaisuus/Migration* 1 (1986), pp. 28-33.
Jallinoja, Riitta. "Miehet ja naiset," in *Suomalaiset: Yhteiskunnan rakenne teollistumisen aikana* (Porvoo, 1980), pp. 222-50.
———— . "Naisten palkkatyön yleistyminen," in *Naisnäkökulmia,* eds. Katarina Eskola, Elina Haavio-Mannila and Riitta Jallinoja (Helsinki, 1979), pp. 17-44.
———— . "Minna Canthin näkemys naisten työstä: oikeus ja velvollisuus," in *Se on kaikki kotiinpäin,* eds. Sirkka Sinkkonen and Eila Ollikainen (Pieksämäki, Finland, 1985), pp. 23-28.
Jutikkala, Eino. "Suomen väkiluvun kasvaminen," in *Suomen talous- ja sosiaalihistorian kehityslinjoja* (Helsinki, 1968), pp. 21-38.
———— . "Suomen teollistuminen," in his *Suomen talous- ja sosiaalihistorian kehityslinjoja* (Helsinki, 1979), pp. 17-41.
———— . "Suuntaus oikealle" and "Yhden puolueen vähemmistöhallitusten aika 1926-1930," in *Kaksi vuosikymmentä Suomen sisäpolitiikkaa 1919-1939,* ed. Päiviö Tommila (Helsinki, 1964), pp. 30-63.
Juva, Mikko. "Kirkko vallankumouksen keskellä," in *Kirkko suomalaisessa yhteiskunnassa 1900-luvulla,* eds. Markku Heikkilä and Eino Murtorinne (Hämeenlinna, Finland, 1977), pp. 42-52.
Kari, Antti. "Imatra Yhdeksäs," in *Canadan Suomalainen Järjestö 25 vuotta, 1911-1936* (Sudbury, Ontario), pp. 9-11.
Kena, Kirsti. "Kirkko itsenäistyneessä Suomessa," in *Kirkko suomalaisessa yhteiskunnassa 1900-luvulla,* eds. Markku Heikkilä and Eino Murtorinne (Hämeenlinna, Finland, 1977), pp. 53-68.

Korppi-Tommola, Aura. "Naisten kasvatuksen ja koulutuksen tutkimus," in *Naiskuvista todellisuuteen*, eds. Päivi Setälä *et al.* (Hämeenlinna, Finland, 1984), pp. 136-51.

Mannila-Kaipaincn, Johanna. "Palvelijan työn merkitys naisten vapauttamiselle. 'Siisti, rehellinen kotiapulainen saa paikan'," in *Naiskuvista todellisuuteen*, eds. Päivi Setälä *et al.* (Hämeenlinna, Finland, 1984), pp. 120-35.

Manninen, Merja. "Kaupunkilaisnaisen asema Suomessa Ruotsin vallan aikana," in *Naiskuvista todellisuuteen*, eds. Päivi Setälä *et al.* (Hämeenlinna, Finland, 1984), pp. 43-67.

Murtorinne, Eino. "Kirkon seitsemän vuosikymmentä," in *Kirkko suomalaisessa yhteiskunnassa 1900–luvulla*, eds. Heikkilä, Markku and Murtorinne, Eino (Hämeenlinna, Finland, 1977), pp. 7-25.

Numminen, Jaakko. "Yhdistymisvapaus ja aatteellinen järjestäytyminen," in *Suomalaisen kansanvallan kehitys*, ed. Pentti Renvall (Porvoo, 1965), pp. 111-23.

Pentikäinen, Samuli. "Maaseudun uskonnollinen elämä," in *Talonpoikaisperinne kunnan kulttuuripolitiikassa* (Kokkola, Finland, 1974), pp. 24-32.

Perttilä, Mikko. "Naisten poliittisen äänioikeuden toteuttaminen," in *Naiskuvista todellisuuteen*, eds. Päivi Setälä *et al.* (Hämeenlinna, Finland, 1977), pp. 153-64.

Pirinen, Kauko. "Kirkon oikeudellisen aseman ja järjestysmuodon kehitys," in *Kirkko suomalaisessa yhteiskunnassa 1900–luvulla*, eds. Markku Heikkilä and Eino Murtorinne (Hämeenlinna, Finland, 1977), pp. 105-22.

Ruutu, Martti. "Koululaitoksen muuttuminen ja sen muuttava vaikutus yhteiskuntaan," in *Suomalaisen kansanvallan kehitys*, ed. Pentti Renvall (Porvoo, 1965), pp. 75-92.

Seppo, Juha. "Kansankirkkona uskonnonvapauslain toteuduttua," in *Kirkko suomalaisessa yhteiskunnassa 1900–luvulla*, eds. Markku Heikkilä and Eino Murtorinne (Hämeenlinna, Finland, 1977), pp. 69-81.

Sinkkonen, Sirkka. "Hoitotyö-universaalia naisten työtä," in *Se on kaikki kotiinpäin*, eds. Sirkka Sinkkonen and Eila Ollikainen (Pieksämäki, Finland, 1985).

Sollamo, Raija. "Nainen kirkon palvelijattarena," in *Se on kaikki kotiinpäin*, eds. Sirkka Sinkkonen and Eila Ollikainen (Pieksämäki, Finland, 1985), pp. 76-86.

Suolinna, Kirsti. "Lestadiolaisuus ja agraarin väestön puolustusmekanismi," in *Maailmankuvan muutos tutkimuskohteena*, eds. Matti Kuusi, Risto Alapuro and Matti Klinge (Helsinki, 1977), pp. 112-20.

Taipale, Vappu. "Nainen ja lääketiede" in *Toisenlainen tasa-arvo*, eds. Sirkka Sinkkonen and Eila Ollikainen (Pieksämäki, Finland, 1982), pp. 96-99.

Valtonen, Tapani. "Väkiluvun ja ikärakenteen kehitys" in *Suomalaiset: Yhteiskunnan rakenne teollistumisen aikana*, eds. Risto Alapuro, Matti Alestalo, Riitta Jallinoja, Tom Sandlund and Tapani Valkonen (Porvoo, 1980), pp. 10-35.

Veikkola, Juhani. "Kansa katkoo kahleitaan — miten käy kansankirkon," in *Kirkko suomalaisessa yhteiskunnassa 1900-luvulla*, eds. Markku Heikkilä and Eino Murtorinne (Hämeenlinna, Finland, 1977), pp. 26-41.

ENGLISH

Alho, L. "The Finns," in *Strangers Entertained: A History of the Ethnic Groups of British Columbia*, ed. John Norris (Vancouver, 1971), pp. 135-6.

Anderson, Alan B. and Niskala, Brenda. "Finnish Settlements in Saskatchewan: Their Development and Perpetuation," in *Finnish Diaspora I: Canada, South America, Africa, Australia and Sweden*, ed. Michael G. Karni (Toronto, 1981), pp. 155-82.

Aromaa-Koskinen, Vuokko. "Assimilation or Isolation – The Dilemma of Finnish American Working Class Women in 1920's and 1930's," in *Toward Equality: Proceedings of the American and Finnish Workshop on Minna Canth*, eds. Sirkka Sinkkonen and Anneli Milen (Kuopio, Finland), pp. 35-48.

Avery, Donald. "Canada's Immigration Policy and the Foreign Navy, 1874-1914," *Historical Papers* (1972), pp. 132-56.

_____ . "European Immigrant Workers in Western Canada, 1900-1930: A Case Study of the Ukrainian Labour Press," in *The Press of Labor Migrants in Europe and North America 1880's to 1930's*, eds. Christiane Harzig and Dirk Hoerder (Bremen, West Germany, 1985), pp. 287-309.

Barber, Marilyn J. "Below Stairs: the Domestic Servant," *Material History Bulletin* 19 (Ottawa, 1984), pp. 37-46.

_____ . "The Women Ontario Welcomed: Immigrant Domestics for Ontario Homes, 1870-1930," *Ontario History* LXXII, no. 3 (September 1980), pp. 148-72.

_____ . "Sunny Ontario for British Girls, 1900-30," in *Looking into My Sister's Eyes: an Exploration in Women's History*, ed. Jean Burnet (Toronto, 1986), pp. 55-73.

_____ . "An Introduction," in *Stranger's Within Our Gates* by J. S. Woodsworth (Toronto, 1977), pp. vii-xxiii.

Carrothers, W. A. "The Immigration Problem in Canada," *Queen's Quarterly* 36 (1929), pp. 517-31.

Cross, Michael. "The Shiner's War: Social Violence in the Ottawa Valley in the 1830's," *Canadian Historical Review* LIV (March 1973), pp. 1-26.

Darroch, Gordon A. and Ornstein Michael D. "Ethnicity and Occupational Structure in Canada in 1871: The Vertical Mosaic in Historical Perspective," *Canadian Historical Review* LXI (September, 1980), pp. 305-33.

De Lottinville, Peter. "Joe Beef of Montreal: Working Class Culture and the Tavern, 1869-1889," *Labour/Le Travail* 8/9 (1981/1982), pp. 9-40.

Dodd, Diane. "The Hamilton Birth Control Clinic of the 1930's," *Ontario History* LXXV, no. 1 (March 1983), pp. 71-86.

Dreisziger N. F. "Immigrant Lives and Lifestyles in Canada, 1924-1939," *Hungarian Studies Review* VIII, no. 1 (Spring 1981), pp. 61-83.

Drystek, Henry F. "'The Simplest and Cheapest Mode of Dealing with Them': Deportation from Canada before World War II," *Histoire Sociale/Social History* XV, no. 30 (November 1982), pp. 407-41.

Engman, Max. "Migration from Finland to Russia during the Nineteenth Century," *Scandinavian Journal of History* 3 (1978).

"Ethnicity and Femininity" special issue of *Canadian Ethnic Studies* XIII, no. 1 (1981).

Godler, Zlata. "Doctors and the New Immigrants," *Canadian Ethnic Studies* IX, no. 1 (1977), pp. 6-17.

Haavio-Mannila, Elina and Kari, Kyllikki. "Changes in the Life Patterns of Families in the Nordic Countries," *Yearbook of Population Research in Finland* XVIII (1980), pp. 7-34.

Hamilton, L. "Foreigners in the Canadian West," *Dalhousie Review* 7 (1938), pp. 448-59.

Harney, Robert F. "Men Without Women: Italian Migrants in Canada, 1885-1930," in *The Italian Immigrant Woman in North America*, eds. Betty Boyd Caroli, Robert F. Harney and Lydio F. Tomasi (Toronto, 1978), pp. 79-101.

Höglund, William A. "Breaking with Religious Tradition: Finnish Immigrant Workers and the Church, 1890-1915," in *For the Common Good: Finnish Immi-*

grants and the Radical Response to Industrial America (Superior, Wisconsin, 1977), pp. 23-64.

Holmio, Armas K. E. "The Beginnings of Finnish Church Life in America," in *The Faith of the Finns* ed. Ralph J. Jalkanen (East Lansing, Michigan, 1972).

Hurd, W. B. "A Case for a Quota," *Queen's Quarterly* 36 (1928), pp. 145-59.

Iacovetta, Franca. "From Contadina to Worker: Southern Italian Immigrant Working Women in Toronto, 1947-62," in *Looking into My Sisters Eyes: an Exploration in Women's History* (Toronto, 1986), pp. 195-222.

Jalava, Mauri, A. "Scandinavians as a Source of Settlers for the Dominion of Canada: The First Generation, 1867-1897," in *Scandinavian-Canadian Studies*, ed. Edward. W. Laine (Ottawa, 1983), pp. 3-14.

———. "Finnish Cultural Associations in Ontario, 1945-80," *Polyphony* 3, no. 2 (Fall 1981), pp. 104-109.

Kaprielian, Isabel. "The Women," *Polyphony* 4, no. 2 (Fall/Winter 1982), pp. 53-60.

Karvonen, Hilja. "Three Proponents of Women's Rights in the Finnish-American Labour Movement from 1910-1930: Selma Jokela McCone, Maiju Nurmi and Helmi Mattson," in *For the Common Good: Finnish Immigrants and the Radical Response to Industrial America* (Superior, Wisconsin, 1977), pp. 195-216.

Kealey, Gregory, S. "The State, the Foreign Language Press, and the Canadian Labour Revolt of 1917-1920," in *The Press of Labour Migrants in Europe and North America 1880's to 1930s,* eds. Christiane Harzig and Dirk Hoerder (Bremen, 1985), pp. 311-45.

Kealey, Linda. "Canadian Socialism and the Woman Question, 1900-1914," *Labour/Le Travail* 13 (1984), pp. 77-100.

Kero, Reino. "Emigration from Finland to Canada before the First World War," *Lakehead University Review* IX, no. 1 (Spring 1976), pp. 7-16.

Kidd, Bruce. "The Workers' Sports Movement in Canada, 1924-40: The Radical Immigrants' Alternative," *Polyphony* 7, no. 1 (1985), pp. 80-88.

Kolehmainen, John. "Harmony Island: A Finnish Utopian Venture in British Columbia," *British Columbia Historical Quarterly* V, no. 2 (April 1941), pp. 111-23.

Kouhi, Christine. "Labour and Finnish Immigration to Thunder Bay, 1876-1914," *The Lakehead University Review* IX, no. 1 (Spring, 1976), pp. 17-40.

Knuttila, Alli and Denet, Elvi. "New Finland Sewing Society," in *Life in the New Finland Woods*, ed. Nancy Schelstraete (Rocanville, 1982), pp. 52-53.

Krats, Peter, V. "Suomalaiset Nikkelialueella: Finns in the Sudbury Area, 1883-1939," *Polyphony* 5, no. 1 (1983), pp. 37-48.

Kukkonen, Walter. "Process and Product: Problems Encountered by the Finnish Immigrants in the Transmission of Spiritual Heritage," *Finnish Experience in the Great Lakes Region: New Perspectives*, eds. Michael G. Karni *et al.* (Turku, 1975), pp. 130-42.

———. "The Influence of Revival Movements of Finland on the Lutheran Churches in North America," in *The Faith of the Finns*, ed. Ralph J. Jalkanen (East Lansing, Michigan, 1972), pp. 90-104.

Laine, Edward, W. "Finnish-Canadian Radicalism and Canadian Politics: The First Forty Years, 1900-1940," in *Ethnicity, Power and Politics in Canada*, eds. Joergen Dahlie and Tissa Fernando (Toronto, 1981), pp. 94-112.

———. "Archival Resources Relating To Finnish Canadians," *Archivaria* 7 (Winter 1978), pp. 110-16.

———. "'Kallista Perintöä – Precious Legacy!': Finnish-Canadian Archives, 1882-1985," *Archivaria* 2 (Summer 1986).

Lamppa, Marvin. "Embers of Revival: Laestadian Schisms in Northeast Minnesota, 1900-1940," in *Finnish Diaspora II: United States*, ed. Michael G. Karni (Toronto, 1981), pp. 193-212.

Leacock, Stephen. "Canada and the Immigration Problem," *National and English Review* (April, 1911), pp. 316-27.

Lerner, Gerda. "Placing Women in History: A 1975 Perspective," in *Liberating Women's History: Theoretical and Critical Essays*, ed. Bernice A. Carroll (Chicago, 1976), pp. 357-67.

_____ . "New Approaches to the Study of Women in American History," *Journal of Social History* IV, no. 4 (Fall, 1969), pp. 333-56.

Leslie, Genevieve, "Domestic Service in Canada, 1880-1920," in *Women at Work, 1850-1930*, eds. Janice Acton *et al.* (Toronto, 1974), pp. 71-125.

Lindström-Best, Varpu, ed. "Finns in Ontario," *Polyphony* 3, no. 2 (Fall 1981).

_____ . "The Impact of Canadian Immigration Policy on Finnish Immigration, 1890-1978," *Siirtolaisuss/Migration* 2 (1981), pp. 5-15.

_____ . "The Socialist Party of Canada and the Finnish Connection, 1905-1911," in *Ethnicity, Power and Politics in Canada*, eds. Joergen Dahlie and Tissa Fernando (Toronto, 1981), pp. 113-22.

_____ . "Central Organization of the Loyal Finns in Canada," *Polyphony* 3, no. 2 (Fall 1981), pp. 97-103.

_____ and Seager Allen. "*Toveritar* and Finnish Canadian Women, 1900-1930," in *The Press of Labour Migrants in Europe and North America 1880's to 1930s*, eds. Christiane Harzig and Dirk Hoerder (Bremen, 1985), pp. 243-64.

_____ . "Fist Press: A Study of the Finnish Canadian Handwritten Newspapers," in *Roots and Realities Among Eastern and Central Europeans*, ed. Martin Kovacs (Edmonton, 1983), pp. 129-34.

_____ . "'I Won't Be a Slave!' – Finnish Domestics in Canada, 1911-30," in *Looking into My Sister's Eyes*, ed. Jean Burnet (Toronto, 1986), pp. 33-53.

_____ . "Tailor-Maid: the Finnish Immigrant Community of Toronto before the First World War," in *Gathering Place: Peoples and Neighbourhoods of Toronto, 1834-1945*, ed. Robert F. Harney (Toronto, 1985), pp. 205-38.

Lower, A. "The Case Against Immigration," *Queen's Quarterly* 37 (1930), pp. 592-602.

Mar, Pamela and Poikonen, Henry. "From Segregation to Integration: The Story of Some of Our Early Community Groups," in *Retrospective: The First Century* ed. E. B. Norcross (Nanaimo, British Columbia, 1979), pp. 89-91.

McCuaig, Katherine. "'From Social Reform to Social Service.' The Changing Role of Volunteers: the Anti-tuberculosis Campaign, 1900-30," *Canadian Historical Review* LXI, no. 4 (December, 1980), pp. 480-501.

McLaren, Angus. "Birth Control and Abortion in Canada, 1870-1920," *Canadian Historical Review* LIX, no. 3 (1978), pp. 317-340.

_____ . "What Has This to Do with Working Class Women? Birth Control and the Canadian Left, 1900-1939," *Histoire Sociale/Social History* XIV 28 (November 1981), pp. 435-54.

Miller, Sally M. "Other Socialists: Native-born and Immigrant Women in Socialist Party of America, 1901-1917," *Labour History* 24, no. 1 (Winter 1983).

Mitchell, Juliet. "Four Structures in Complex Unity," in *Liberating Women's History: Theoretical and Critical Essays*, ed. Bernice A. Carroll (Chicago, 1976), pp. 385-99.

Mitchinson, Wendy. "The WCTU: 'For God, Home and Native Land': A Study in Nineteenth Century Feminism," in *A Not Unreasonable Claim: Women and Reform in Canada 1880s-1920s*, ed. Linda Kealey (Toronto, 1979), pp. 151-67.

Morrison, Jean. "Ethnicity and Violence: The Lakehead Freight Handlers before World War I," in *Essays in Canadian Working Class History*, eds. Gregory Kealey and P. Warrian (Toronto, 1976), pp. 143-60.

―――― . "Ethnicity and Class Consciousness: British, Finnish and South European Workers at the Canadian Lakehead Before World War I," *The Lakehead University Review* IX, no. 1 (Spring 1976), pp. 41-55.

Newton, Janice. "Women and *Cotton's Weekly:* A Study of Women and Socialism in Canada, 1909," *Resources for Feminist Research* (Fall 1980), pp. 58-60.

Nicholson, Murray W. "Peasants in an Urban Society: the Irish Catholics in Victorian Toronto," in *Gathering Place: Peoples and Neighbourhoods of Toronto, 1834-1945*, ed. Robert F. Harney (Toronto, 1985), pp. 47-73.

Ollila, Douglas J. "The Finnish American Church Organization," in *Old Friends – Strong Ties*, eds. Tauri Aaltio *et al.* (Vaasa, Finland, 1976), pp. 145-74.

Orta, Timo. "Finnish Emigration Prior to 1893: Economic, Demographic and Social Backgrounds," in *The Finnish Experience in the Western Great Lakes Region: New Perspectives*, eds Michael G. Karni, Matti E. Kaups and Douglas J. Ollila (Turku, 1975), pp. 21-35.

Pahkala, Annette. "Delivering Babies: Midwives," in *Life in the New Finland Woods*, ed. Nancy Mattson Schelstraete (Rocanville, Sask., 1982), p. 45.

Papp, Susan. "Oral History: Reflections of the Members of Three Waves of Hungarian Immigrants in Ontario," in *Roots and Realities among Eastern and Central Europeans*, ed. Martin L. Kovacs (Edmonton, 1983), pp. 155-64.

Perin, Roberto. "Clio as an Ethnic: The Third Force in Canadian Historiography," *Canadian Historical Review* LXIV, no. 4 (December 1983), pp. 441-67.

―――― . "Religion, Ethnicity and Identity: Placing the Immigrant within the Church," *Religion/Culture: Comparative Canadian Studies* VII (1985), pp. 212-29.

Petroff, Lillian. "The Macedonian Community in Toronto to 1930: Women and Emigration," *Canadian Women's History Series* V (Toronto, 1977).

Pucci, Antonio. "Canadian Industrialization versus the Italian Contadini in a Decade of Brutality, 1902-1912," in *Little Italies in North America*, eds Robert F. Harney and Vincenza Scarpaci (Toronto, 1981), pp. 182-207.

Radforth, Ian. "Finnish Lumber Workers in Ontario, 1919-46," *Polyphony* 3, no. 2 (Fall, 1981), pp. 23-34.

Ramkhalawansingh, Ceta. "Women during the Great War," in *Women at Work, 1870-1930*, eds. Janice Acton *et al.* (Toronto, 1974), pp. 261-307.

Rasmussen, Mark. "Finnish Settlement in Rural Thunder Bay, Ontario, Canada," *Siirtolaisuus/Migration* 2 (1983), pp. 3-15.

Repo, Satu. "Rosvall and Voutilainen: Two Union Men Who Never Died," *Labour/Le Travail* 8/9 (1981/1982), pp. 79-102.

―――― . "The Big Shop: Finnish Immigrant Tailors in Toronto," *This Magazine* 9, no. 5/6 (November-December, 1975), pp. 30-32.

Ross, Carl. "Finnish American Women in Transition, 1910-1920," in *Finnish Diaspora II: United States*, ed. Michael G. Karni (Toronto, 1981), pp. 239-55.

―――― . "Minna Canth: her political, social and cultural significance in Finland and America," in *Toward Equality: Proceedings of the American and Finnish Workshop on Minna Canth*, eds. Sirkka Sinkkonen and Anneli Milen (Kuopio, 1986), pp. 9-20.

―――― . "Minna Canth: Her political, social and cultural significance in Finland," in *Women Who Dared: The History of Finnish American Women*, eds. Carl Ross and K. Marianne Wargelin Brown (St. Paul, Minnesota, 1986), pp. 103-11.

Rotenberg, Lori. "The Wayward Worker: Toronto's Prostitute at the Turn of the Century," in *Women at Work, 1870-1930*, eds. Janice Acton *et al.* (Toronto, 1974), pp. 33-69.

Saarinen, Oiva, W. "Finns in Northeastern Ontario with Special Reference to the Sudbury Area," *Laurentian University Review* 15, no. 1 (1982), pp. 41-54.

_____ . "Geographical Perspectives of Finnish Canadian Immigration and Settlement," *Polyphony* 3, no. 2 (Fall 1981), pp. 16-22.

Sangster, Joan. "Finnish Women in Ontario, 1890-1930," *Polyphony* 3, no. 2 (Fall 1981), pp. 46-54.

_____ . "The Communist Party and the Woman Question, 1922-1929," *Labour/Le Travail* 15 (Spring 1985), pp. 25-56.

Seager, Allen. "Migration and Proletarianization: Aspects of Finnish Immigrant Experience in Western Canadian Coal Mining, 1880-1940," *Siirtolaisuus/Migration* 2 (1983), pp. 7-15.

_____ . "Finnish Canadians and the Ontario Miners Movement," *Polyphony* 3, no. 2 (Fall, 1981), pp. 35-45.

Seller, Maxine S. "The 'Women's Interests' Page of the *Jewish Daily Forward*: Socialism, Feminism and Americanization in 1919," in *The Press of Labor Migrants in Europe and North America 1880's to 1930's*, eds. Christiane Harzig and Dirk Hoerder (Bremen, West Germany, 1985), pp. 221-42.

Smith, Hilda. "Feminism and the Methodology of Women's History," in *Liberating Women's History: Theoretical and Critical Essays*, ed. Berenice A. Carroll (Chicago, 1976), pp. 368-84.

Soikkanen, Hannu. "Revisionism, Reformism and the Finnish Labour Movement before the First World War," *Scandinavian Journal of History* 3 (1978), pp. 347-60.

Sokolsky, Zoriana Yaworsky. "The Beginnings of Ukrainian Settlement in Toronto, 1891-1939," in *Gathering Place: Peoples and Neighbourhoods of Toronto, 1834-1945*, ed. Robert F. Harney (Toronto, 1985), pp. 279-302.

Stjärnstedt, Riitta. "Finnish Women in North American Labour Movement," in *Finnish Diaspora II: United States*, ed. Michael G. Karni (Toronto, 1981), pp. 257-76.

Strong-Boag, Veronica. "The Girl of the New Day: Canadian Working Women in the 1920's," in *The Consolidation of Capitalism 1896-1929*, eds. Michael S. Cross and Gregory S. Kealey (Toronto, 1983), pp. 169-211.

Sturino, Franc. "Family and Kin Cohesion among South Italian Immigrants in Toronto," in *The Italian Immigrant Woman in North America*, eds. Betty Boyd Caroli, Robert F. Harney and Lydio F. Tomasi (Toronto, 1978), pp. 288-311.

_____ . "The Role of Women in Italian Immigration to the New World," in *Looking into My Sister's Eyes: an Exploration in Women's History*, ed. Jean Burnet (Toronto, 1986), pp. 21-33.

Swyripa, Frances. "Outside the Bloc Settlement: Ukrainian Women in Ontario during the Formative Years of Community Consciousness," in *Looking into My Sister's Eyes: an Exploration in Women's History*, ed. Jean Burnet (Toronto, 1986), pp. 155-78.

Van Cleef, Eugene. "Finnish Settlements in Canada," *The Geographical Review* XLII, no. 2 (1952), pp. 253-66.

Van der Vynckt, Susan and Kasnitz, Deborah. "Immigrant Women and Family Planning in Australia," *Ethnic Studies* (Australian) 2, no. 1 (1978), pp. 35-47.

Varjo, Uuno. "Communities as Factors of Social Geography: The Finnish Rural Settlements in the Vicinity of Thunder Bay, Ontario," *Siirtolaisuus/ Migration* 1 (1986), pp. 1-8.

Vecoli, Rudolph J. "Contadini in Chicago: A Critique of the Uprooted," *Journal of American History* 51 (1964), pp. 404-15.

————. "Padroni Slaves or Primitive Rebels?" in *Perspectives in Italian Immigration and Ethnicity*, ed. S. M. Tomasi (New York, 1977), pp. 25-49.

Ware, Helen. "Immigrant Fertility: Behaviour and Attitudes," *International Migration Review* 9 (Fall 1975), pp. 361-79.

Wargelin Brown, K. Marianne "A Closer Look at Finnish-American Immigrant Women's Issues, 1890-1910," in *Finnish Diaspora II: United States*, ed. Michael G. Karni (Toronto, 1981), pp. 213-37.

————. "Canth's sojourn in America, "in *Women Who Dared: The History of Finnish American Women*, eds. Carl Ross and K. Marianne Wargelin Brown (St. Paul, Minnesota, 1986), pp. 112-22.

————. "Trailblazers in Finland for Women's Rights: A Brief History of Feminism in Finland," in *Women Who Dared: The History of Finnish American Women*, eds. Carl Ross and K. Marianne Wargelin Brown (St. Paul, Minnesota, 1986), pp. 1-13.

————. "The Legacy of Mummu's Granddaughters: Finnish American Women's History," in *Toward Equality: Proceedings of the American and Finnish Workshop on Minna Canth*, eds. Sirkka Sinkkonen and Anneli Milen (Kuopio, Finland, 1986), pp. 49-83.

————. "A Closer Look at Finnish American Women's Issues," in *Women Who Dared: The History of Finnish American Women*, eds. Carl Ross and K. Marianne Wargelin Brown (St. Paul, Minnesota, 1986), pp. 83-102.

Wilkinson, Shelagh and Verthuy Mair eds. "Multiculture," *Canadian Woman Studies/les cahiers de la femme* 4, no. 2 (Winter 1982).

Wilson, Donald J. ed., "The Finnish Experience," *Lakehead University Review* (Spring, 1976).

————. "Matti Kurikka and the Settlement of Sointula, British Columbia, 1901-1905," *Finnish Americana* 3 (1980), pp. 6-29.

————. "Matti Kurikka: Finnish Canadian Intellectual," *B. C. Studies* 20 (Winter 1973-74), pp. 50-65.

————. "A Synoptic view of *Aika*, Canada's First Finnish Language Newspaper," *Amphora* 29 (March 1980), pp. 9-14.

————. "The Canadian Sojourn of a Finnish-American Radical," *Canadian Ethnic Studies* xvi, no. 2 (1984), pp. 102-15.

————. "Finns in British Columbia before the First World War" *Polyphony* 3, no. 2 (Fall, 1981), pp. 54-64.

————. "Matti Kurikka and A. B. Mäkelä: Socialist Thought Among Finns in Canada, 1900-1932," *Canadian Ethnic Studies* x, no. 2 (1978), pp. 9-21.

Woycenko, Ol'ha. "Community Organizations," in *A Heritage in Transition: Essays in the History of Ukrainians in Canada*, ed. Manoly R. Lupul (Toronto, 1982), pp. 173-94.

Zucchi, John E. "Italian Hometown Settlements and the Development of an Italian Community in Toronto, 1875-1935," in *Gathering Place: Peoples and Neighbourhoods of Toronto, 1875-1940*, ed. Robert F. Harney (Toronto, 1985), pp. 121-46.

Unpublished Theses and Papers

FINNISH

Huhta, Miika. "Siirtolaisuus Suomesta Kanadaan ennen ensimmäistä maailmansotaa ja suomalaisten sijoittuminen Kanadaan" (Pro Gradu Paper, University of Turku, Finland, 1982).
Stjärnstedt, Riitta. "Naiset amerikansuomalaisessa työväenliikkeessä vuoteen 1920" (Pro Gradu Paper, University of Turku, Finland, 1981).
Väänänen, Marjatta. "Suomen ensimmäiset parlamenttinaiset," manuscript presented by the Minister of Culture (Helsinki, 1977).

ENGLISH

Alanen, Arnold R. "Finns and Other Immigrant Groups in the American Upper Midwest: Interactions and Comparisons," Paper presented at Finn Forum III, Turku, 1984.
Allen, Martha Isobel. "A Survey of Finnish Cultural, Economic and Political Developments in the Sudbury Districts of Ontario." M.A. thesis, University of Western Ontario, 1954.
Bayley, Charles M. "The Social Structure of the Italian and Ukrainian Immigrant Communities in Montreal, 1935-1937." M.A. thesis, McGill University, 1939.
Cross, Dorothy S. "The Irish in Montreal, 1867-1896." M.A. thesis, McGill University, 1969.
Hummasti, Paul George. "Finnish Radicals in Astoria, Oregon, 1904-1940: A Study in Immigrant Socialism." Ph.D. diss., University of Oregon, 1975.
Jalava, Mauri M. "'Radicalism or a New Deal'?: The Unfolding World View of the Finnish Immigrants in Sudbury, 1883-1932." M.A. thesis, Laurentian University, 1983.
Karlinsky, Janice B. "The Pioneer Women's Organization: A Case Study of Jewish Women in Toronto." M.A. thesis, University of Toronto, 1979.
Kaprielian, Isabel. "Women at Work: the Case of Finnish Domestics and Armenian Boardinghouse Operators." Unpublished manuscript, Toronto, May 1984.
Krats, Peter V. "Sudburyn Suomalaiset: Finnish Immigrant Activities in the Sudbury Area, 1883-1939." M.A. thesis, University of Western Ontario, 1980.
Lindström-Best, Varpu. "Finnish Immigrants and the Depression: A Case Study of Montreal." Ph.D. II term paper, York University, 1981.
Martynowych, Orest T. "Village Radicals and Peasant Immigrants: The Social Roots of Factionalism Among Ukrainian Immigrants in Canada, 1896-1918." M.A. thesis, University of Manitoba, 1978.
McCandless, Dianne. "Finnish Immigrants – Single Women." Undergraduate term paper, Lakehead University, 1980.
Ollila, Douglas J. "The Formative Period of the Finnish Evangelical Lutheran Church in America or Suomi Synod." Ph.D. diss., Boston University, 1963.
Penti, Marsha. "The Role of Ethnic Folklore Among Finnish American Returnees." Ph.D. diss., Indiana State University, 1983.
Radforth, Ian W. "Bushworkers and Bosses: A Social History of the Northern Ontario Logging Industry, 1900-1980." Ph.D. diss., York University, 1985.
Rasmussen, Mark. "The Geographic Impact of Finnish Settlement on the Thunder Bay Area of Northern Ontario." M.A. thesis, University of Alberta, 1978.

Roberts, Barbara Ann. "Purely Administrative Proceeding: The Management of Canadian Deportation, Montreal, 1900-1935." Ph.D. diss., University of Ottawa, 1980.

Saarinen, Oiva and Tapper G. O. "The Beaver Lake Finnish-Canadian Community: A Case Study of Ethnic Transition as Influenced by the Variables of Time and Spatial Networks, Ca. 1907-1983." Presented at Finn Forum III, Turku, 1984.

Salo, A. H. "Kalevan Kansa Colonization Company: Finnish Millenarian Activity in B. C." M.A. University of British Columbia, 1978.

Seager, Charles Allen. "A Proletariat in Wild Rose Country: The Alberta Coal Miners, 1905-1945." Ph.D. diss., York University, 1981.

Sillanpää, Lennard. "The Political Behaviour of Canadians of Finnish Descent in the District of Sudbury." Licentiate thesis, University of Helsinki, 1975, rev. in 1976.

Index

Aallotar (Maiden of the Waves), 23, 57, 140, 142, 152
Abbey, Saskatchewan, 69
Abitibi, Quebec, 36
Aho, Arthur, 27
Aho, Maria, 27
Äijö, Sulo, 106
Aika (Time), Sointula, British Columbia, 75, 145
Akateeminen Karjala Seura (Academic Karelia Society), 117
Alberta, 29-30, 32, 34-36, 70, 136, 159
Algoma District, Ontario, 29
Anderson, Lyyli, 81
Anglicans, 130
Avery, Donald, 2

Baptists, 130
Battle River, Alberta, 82
Bayley, Bill, 141
Beauharnois, Quebec, 36
Beaver Lake, Ontario, 25, 73
Bebel, August, 145
Bellevue, Alberta, 159
Bernstein, Eduard, 19
"Big Selma," 106
Blairmore, Alberta, 159
Bobrikov, Nikolai, 15
Boston, Mass., 93
Boston's Congregationalist Seminary, 132
British Columbia, 23-24, 29-32, 34-36, 38, 88, 122, 140-41, 144, 154
British Isles, 89-90
Buhay, Becky, 159-60
Burnet, Jean, 4

Calgary, Alberta, 37
Calumet, Michigan, 120
Canadan Uutiset, Port Arthur, Ontario, 68, 78-79, 108, 135, 148, 155
Canadian Federation of Women's Labour League (WLL), 74, 159
Canadian Pacific Railway (CPR; *siipiiaari*), 22-24
Canadian Socialist Federation (CSF), 147
Canth, Minna, 17, 95
Carlin station, British Columbia, 31
Chicago, Illinois, 93, 133
Chicoutimi, Quebec, 36
Christian Workers' Mission, Toronto, 132
Church of All Nations (*Queenin kirkko,* The Queen Street Church), 133-35
Churchill, Manitoba, 7
Cleveland, Ohio, 81, 133
Cobalt, Ontario, 36, 73, 87, 147, 158
Cochrane, Ontario, 36, 105, 112
Comintern, 157-58
Communist Party (of Finland), 21
Communist Party of Canada, 156-57
Communist Party's Women's Bureau, 159
Comox-Atlin District, British Columbia, 30
Congregationalist Church (Tibet), 127
Congregational Sewing Society (New Finland), 121-22
Congregationalists, 130, 132
Conneaut, Ohio, 123
Copper Cliffin Nuorisoseura (Young People's Organization of Copper Cliff), 142-43

56775

Lindestrom-Best, Varpu

Defiant sisters: a social
history of Finnish immigrant
women in Canada

Printed in Canada